T0355256

Roads to Freedom

Roads to Freedom
Prisoners in Colonial India

Mushirul Hasan

OXFORD
UNIVERSITY PRESS

OXFORD
UNIVERSITY PRESS

Oxford University Press is a department of the University of Oxford.
It furthers the University's objective of excellence in research, scholarship,
and education by publishing worldwide. Oxford is a registered trademark of
Oxford University Press in the UK and in certain other countries.

Published in India by
Oxford University Press
YMCA Library Building, 1 Jai Singh Road, New Delhi 110 001, India

© Oxford University Press 2016

The moral rights of the author have been asserted.

First Edition published in 2016

ISBN-13: 978-0-19-945883-7
ISBN-10: 0-19-945883-9

Typeset in Adobe Jenson Pro 11/13
by Tranistics Data Technologies, New Delhi 110 044
Printed in India by Replika Press Pvt. Ltd

For Zoya

Contents

Acknowledgements

I am enormously grateful to the Jawaharlal Nehru Memorial Fund for appointing me as the Jawaharlal Nehru Fellow (2013–15). This book and a companion volume, *When Stone Walls Cry: The Nehrus in Prison*, also being published by the Oxford University Press, have grown out of my project on political prisoners in colonial India. Work on these two books was completed in the course of this fellowship. Some of these chapters were presented as lectures and I am grateful to the organizers and audience for their comments. These include the Nehru Memorial Museum and Library, the National Archives of India, Jamia Millia Islamia, and Delhi University, all in New Delhi, and Calcutta University, among others.

A book such as this has involved considerable archival work. I have relied considerably on the goodwill and generous help of librarians and staff of several libraries. My greatest thanks are owed to the staff of the National Archives of India and the Uttar Pradesh State Archives, Lucknow, for their help in finding documents and materials for this book. I am greatly indebted to the staff of the Nehru Memorial

Museum and Library and the India International Centre Library, New Delhi, for their constant help in finding materials and documents.

I am especially grateful to Nitasha Devasar, Gyanesh Kudaisya, and Nishat Zaidi for their support at various stages of this project. I want to thank the Oxford University Press for its sympathetic and efficient handling of the production of this book.

I would like to thank members of my family—Abida Hasan, Mujeebul Hasan, Shaaz Hasan, Shahzad Hasan, Zakia Hasan, Abbas Kazim, Naazli Naqvi, Salma Rizvi, Samir Rizvi, Samina Rizvi, Mohammed Tariq Siddiqi, Kahkashan Siddiqi, Khusro Siddiqi, Saadi Atiq Siddiqi, and Sameen Siddiqi—who have over the years given me great support, comfort, and affection.

The book is dedicated to Zoya who has sustained me in more ways than I can enumerate and also made this book happen.

1.   Introduction

'The Prisoner's Paradise'

This too I know—and wise it were,
    If each could know the same—
That every prison that men build
    Is built with bricks of shame,
And bound with bars lest Christ should see
    How men their brothers maim.

With bars they blur the gracious moon,
    And blind the goodly sun;
And they do well to hide their Hell,
    For in it things are done
That neither Son of God nor son of Man,
    Ever should look upon!

With midnight always in one's heart,
    And twilight in one's cell,

We turn the crank, or tear the rope,
    Each in his separate Hell,
And the silence is more awful far
    Than the sound of a brazen bell.

And never a human voice comes near,
    To speak a gentle word:
And the eye that watches through the door
    Is pitiless and hard:
And by all forgot, we rot and rot,
        With soul and body marred.

—Oscar Wilde, 'The Ballad of Reading Gaol' (1898)[1]

Rosa Luxemburg (1871–1919) remarked that the violence of the oppressed is in no way comparable to the violence of the oppressor.[2] One is justified and the other is not. On 26 January 2013, the *Los Angeles Times* reported 55 persons dying in a prison riot in Venezuela—this was the fourth incident of violence in less than two years. Usually, this kind of violence occurs wherever the courts are undermanned, the backlog of cases enormous, and the prisons overcrowded. In the same year, in Israel, 3,000 Palestinians staged a one-day hunger strike against the suspicious death of an inmate. The protests it sparked raised international concerns.[3] In December 2013, global Sikh organizations sought the intervention of the United Nations for the release of 118 political prisoners (Sikh) lodged in various Indian jails. *The Hindu* reported on 14 February 2014 that in the central and district jails in Jharkhand, 1,100 to 1,500 prisoners, mostly Maoists, had gone on hunger strike . The Communist Party of India (Maoist) observed a *bandh* in their support. Such incidents take place with unfailing regularity, and yet the state functionaries have not addressed the essential issue of locking up people and, figuratively, throwing away the key.[4] As independent India's first prime minister, when Jawaharlal Nehru (1889–1964) was called upon to

---

[1] Stuart Mason, *Oscar Wilde* (London, 1972), pp. 836–7.

[2] Mary-Alice Waters (ed.), *Rosa Luxemburg Speaks* (New York: Pathfinder Press, 1970), p. 29.

[3] *The Hindu*, 25 February 2013.

[4] Kuldip Nayyar, *Beyond the Lines: An Autobiography* (New Delhi: Roli, 2012), p. 239. See also, Rani Dhavan Shankardass, *Of Women 'Inside': Prison Voices from India* (New Delhi: Routledge, 1912), pp. 19, 281.

initiate reforms, he suggested that very few of the nobler things of the world could enter jail—truth, mercy, love, etc., are stopped at the gate. His sole consolation was that the authorities could not keep God and His nature out of jail.[5]

Escape from prison is also a common occurrence. In 2013, more than 1,000 detainees in Libya, probably inspired by the bitter and violent engagement between the army and the Muslim Brotherhood in neighbouring Egypt, escaped from a prison near Benghazi.[6] On 12 February 2013, *The Hindu* reported that the 3,700 inmates of barrack number 4, called Chhota Chakkar, had dug an 18-foot tunnel in the Sabarmati Central Jail. The escape bid exposed the poor monitoring and overcrowding—the prison had 900 inmates over and above its capacity, which made a mockery of justice. The problem in the United States of America is of a different nature. One in every 100 adults in that country is in prison,[7] and experts discuss the impact of harsh punishments and, in particular, long mandatory sentences.[8]

According to M. K. Gandhi, who spent more time in prison than any Indian, the prison system was almost, if not altogether, devoid of humanity. He told his British audience in 1931: 'We are prisoners. You Englishmen and Englishwomen are our jailors. You have to realize your responsibility, just as we have to render an account of ourselves, you as jailors will also have to render an account of yourselves.'[9] Gandhi underlined this point because the atavism of cruelty was far too deeply ingrained in wardens and jailors.

Jail conditions, despite the public outcry, are beyond scrutiny and reason, with the result that the lives of prisoners have not changed

[5] S. Gopal (ed.), *Selected Works of Jawaharlal Nehru* (*SWJN*) (New Delhi: Jawaharlal Nehru Memorial Fund, 1972), p. 323.

[6] *The Sunday Express*, 28 July 2013.

[7] Adam Liptak, '1 in 100 U.S. Adults Behind Bars, New Study Says', *New York Times*, 28 February 2008.

[8] Adam Liptak, 'Inmate Count in U.S. Dwarfs Other Nations', *New York Times*, 23 April 2008.

[9] Gandhi to Ajmal Khan, 14 April 1922, Rene Fulop-Miller, *Lenin and Gandhi* (London: G.P. Putnam's Sons, first English edn, 1927), pp. 309–10. See also, 'Speech at Meeting of Commonwealth of India League, 30 Oct. 1931', *The Collected Works of Mahatma Gandhi* (*CWMG*), vol. XLVIII (Publications Division, Ministry of Information and Broadcasting, Government of India), pp. 249–50.

much even today. People 'outside' do not want to hear about people 'inside'. Stories of rape, extortion, and corruption are not infrequently associated with Delhi's colossal Tihar Jail, the largest and most well known in Asia. Even though international law regards prohibition of torture a *jus cogens* norm, custodial torture is rampant.[10] This is documented by the 2009 report of the Asian Centre of Human Rights.[11] India has neglected to even ratify the United Nations Convention against Torture and Other Cruel, Inhuman or Degrading Treatment or Punishment (Convention against Torture, or CAT). The political classes have not paid heed to the row over according the status of 'political prisoner' to Maoists and the demand by an international committee for the unconditional release of all political prisoners. As a result, jails continue to be a site of horrendous violation of contemporary human rights, norms, and standards.

Surendranath Banerjea (1848–1925), one of the architects of the Swadeshi Movement in Bengal, remarked that 'a bad law in the hands of rulers owing no responsibility to the people is apt to be worked in a manner that often creates grave public dissatisfaction'.[12] Indeed, this applied to the codification process that involved transplanting English law, complete with lawyers and judges.[13] And though free India has longed for laws divested of colonial association and adapted to the changing times, Act 45 of 1860 and the Prison Act of 1894 are still in place.[14] Consequently, the ambiguities of the colonial system itself have weighed down the justice system.[15] The 'official' thinking is the same; the attitude of jail superintendents resembles that of the British. A truly general humanistic approach is missing with the result that the restructuring of jails is, in spite of everything, a tender plant. Consider, for example,

[10] Nitya Ramakrishnan, *In Custody: Law, Impunity and Prisoner Abuse in South Asia* (New Delhi: Sage Publications, 2013).

[11] Vahida Nainar and Saumya Uma, *Pursuing Elusive Justice: Mass Crimes in India and Relevance of International Standards* (Delhi: Oxford University Press, 2013), p. 335.

[12] Surendranath Banerjea, *A Nation in Making* (Delhi: Oxford University Press, 1963; reprint), p. 144.

[13] David Skuy, 'Macaulay and the India Penal Code of 1862', *Modern Asian Studies*, vol. 32, no. 3 (1998): 513–14.

[14] Parliament and the state legislatures have amended from time to time several acts of The Code of Criminal Procedure.

[15] Shankardass, *Of Women 'Inside'*, p. 12.

overcrowding and the consequent problems it leads to. In July 2012, the available capacity in Indian jails was 343,169, but the occupancy rate went beyond 112.2 per cent. The Moradabad Central Jail in Uttar Pradesh (UP) was so chock-a-block that there was not enough space for the inmates to sleep. So they slept in shifts. Each morning when they went to court for trial, the rest had their share of a six-foot by two-foot cell. Aurobindo Ghose (1872–1950) had rightly affirmed: 'India is free but she has not achieved unity, only a fissured and broken freedom.'[16]

When will India abandon the colonial model and learn to treat its prisoners with dignity? Do we need to revisit theories of crime and punishment? Have we run out of ideas in the punishment list, but not in the offence list? If the colonial implant had a specified agenda, what is ours?[17] At this stage of our narrative, it may be useful to put forward the following lines from Oscar Wilde, who was jailed for homosexuality in one of the great scandals of the epoch:

> For they starve the little frightened child
>   Till it weeps both night and day:
> And they scourge the weak, and flog the fool,
>   And gibe the old and grey,
> And some grow mad, and all grow bad,
>   And none a word may say.
>
>   . . .
>
> For only blood can wipe out blood,
>   And only tears can heal …
>
> —'The Ballad of the Reading Gaol'

John Stuart Mill (1806–1873), the nineteenth-century British political thinker, observed that to serve the happiness of others by the absolute sacrifice of one's own was the highest virtue in man. With this perspective in mind, I present an array of familiar Indian faces in a new setting and relate them to the moments of the time. I acquaint the younger generation with their toil and sacrifices, for only against the background of this knowledge can we measure the magnitude of their contribution to nationalist consciousness. I believe one can do their memory no greater service than by making known the facts of their life.

---

[16] Sachidanand Mohanty, *Sri Aurobindo: A Contemporary Reader* (New Delhi: Routledge, 2008), p. 195.

[17] Shankardass, *Of Women 'Inside'*, p. 11.

The Black Waters (*Kala Pani*)

The British Empire had its dark spots. The East India Company and the government under the Crown created their own Gulags by condemning thousands to forced labour, at times for decades, and subjected the prisoners' intellect to their tyranny. Pattison Walker, the first superintendent of the Kala Pani or the Black Waters, reached Port Blair on 10 March 1859 with two hundred convicts.[18] Such officers, mostly British rather than 'Native Jailors',[19] became lawless without restraint and often turned into monstrous tyrants. Thus his successor, Captain Haughton, gave free rein to terror and drove the prisoners to despair under the compulsion of the lash.[20] Given their insolence, racism, and impudence, such officers did not approve of sporadic eruptions by the 'rebels' and by the 'fundamentalists'. Accordingly, they followed the shadow of terror by bringing over the five 'Wahhabi' rebels (*Mujahidan-e Jang-e Azadi*) to the Andaman Islands in the 1860s and '70s. They did not spare the brothers Yahya Ali (1828–1868) and Ahmad-Allah (1808–1881).[21] Nor did they show mercy to Maulana Mohammad Jafar of Thaneswar, a key figure

---

[18] Great Britain first practised penal transportation of convicted criminals in the Americas, and later in Australia between 1788 and 1868. In South Asia, penal settlements existed, but they were abandoned until the reluctance to house the 1857 'rebels' on the mainland led to the re-establishment of the penal settlement at Port Blair in 1858. See Ranjan Chakrabarti, *Terror, Crime and Punishment: Order and Disorder in Early Colonial Bengal* (Kolkata: Reader's Service, 2009), p. 144.

[19] Frederic J. Mouat, *Report of the Jails of the Lower Provinces of the Bengal Presidency, for 1856–57* (Calcutta: John Gray 'Calcutta Gazette' Office, 1857), p. 7. See also Thomas R. Metcalf, *The Aftermath of Revolt: India, 1857–1870* (New Delhi: Manohar, 1990), p. 292.

[20] Jaweed Ashraf, *The Panel Settlement in Andamans, 1858–1870* (New Delhi: Gaur Publishers, 2011), p. xi; Qeyamuddin Ahmad, *The Wahhabi Movement in India* (New Delhi: Manohar, 1994), pp. 215–16; Metcalf, *Aftermath*, p. 292.

[21] 'When I see that spot in Ambala court where I was sentenced to hanging, or when I pass the Ambala jail where I was a prisoner for one and a half years, or move on the roads where after the hanging order we were taken to the jail, then my heart quivers on seeing the omnipotence of God and the thought comes to me on the day of pronouncement of the order of hanging

in the Ambala Trial,[22] though, unlike others, he was caught up in the dialectics of exalting the colonizer and humbling the colonized. Fazl-e Haq Khairabadi (1792–1861), a jurist who followed his father's tradition of emphasizing the rational sciences at the Islamic school in Khairabad,[23] was their big fish. Munir Shikohabadi (1814–1880), also exiled, refers to him as 'the treasure house of scholarship'; others describe his 'excellence in esoteric learning' and his skills as a poet.[24]

Intellectually, Fazl-e Haq gained an enviable standing at a time when the *ulama* and Sufis of north India lived in the shadow of the successors of Shah Waliullah (1703–1762) and his eldest son, Shah Abdul Aziz (1746–1824).[25] Like the Bhakti movements in medieval India, Sufism was often tinged with a kind of social radicalism or anti-feudalism. Fazl-e Haq left government service in disgust to take up employment with the princely states.[26] Added to the litany of complaints, was his critique of the British rule,[27] which led him to tacitly back, without being directly involved in the day-to-day

---

who could have thought that someday I will move about on the same spots without any hindrance and enter the same room of the court as a free man' (Ashraf, *Panel Settlement*, p. 168).

[22] Jafar Thanesari, *Kala Pani wa Tawarikh Ajeeb* (Patna: Khuda Bakhsh Library, n.d., reprint); Waseem Ahmad Saeed, *Kala Pani: Gumnam Mujahidin Jung-e Azadi* (New Delhi: Maulana Azad Academy, 2010); Ghulam Rasool Mehr, *1857 ke Mujahid* (Lahore: Kitab Manzil, n.d.).

[23] In 1850, Khairabad was the 'residence of the families of a good many public officers in our Service, and that of Oude' (P. D. Reeves, ed., *Sleeman in Oudh* [Cambridge: Cambridge University Press, 1971], p. 263).

[24] Mushirul Hasan, *A Moral Reckoning: Muslim Intellectuals in Nineteenth-Century Delhi* (New Delhi: Oxford University Press, 2005), p. 24.

[25] Ayesha Jalal, *Partisans of Allah: Jihad in South Asia* (New Delhi: Permanent Black, 2008), pp. 80–1; Jamal Malik, *Islam in South Asia: A Short History*, (New Delhi: Orient BlackSwan, 2008), pp. 253–4.

[26] Avril A. Powell, *Muslims and Missionaries in Pre-Mutiny India* (London: Curzon Press, 1993), p. 194. See also, Margrit Pernau, *Ashraf into Middle Classes: Muslims in Nineteenth-Century Delhi* (New Delhi: Oxford University Press, 2013), p. 188.

[27] Aziz Ahmad, *Islamic Modernism in India and Pakistan, 1857–1964* (London: Oxford University Press, 1967), p. 28.

planning, the insurrection on 25 August 1857. He paid a heavy price for it. While so many scholars of his kind brokered peace with the authorities, Fazl-e Haq languished in the 'Black Waters' until his death in 1861. Ghalib mourned him as a sublime, highly positive manifestation of selflessness, now forgotten and forsaken. Fazl-e Haq felt cut off from life and from the world in that demoralizing atmosphere. He wrote:

> The excesses of the hard-hearted enemy cast me on the shore of a great saltish sea in a plateau which has a cape (*ras*), also named *ras*. Here the sun always shines straight upon my head. It has difficult mountain passes and hilly roads full of trouble. There are passes in the hills, enveloped by waves of the tumultuous sea whose water is bitter; its breeze is hotter than *simum* and its comforts are more dangerous than poison; its eatables are more bitter than the taste of colocynths and its water more harmful than snake poison. Its sky is a cloud which rains sorrows and its rain clouds shower afflictions and miseries.... It was in this environment that I became a victim of several diseases and severe illnesses. These made me lose my patience; my heart became melancholy: my full moon was dimmed and my honour was lost. I do not know how deliverance and emancipation can be effected from this condition which has made me sorrowful ... so that I might be compensated for.[28]

Scores of people pined away in the Andamans or perished by the dozens in the bloom of manhood through deprivation, disease, or by committing suicide. Thousands were jailed, and many went to the gallows with heads unbowed. A popular saying of the times was, 'the blood of the martyrs will colour the red dawn'. A household saying in the course of the Lahore Conspiracy Case was that 'the graves of the martyrs are places where fairs will be held every year'.[29] Was it worth paying the price? The men of the time had no doubt that it was. Sarat Chandra

[28]   S. Moinul Haq, 'The Story of the War of Independence 1857–8: Being an English translation of Allamah Fadl-Haqq's *Risalah* on the War', *Journal of the Pakistan Historical Society* vol. 5, no. 1 (1957): 23–57. The historian Jamal Malik doubts its authenticity (Malik, *Islam in South Asia*, p. 271n33). See also Fazl-e Haq's *Baghi Hindustan* (in Urdu), translated by Abdul Shahid Khan Sherwani (Lahore: Maktaba-e Qadirya, 1978).

[29]   Surjit Hans, 'The Metaphysics of Militant Nationalism', in *Indian Response to Colonialism in the Nineteenth Century*, edited by Alok Bhalla and Sudhir Chandra (New Delhi: Sterling, 1993), pp. 223–4.

Chatterjee (1876–1938), the Bengali novelist, portrayed their sacrifices in *Pather Dabi* (The Path's Demand). Author Shudha Mazumdar, who was the first Indian woman to promote prison reform, recalls in her memoirs 'the thrill' of secretly poring over it in the still of the night, locking it up in her drawer, and surreptitiously returning the banned book to its owner. In Chittagong, she heard of Surya Sen, the bold 'terrorist' leader, and of the Revolutionary Youth Society.[30] Lala Lajpat Rai (1865–1928) declared that repression, espionage, or 'official terrorism' would not stop or check the surge of the new feeling of patriotism and nationalism; the sentences of death and transportation only fuelled it further.[31] Today, the 'new feeling of patriotism and nationalism' evokes interest and curiosity. Indeed, the indomitable courage of the victims of British cruelty has turned Kala Pani into 'a sacred place of pilgrimage sanctified by the dust of martyrs' feet'.[32]

Overland Prisons

In the early 1890s, the two penal establishments—the Central Jail and the Viper Chain Gang Jail—housed a daily average of 11,804 convicts. In the early twentieth century, 2,662 of them were from UP alone.[33] Gradually, they were joined by prisoners from other areas. In August 1921, each one of the Mappilla (Moplah) rebels, who belonged to the principal Muslim community of fishermen, sailors, and coolies along the Malabar Coast, made the most of the luxury of 500 cubic feet of space, and 27 square feet of superficial area per person. Though the Jail Committee proposed a minimum of 75 square yards (area within the main walls) per inmate, that is, 23.25 acres for a central jail of 1,500 prisoners, jail officials adopted a typically mechanistic and often racial

---

[30] Shudha Mazumdar, *Memoirs of an Indian Woman*, edited with an introduction by Geraldine Forbes (New York: An East Gate Book, 1989), p. 179.

[31] K. L. Tuteja (ed.), *Young India: An Interpretation and a History of the Nationalist Movement from Within* (New Delhi: National Book Trust, 1965), p. 189.

[32] R. Chakrabarti, *Terror, Crime and Punishment*, p. 144. The penal settlement was abolished on 16 August 1945.

[33] Lt-Col C. MacTaggart, *Annual Report of the Condition and Management of the Jails in the United Provinces, for the Year Ending 31 December 1913* (Allahabad, 1914), p. 2.

approach and turned a blind eye to disease, endless toil, isolation, and death. Hence they refused to accept the Savarkar brothers—Ganesh (1879–1945) and Vinayak (1883–1966)—in December 1920.[34] Similarly, they turned down the transfer of Sikh activists in the Gurdwara Agitation.[35]

Three other examples show the indifference of the authorities to the concerns of the prisoners.[36] First, ex-sowar Thakur Singh, son of Prem Singh, wanted to shift from Poona so that his relatives could 'supplement' his 'provincial' diet in the Punjab.[37] In Calcutta, S. S. Batliwala wished for his wife's company, then in Yeravda—sometimes called the 'King's Hotel'.[38] Lakshmi Kant Shukla and Vishnu Saran Dublis, too, longed for the company of their respective spouses.[39] While each of the cases is singular or atypical, the juridical–political responses did not seem capable of distinguishing between a range of human voices. I do no more than to call attention to their voices of lament and celebration, of agony and relief. The thoughts of the creative minds amongst them flew, like leaves chased by the winds, in all directions.

'Let Us Now Praise Famous Men'[40]

Prison, to Aurobindo Ghose, signified an *ashram* (religious heritage). He claimed that God sheltered him; at one point, he found himself in the lap of the World-Mother, cared for like a child.[41] When he was

[34] Home Dept, A., Proceedings, June 1921, file nos 64–83 (all Home Department files have been consulted at the National Archives of India). Ganesh was sentenced on 9 June 1909 to transportation for life; Vinayak in December 1909 for abetment of A.M.T. Jackson's murder at Nasik.

[35] Home Dept, Political, file no. 69/4, 1922.

[36] Dorothy Norman, *Nehru: The First Sixty Years*, vol. 1 (London: The Bodley Head, 1965), p. 226.

[37] Home Dept, Political (I), file no. 44/99, 1943.

[38] Home Dept, Political (I), file no. 43/45, 1941.

[39] Home Dept, Jails, file no. 104/35, 1935. They were convicted in the Kakori Conspiracy Case (1925–7) and played a prominent role in protests in the Naini Central Prison in 1929.

[40] This is a quote by Rudyard Kipling.

[41] Leonard A. Gordon, *Bengal: The Nationalist Movement, 1876–1940* (New Delhi: Manohar, 1979), p. 1118. He was arrested in May 1908 for his revolutionary activities. C. R. Das defended him in the Alipore Bomb Case.

asleep in ignorance, he came to a place of meditation full of holy men and found their company wearisome; when he awoke, God took him to a prison and turned it into a place of meditation and His testing ground.[42] Long attuned to rebellion, to Savarkar the atmosphere of the Cellular Jail in Andaman suggested the possibility of a flaming 'revolt'. However, he looked upon the jail sentence as an opportunity to serve under His Banner. Early in the morning and late in the evening, he used to pass insensibly into a sweet sound sleep after trying a bit of *pranayam*.[43]

Jailgoing became the most sublime of tasks. Thus, Aurobindo Ghose reacted to the arrest of Bipin Chandra Pal (1858–1923), writer–orator, and commended his 'manly, straightforward and conscientious stand for the right as he understood it'. Comforted by Pal coming out of prison with his power and influence doubled, he expected posterity to judge between him and the petty tribunal that treated the actions prompted by his 'honourable scruples' as crimes.[44] Bhagat Singh (1907–1931), who threw a bomb into the Central Legislative Assembly in Delhi on 8 April 1929, had other ideas. He imagined revolution as the inalienable right of mankind and freedom as everybody's birthright.[45] While officials fiddled over his deathbed, Punjab's towns and villages resounded with innumerable songs about his heroism.[46] In much the same vein, martyrdom became a spiritual condition and its attainment the loftiest of all goals.[47] Hence, Lajpat Rai's death, in the course of the agitation against the Simon Commission, led to

[42] Sri Aurobindo, *Tales of Prison Life* (Puducherry: Sri Aurobindo Ashram, 2012, second impression).

[43] Dhananjay Keer, *Veer Savarkar* (Bombay: Popular Prakashan, 1966), p. 112.

[44] *Bande Mataram*, 12 September 1907; Sri Aurobindo, *Bande Mataram* (Pondicherry: Sri Aurobindo Ashram , 1973), pp. 531–2.

[45] Bhagat Singh, *The Jail Notebook and Other Writings*, introduced and edited by Chaman Lal (Delhi: Leftword, 2007).

[46] Home Dept, Political, file no. 201, part XX, 1922; Executive Council Office, file no. 148, 1942; Home Dept, Jails, file no. 7/104, 1933; Home Dept, Political, file no. 44/76, 1934; and Home Dept, Jails, file no. 54, 1935.

[47] To Padmaja and Leilamani Naidu, 2 May 1932, in Makarand Paranjape (ed.), *Sarojini Naidu: Selected Letters, 1890s to 1940s* (Delhi: Kali for Women, 1996), p. 269.

fire and fury in the public arena.[48] It was avenged by the Revolutionary Socialist Republican Army. Again, Bengal extolled Jatindranath Das (1904–1929) and Subhas Chandra Bose (1897–1945), 'the liberator on a white horse, a rather incongruous Joan of Arc'.[49] He had been imprisoned from 1924 to 1927, and then again in 1930. Sympathy, honour, and accolades are what he got for his persecution.

This book does not trace the long and arduous path to freedom. I have instead focused on political prisoners who aimed to illuminate and enrich the world with their deeds, and others who ascribed, as Aurobindo Ghose did, both their release from prison and their renewed activity to divine power. Yet, 'even the heroes and heroines and the faith that moved them have been downgraded as sentiments of little value', writes Chandralekha Mehta, daughter of Vijaya Lakshmi Pandit (Swarup Nehru).[50] They find a place in my narrative. I discuss their life stories, about which so little has appeared in print, and link them to the political stir from the 1920s onwards. In all this, Gandhi's radiant figure stands out against the dark background of British rule.

[48] At the time of the arrival of the Simon Commission in February 1927, leaders burned the effigies of Lord Birkenhead (1872–1930), the Secretary of State for India, and Ramsay MacDonald (1866–1937), author of the Communal Award. For reactions to Lajpat Rai's martyrdom, see Jawaharlal Nehru, *An Autobiography* (London: Allen & Unwin, 1936), p. 174, and Aruna Asaf Ali, *Fragments from the Past: Select Writings and Speeches* (New Delhi: Patriot Publishers, 1989), p. 101. A Calcutta newspaper combined its eulogy with fear: 'At the very moment when Lajpat Rai was sentenced to 2 years' imprisonment, it became clear that the frantic dance started by the ruling Power, in harmony with the tune of India's awakening, has now turned into a death-dance. This dance has now become transformed into a death-dance' (*Banglar Katha*, 24 March 1922, *Report on Indian Newspapers and Periodicals in Bengal*, week ending 1 April 1922, in *Indian Newspaper Reports c. 1868–1942*, from the British Library, London, microfilm, part 1: Bengal, 1874–1903 [hereafter *Report*, Bengal]).

[49] R. P. Noronha, *A Tale Told by an Idiot* (New Delhi: Vikas Publishing House, 1976), p. 17; K. N. Panikkar (ed.), *Towards Freedom: Documents on the Movement for Independence in India*, 1940 (New Delhi: Indian Council of Historical Research [ICHR] and Oxford University Press, 2009), part 1, p. 344.

[50] Chandralekha Mehta, *Freedom's Child: Growing Up during Satyagraha* (UK: Penguin Books, 2008), p. xxi.

Why did people traverse the jail road when they could have achieved personal glory and advancement by taking a less hazardous route? What encouraged their fraternal attachment and their lifelong striving? Why did the young Gandhi forsake his European clothing and adopt the loincloth? What led Motilal Nehru (1861–1931) and his son Jawaharlal Nehru to chasten life and character by adopting the discipline of self-abnegation? Why did the Ali brothers (Shaukat and Mohamed) give up European attire to wear crescent moons on their grey caps and the *Khuddam-e Kaaba* (Servants of Kaaba) badges? News spread far and wide that the once-fashionably dressed Shaukat Ali (1873–1938) had taken to wearing a loose, long green coat of peculiar cut, and that his shaggy beard symbolized his protest against Europe and Christendom.[51] Why did they come out of jail just as brave as they went in?[52] Why did Mazharul Haq (1866–1930), who was with Gandhi in England and returned to India by the same boat in 1891, give up his *chhota peg*, wear a beard, and abandon his palatial bungalow to live in a *kuchcha* house near the Ganga at Digha Ghat?[53] Bihar's leading barrister 'grew as fond of the ascetic life as he was of princely life', stated Gandhi. His wife, a member of Bombay's Tyabji family, offered to him her choicest four bangles made of pearls and rubies. The Mahatma was overwhelmed with joy when she produced the bangles and thanked God that He had brought him in touch with the Tyabji family.[54]

Why did Chitta Ranjan Das (1870–1925) give up his princely lifestyle? Was such the agony of servitude? Did he give up his individual freedom for a common, national, freedom? Finally, what does one make of Khan Abdul Ghaffar Khan's (1890–1988) fetters, grinding

[51] Mohamed Ali, *My Life—A Fragment: An Autobiographical Sketch of Maulana Mohamed Ali*, edited and annotated by Mushirul Hasan (New Delhi: Manohar, 1999), p. 88; Mohamed Ali to F. S.A. Slocock, 29 January 1917, in *Mohamed Ali in Indian Politics: Select Writings, 1920–23*, vol. 2, edited by Mushirul Hasan (New Delhi: Atlantic Publishers, 1983), pp. 13–14; and A. M. Dariabadi, *Insha-e Majid* (Calcutta, 1991), p. 479.

[52] Home Dept., Political, file no. 303, 1921.

[53] Syed Mahmud, 'Looking Back', in *1921 Movement Reminescences* (New Delhi: Publications Division, Ministry of Information and Broadcasting, Government of India, 1971), p. 143.

[54] *CWMG*, vol. XXII, p. 54.

prison labour, and solitary confinement? My intention in this book is to indicate the direction in which the reader must search for solutions to the very complex problems of the Anglo-Indian encounter.

I hint at another crucial debate. For the most part, political prisoners were like a red rag to the bull. A mere mention of them invited the risk of instant loss of attention and audience. But alternative currents of thought on the political existed as well.[55] For instance, the colonial legal lexicon that defined all political activities as 'sedition' was aptly contested by, among others, the Marxists who reasoned that it was no offence to violate the colonial law because it benefited British capital and Indian owners of large property.[56] I try to confront such assertions, look at the change of tone and emphasis, and set out, in a quick historical survey, how they came to be produced.

'If my country can do without me, I can do without her. The world is large enough.' This is Hugo Grotius (1583–1645), a jurist in the Dutch Republic who escaped from imprisonment.[57] Yet his sentiments and personal fate must not lead us to believe in this being either the outlook or the fate of Indian prisoners. Three facts changed from the last quarter of the nineteenth century: the emergence of colonialism with its own decrees, many of which were formulated in the light of the experience of the 1857 revolt; the clash of ideologies, which the Indian National Congress (INC), founded in December 1885, exemplified and that were linked to notions of power and authority; and the social and cultural resurgence, starting with the Brahmo Samaj Movement in Bengal, which produced the encounter with the West. I endeavour to evaluate these interconnections without losing sight of the regime of institutional segregation, the modes of control, as well as the resentment they bred.

Studies and Interpretations

The prisoner lay on the bare floor of his seven foot by eight foot death cell, gazing intensely at the ceiling as if trying to pierce through its concrete solidity to the vast canopy of the sky beyond. He had a feeling he

[55] Note by W. S. Marris, 19 October 1919, Home Dept, Political, Proceedings, April 1921, file nos 32–340.

[56] Suchetana Chattopadhyay, *An Early Communist: Muzaffar Ahmad in Calcutta, 1913–1929* (New Delhi: Tulika Books, 2011), p. 241.

[57] Franz L. Neumann, 'The Intelligentsia in Exile', in *Critical Sociology*, edited by Paul Connerton (New York: Penguin Books, 1976), p. 423.

could see the thin, white layer of cloud lined against its blue immensity. He lay like that for almost an hour, intent and motionless.[58]

Eric Hobsbawm (1917–2012) argued long ago that criminality is a form of protest, and banditry is its most common form in class-divided agrarian societies. Social scientists have have studied the situation in India to build on this argument to examine colonial notions of law and justice as they applied to criminality, and utilized, moreover, ethnographic literature to decipher the meanings behind criminal tribes and classes and dispute their representation as habitual offenders.

Earlier, scholars like Donald Clemmer and Gresham Sykes, to mention just a few, gave birth to ethnographic prison sociology as a discipline[59] and connected long durations in prison to depression and changes in brain physiology, all of which could make inmates of a prison malleable, sensitive, and vulnerable to the influence of those controlling the environment. In recent decades, some others have analysed the jail regime and its linkages with law, notions of criminality, and principles of justice, and drawn parallels between Britain and its colonies, both in the conceptualization of the 'criminal classes' and in the management of prisoners. Satadru Sen turns to the Andaman Islands, while Anderson delineates the biological and cultural interpretations, and the use of the

[58] Fakhar Zaman, *The Prisoner: A Novel*, translated from Punjabi by Khalid Hasan (Lahore: Book Traders, 1994), p. 7.

[59] The founding of ethnographic prison sociology as a discipline, from which most of the meaningful knowledge of prison life and culture stems, is commonly credited to two key texts: Donald Clemmer's *The Prison Community*, published in 1940 and republished in 1958; and Gresham Sykes' *The Society of Captives*, also published in 1958. Clemmer's text, based on his study of 2,400 convicts over three years propagated the notion of the existence of a distinct inmate culture and society with values and norms antithetical to both the prison authority and the wider society. In this world, for Clemmer, these values, formalized as the 'inmate code', provided behavioural precepts that united prisoners and fostered antagonism to prison officers and the prison institution as a whole. He termed the process whereby inmates acquired this set of values and behavioural guidelines as they adapted to prison life 'prisonization', defined as the 'taking on, in greater or lesser degree, the folkways, mores, customs and general culture of the penitentiary'. However, while Clemmer argued that all prisoners experienced some degree of prisonization, this was not a uniform process and factors such as the extent

criminals' bodies in the creation of racial hierarchies that are based on physical attributes.[60] Radhika Singha has explored the emergence of colonial criminal law, discussed in its light the *thugee* and dacoity operations, and deciphered the language of lawmakers and reformers. She shows a perceptive understanding of their intent. Her study of changes in penal policy is instructive. On this score the evidence she marshals is undeniably compelling.[61] So is the broad outline of the change in perspective.

Another, and wider, application of the earlier writings on colonialism is Elizabeth Kolsky's study of 'white violence' and the Code of Criminal Procedure that gave to all British subjects the same privileges and protections regardless of their occupation or class background. The law thus provided 'non-official' British residents in India immunity from civil and criminal prosecution. Through such preferential treatment the 'law defined and defended what in social reality were unstable and porous boundaries, thereby making fuzzy distinctions between the colonized and the colonizer into something that was more black and white'. The author also traces the tension between British settlers in India, who were not connected to the East India Company (before 1857) or to the British Crown thereafter, and the official British or company establishment, exemplified by the debate surrounding the Ilbert Bill,[62] and the role played by race in the construction of the late nineteenth-century judicial system in India.[63]

Taylor C. Sherman opens a new window on the 'coercive network' to recognize the value of interconnected institutions, laws, and practices

---

to which a prisoner involved himself in primary group relations in the prison and the degree to which he identified with the external society, all had a considerable impact.

[60] Clare Anderson, *Legible Bodies: Race, Criminality and Colonialism in South Asia* (Oxford: Berg, 2004); Satadru Sen, *Savagery and Colonialism in the Indian Ocean: Power, Pleasure and the Andaman Islanders* (London: Routledge, 2012) and *Disciplining Punishment: Colonialism and Convict Society in the Andaman Islands* (New Delhi: Oxford University Press, 2000).

[61] Radhika Singha, *A Despotism of Law: Crime and Justice in Early Colonial India* (New Delhi: Oxford University Press, 1998).

[62] A bill introduced in 1883 by Lord Ripon to allow Indian judges and magistrates the jurisdiction to try British offenders in criminal cases at the district level—something that was not permitted at the time.

[63] Elizabeth Kolsky, *Colonial Justice in British India: White Violence and the Rule of Law* (Cambridge: Cambridge University Press, 2010), p. 230.

that constituted the state's coercive repertoire. With the focus on some interlinked studies, such as the Punjab disturbance of 1919, he turns his gaze to the increasing diversity of penal practices, the unpredictability and contingency of coercive practices, the nature of state violence, the inconsistency of coercive policies, and their patchy implementation. There are insights into punishment and its essentially spectacular purposes that transformed penal practices into political spectacle.[64]

In *Colonizing the Body* and other major researches, which every now and then rely upon the findings of anthropological excursions, David Arnold points to crime and politics being inseparable from the colonial regime: serious crime implicitly defied state authority and turned out to be, possibly, a prelude to rebellion; political resistance took the form of 'crime' or was the likely occasion for it. The resources and skills developed in combating the one were freely employed in defeating the other.[65]

Ujjwal Kumar Singh in *Political Prisoners in India* illuminates 'the permanence and ruptures in the nature of penal sanctions imposed by the state against its antagonists in colonial and independent India.'[66] He links the prison with the imposing framework of disciplining and strategies of power, and points to jail rules serving to establish the superiority and inviolability of imperial power.[67] Of great consequence is his argument that free India's penal strategies overlooked legality and constitutionalism, which were integral to the critique of colonial structures. The Nehruvian era itself began with state coercion in Telangana and nearly stretched to the eruption of the Naxalite movement, which derived its name from the village Naxalbari in Bengal that became famous for being the site of a Maoist peasant uprising in 1967. This period in history was also witness to institutional structures wielding authority, the techniques of power, and the disciplinary management of the population.[68]

Rani Dhavan Shankardass questions the exercise of criminal punishment by the state carried out within the framework of a

[64] Taylor C. Sherman, *State Violence and Punishment in India* (London: Routledge, 2010).

[65] David Arnold, *Police Power and Colonial Rule: Madras, 1859–1947* (Oxford: Oxford University Press, 1986), p. 3.

[66] Ujjwal Kumar Singh, *Political Prisoners in India* (New Delhi: Oxford University Press, 1998).

[67] U.K. Singh, *Political Prisoners in India*, p. 5.

[68] U.K. Singh, *Political Prisoners in India*, p. 206.

legal system. The prison is, in her frame, a suitable focal point for determining punishment because it houses those who are the subjects of punishment. 'It is,' she writes, 'the location from which policymakers have been able to reinforce the widely held liberal–legalistic view that prison is the punishment system par excellence from amongst many punishment forms that those in authority have meted out to offenders.'[69] In her second major book, Shankardass discusses the *legalities* that determined prisoners' guilt (or in other words, the realities of the before and after relating to them). Women prisoners are a 'special category' that required a more than exclusive focus.[70]

Finally, beyond all these writings in various spheres, which are organically interdependent because they express a single set of conceptions, we must remember the vast area of oral discussion that the study of prisons involves. Herein, indeed, we may see the cause, as well as the content, of the supportive and illustrative evidence. From another point of view, I have made use of the literary genre that embraces the political and non-political aspects of my story. The creative writings of many political prisoners have not been discussed in any work before. The creative writings, in fact, weave numberless threads into a single design. As for political and biographical details, I have stressed on relationships and conveyed to the reader an appreciation of the role of personal affiliations and attachments.[71]

If we consider our subject chronologically, we find that it falls into three distinct periods: the beginning of the jail regimentation after the Wahhabi conspiracy; the post-1857 phase, when the institutionalization of the jail regime took place; and the Gandhian era, which brought to the fore a special category of 'political prisoners' and the steady flow of prisoners into British jails. On the eve of the transfer of power governmental activity was reduced to the bare minimum.

[69] Rani Dhavan Shankardass, *Punishment and the Prison: Indian and International Perspectives* (New Delhi: Sage Publications, 2000), p. 19.

[70] Shankardass, *Of Women 'Inside'*, p. 279.

[71] Mushirul Hasan, *Faith and Freedom: Gandhi in History* (New Delhi: Niyogi Books, 2013).

2. 'Sunlight on a Broken Column'

To exchange the common herding of prisoners of all descriptions for careful classification, to substitute a strict and useful industry for idleness, or for a light and ill-directed labour to provide that the life which is irksome should not also be unhealthy, and that the congregation of the vicious should not be a school of vice, are all objects, for the first approach to which buildings must be erected, machinery formed, and establishments, and checks upon establishments contrived, and in the perfect attainment and maintenance of which great disappointment has, after every effort and expense, in many countries ensued.[1]

Prisons existed in the thirteenth century without the paraphernalia of jailors, superintendents, and warders. As a disgraced courtier, Ziauddin Barani suffered the ignominy of a jail sentence for plotting the overthrow of his contemporary Tughlaq ruler, Mohamed bin Tughlaq. The

---

[1] *Report of the Committee on Prison Discipline to the Governor General of India in Council* (London: Baptist Mission Press, 1838), p. 1.

Mughal system of justice dealt with crime, as it was understood then; the emperor and his nobles punished enemies or *baghis* (rebels) by consigning them to the dungeon under the charge of an officer within the confines of forts and palaces, or had them sent away to a far-off land. Emperor Jahangir (1569–1627) ordered Vir Singh Deo, a Bundela chief and the ruler of Orchha, now in Madhya Pradesh, to imprison his nephew in the Gwalior fort.[2] He also put Guru Hargobind in the Gwalior Jail for three years from 1609 to 1612. Aurangzeb (1618–1707) had his brother Murad Baksh beheaded on 4 December 1661, and, as a final indignity, had him buried in the Traitors' Cemetery reserved for state prisoners in the Gwalior Fort. Francois Bernier (1625–1688), the French physician who travelled to India, wrote: 'After having consigned Morad-Bakche to Gwalior, he went to Dehli, where he began in good earnest … to assume all the acts, and exercise all the prerogatives, of a legitimate King.'[3] J. B. Tavernier (1605–1689), a French gem merchant, confirmed that the Mughals sent princes and nobles for 'safe custody' to Gwalior. Francois Bernier mentioned that they were doused with infusion of opium.[4] Father Monserrate, a Jesuit priest from Portugal who arrived at Akbar's court in 1580, said that the prisoners would 'rot away in chains and filth.'[5] Edward S. Holden characteristically concluded that there was 'something not totally unfamiliar in this Orientalist nature freely displayed under strange and outlandish conditions.'[6]

An important step in British India was codification of prison laws, of which the Indian Penal Code is an example. It was in the first

[2] Henry Beveridge (ed.) and Alexander Roger (trans.), *Tuzuk-i Jahangiri*, vol. 1 (Delhi: Munshiram Manoharlal, 1968), p. 111.

[3] Francois Bernier, *Travels in the Mogul Empire, 1656–1668*, translated by A. Constable, revised by V. A. Smith (Oxford: Oxford University Press, 1934), p. 85.

[4] Jean-Baptiste Tavernier, *Travels in India*, vol. 1, translated by V. Ball, edited by William Crooke (New Delhi: Oriental Books Reprint Corp., reprint, 1977), p. 52. Edward Terry, in *Travellers' India*, edited by H. K. Kaul (New Delhi: Oriental Books Reprint Corp. 1977), p. 213.

[5] *The Commentary of Father Monserrate on His Journey to the Court of Akbar*, translated from the original Latin by J. S. Hoyland, annotated by S. N. Banerjee (London: Humphrey Milford, Oxford University Press, 1922), p. 211.

[6] Edward S. Holden, *The Mughal Emperors of Hindustan* (London: Archibald Constable & Co. 1893), p. 131.

instance drafted by the Indian Law Commission appointed under the Charter Act of 1833. The Code became law in 1860, and, supplemented by the Code of Criminal Procedure, introduced some degree of uniformity in the administration of criminal justice. Codification was ultimately extended to practically every branch of administration in the form of manuals encompassing the law on the subject as well as rules and regulations, for example, on land acquisition, police, jails, registration, stamps, and excise.[7]

The justice and police departments rested on the watchmen, mostly hereditary, under the direction of *tehsildar*s, the collector, and the magistrate. In the Bombay and Madras presidencies, the police system depended chiefly on the country's ancient usages. In fact, the Indian Police Commission (1902–3) pinned its faith in the headmen and the *panchayat*s for disposing of petty cases. It assumed that the criminal law rested on the people, and they would support its provisions once law enforcement improved. So the administrators set for themselves the aim of fostering and maintaining self-reliance and self-help with regard to policing and other matters of local importance. By these means, they hoped to defend the status quo.[8]

In colonial times, prison management was linked to the metropolitan concepts of reform in Western Europe, but it was not so in the 1830s. Following the annexation of Sind in 1843, Charles Napier (1782–1853), the governor, put together a regular police force and generated much data on enforcing 'discipline'. This exercise came in for criticism on the grounds that the mechanism thus evolved would undermine the autonomy of village communities that had survived centuries of change. In the system being envisaged, the powers of village elders and panchayats were to be usurped by the district officer or the police.[9] None

---

[7] This summary is based on L.S.S. O'Malley, *The Indian Civil Service, 1601–1930* (London: John Murray, 1931), pp. 95, 97.

[8] *History of Police Organization in India and Indian Village Police* (University of Calcutta, 1913), p. 46. This was for circulation among teachers and students only.

[9] Romesh Dutt, 'Administration of Justice in India', *India, Ceylon, Straits Settlements, British North Borneo, Hong-Kong* (London: Kegan Paul, 1899), pp. 316, 317; W. H. Sleeman, *Rambles and Recollections of an Indian Official* (London: J. Hatchard and Son, 1844; reprint, 1993), pp. 544–61.

the less, the Police Commission in 1860 stressed discipline as a part of administering the law, and a most important part at that. For that reason, it deployed every argument that applied in 'advanced' countries, and while it recognized the circumstantial differences, it recommended that the measure of benefit to be derived from any improvement in the prison department would be as great in India as in the wealthy and 'enlightened' nations.[10] In Bengal, therefore, jails were treated as a separate department under a non-judicial inspector-general.

Besides sizing up the judicial system, plans were mapped to punish, subjugate, and subordinate the 'recalcitrant' elements. One of the earliest descriptions of their racial/ethnic characteristics is available in the handbooks for the Indian Army in 1894. They grew out of other works and called attention to other writings. Their publication had a special bearing upon subjects that engaged the Army and the administration.[11]

Ethnographers invented an entire category of Criminal Tribes 'to reorder the identity of the offender in a more uniform and standardized way and thus to mark him out more rigorously from the rhythm of society'.[12] There was, thus, on the statute book the Criminal Tribes Act of 1911, under the provisions of which members of such tribes could be concentrated in settlements where they could be subjected to 'adequate supervision' even as they were 'helped' in gaining a livelihood. In the mid-1920s, there were 4,000,000 of 'these troublesome and unattractive people'. It was said of them that the whole structure of their social habits was conceived upon the basis of crime, and that burglary or theft was their hereditary occupation.[13] Thus the Kolis were designated as one of 'the most turbulent and predatory tribes … addicted to highway and house dacoity and robbery, house-breaking and thefts, cattle lifting, thefts of standing crops and field produce'.[14]

[10] *Report of the Committee on Prison Discipline*, p. 72.

[11] Mushirul Hasan (ed.), *Writing India: Colonial Ethnography in the Nineteenth Century* (New Delhi: Oxford University Press, 2012).

[12] Madhurima Sen, *Prisons in Colonial Bengal, 1838–1919* (Kolkata: Thema Books, 2007), p. 14.

[13] Earl of Ronaldshay, *India: A Bird's-Eye View* (London: Constable & Company Ltd., 1924), pp. 203–4.

[14] *Notes on Criminal Classes in the Bombay Presidency* (Bombay: Government Central Press, 1908), p. 103.

Additionally, using anthropometry and fingerprints, prisoners (before their conviction) were given a card that specified their religion, caste, and sect.[15] Modern dactyloscopy, in effect, helped the government register and investigate criminal activity. By 1920, a million and a quarter fingerprint slips or forms were filed at eight provincial police headquarters.[16] Thousands were arrested and sent for trial before a magistrate, charged with petty thefts that really did not call for police interference as a matter of course. 'Our legal definitions of men,' pronounced Bengal's Lieutenant-Governor, 'are too rigid to suit human nature in the East.'[17]

Dactyloscopy, or the method of studying fingerprints to establish identification, was not enough. Prisoners were measured, quantified, and circumscribed into categories.[18] Categories A, B, and C existed beforehand. In this manner, Bihar's Bankipur Jail housed upper-class prisoners; the rest were, in accordance with the categorization, put in Camp Jail.[19] In theory, character, past history, standard of living, nature of offence, social status, and education entitled a prisoner 'A' class categorization, but, in practice, judges downgraded them either to the 'B' or 'C' status.[20] Thus, Vinay's so-called crime in Munshi Premchand's *Rangbhumi* was that he saved a helpless young woman from the clutches of a district officer. The officer brought a lawsuit for theft, and had him jailed. The court was blind; the judge did what the district officer told him to do. Given his self-esteem, Vinay refused to take the bait of escaping from jail. His life, he said, was not so precious to him.[21]

Vinay's example is apt. But there are other cases as well. For example, a mixed group of small farmers, agricultural labourers, and unskilled

---

[15] Home Dept, Police A, Proceedings, December 1900, file nos 57–58.

[16] Douglas G. Browne and Alan Brock, *Fingerprints: Fifty Years of Scientific Crime Detection* (London: George G. Harrap & Co. Ltd, 1953), pp. 86–7.

[17] Bampfylde Fuller, *Studies of Indian Life and Sentiment* (London: John Murray, 1910), p. 285.

[18] U. K. Singh, *Political Prisoners in India*, p. 18.

[19] Rajendra Prasad, *Autobiography* (Delhi: Asia Publishing House, 1957), p. 541.

[20] M. N. Roy, *Fragments of a Prisoner's Diary: Crime and Karma: Cats and Women* (Calcutta: Renaissance Publishers Private Ltd, 1950), p. 20.

[21] Premchand, *Rangbhumi: The Arena of Life*, translated by Christopher King, with an introduction by Alok Rai (New Delhi: Oxford University Press), p. 224.

workers were drawn into 'crime' by their circumstances and not because they had a 'criminal bent of mind'. Jharkhand's tribal and *kisan* organizer, Swami Sahajanand (1889–1950), came across kisans cutting wood, and when they were stopped and then resisted to the point of violence and someone's death, they inevitably became involved in a criminal life. The prisoners he met would not have lost their lands or been caged had they benefited from proper legal advice. On the contrary, almost everyone connected with the legal machinery indulged in fraud and deception and brought into play other dishonest means to dupe them.[22] During the early1920s, jail wardens used the thumb impression of Khilafat volunteers as evidence of their apology.[23] Jawaharlal Nehru came across a young convict overseer whose only 'offence' was that his companions cheated him while playing a game of marbles. They had high words and a fight. Some bricks were hurled and a death occurred.[24]

Managing the Prisoner

The number of prisoners in Bengal and the North Western Provinces (NWP) went up from 40,914 in 1835 to 47,736 in 1842. In Bengal, scarcity of food and a rise in food grain prices increased their number by over 4,000 in 1888–9. In 1890, central and district jails and lock-ups numbering 746 housed 495,820 prisoners. The two penal establishments in the Andaman and Nicobar Islands contained, in 1890–1, a daily average of 11,804 convicts.[25]

Syed Ahmad Khan referred to a jailbreak in Moradabad on 19 May 1857.[26] To prevent such incidents, the British tightened management. An important step in this direction was the building of new jails. So,

[22] Walter Hauser (ed.), *Swami Sahajanand and the Peasants of Jharkhand: A View from 1941* (New Delhi: Manohar, 2005), pp. 109, 167.

[23] *Bangavasi* (Calcutta), 31 December 1922, *Report on Indian Newspapers and Periodicals in Bengal, 1922.*

[24] Prison Diary, 5 June 1930, *SWJN*, vol. 4, p. 359.

[25] W. W. Hunter, *The Indian Empire: Its Peoples, History, and Products* (London: Smith Elder & Co., Indian Reprint, 1973), p. 560.

[26] Sir Syed Ahmad Khan, *History of the Bijnor Rebellion*, translated with notes and introduction by Hafeez Malik and Morris Dembo (Delhi: Idarah-e Adabiyat-e Dehli, 1982), p. 7.

Agra had its first in 1862, followed by Shahjahanpur, Kanpur, and Fatehpur. Renovating old prisons and making them more secure was next on the agenda.[27] Hence Calcutta's Alipore Jail cost the Indian exchequer Rs 10,039,713.2 in 1910.[28] The Nasik and Kanchrapara Jails were built at a cost of Rs 200,000.[29] The Hazaribagh Jail was a financial liability, but it performed the useful purpose of preventing 'sedition' and 'rebellion' among the 'criminals'.[30]

The Great War speeded up the process of internment and imprisonment. Conspiracy cases became frequent, usually resulting in death sentences or life terms. Virendranath Chattopadhyaya (Chatto), brother of Sarojini Naidu (1879–1949), gave up his unedifying middle-class way of life and engaged in revolutionary propaganda in London, Paris, and Berlin, where the Berlin Committee for Indian Independence was established in 1915. He worked closely with Savarkar and Mme Bhikaji Rustom K. R. Cama (1861–1936).[31] The English novelist Somerset Maugham (1874–1965) portrayed him as 'Chandarlal' in his short story 'Giulia Lazzari'.

Various government committees suggested improvements in the management of jails, but the superintendents did not entertain or practise the higher aim of reformation.[32] Instead, they used coercion and severity to make prisons a terror to 'evildoers'. A slight change in their attitudes was forced by the revolutionaries and other militant nationalists, many of whom protested against the treatment meted out to them. The Sedition Committee's Report in 1918 illustrates their panic and hysterical reactions.[33] By that time, the number of

[27] R. Chakrabarti, *Terror, Crime and Punishment*, pp. 108–9.

[28] Madhurima Sen, *Prisons in Colonial Bengal*, pp. 33, 34.

[29] *Dainik Basumati*, 28 January 1922, *Report*, Bengal, week ending 4 February 1922.

[30] Note by J. H. DuBoulay, 16 December 1916, Home Dept, Political A, July 1917, file nos 490–509.

[31] Milton Israel, *Communications and Power: Propaganda and the Press in the Indian Nationalist Struggle, 1920–1947* (Delhi: Oxford University Press, 1994), pp. 262–3.

[32] Kaul, *Travellers' India*, p. 204.

[33] D. K. Lahiri Choudhry, 'Sinews of Panic and the Nerves of Empire: The Imagined State's Entanglement with Information Panic, India c. 1880–1912', *Modern Asian Studies*, vol. 38, no. 4 (2004).

prisoners had risen in certain areas. By 1913, 691 male convicts and 3 women had entered the dark recesses of the Umballa (Ambala) Jail.[34] Following World War I, there occurred a surge in the number of prisoners, particularly as a result of the April 1919 disturbances and the convictions in Martial Law cases. Across the Punjab, a 21.4 per cent increase in jail population took place over the previous year.[35] Lahore's jail population doubled during the Rowlatt Satyagraha. After a decade or so, the numbers rose to over 2,500 and, on a single day in 1931, to 2,999, due to the chaos created by a regional formation, the Ahrars,[36] against the Maharaja of Kashmir. Hence Punjab budgeted for a new jail for 1,500 prisoners at Multan, two subsidiary jails to replace the condemned 'Serial' jails in Gujarat and Kasur respectively, and one for 600 adolescents at Lahore. Three new jails were built between 1927 and 1933 to keep prisoners in 'safer' places.[37]

An increase in jail population also took place in the late 1920s and early 1930s.[38] Many of the 'new' prisoners were housed in the Detention Camp at Deoli, an ancient small town located 50 to 60 kilometres from Rajasthan's Kota district, in the wilderness of the desert. Set up to bring in the 'rebels' of 1857, it had just barracks and rooms. Helping the British guards were Nepalese and Garhwali soldiers. In 1936, when the new barracks and rooms were constructed, the administration tightened security, and, at the end of 1940, brought by train a number of detainees from the Agra Central Jail to Kota , and then by bus into Deoli. This included Z. A. Ahmed, 'a great intellectual, mass leader and orator'.[39] He wrote:

[34] Archibald B. Spens, *A Winter in India: Light Impressions of Its Cities, Peoples and Customs* (London: Stanley Paul & Co., 1913), p. 57.

[35] *Report on the Administration of the Punjab and Its Dependencies for 1919–20* (Lahore: Govt. Printing Press, 1921), p. 44.

[36] Literally 'free'; 'free men'. They supported the Congress during Civil Disobedience.

[37] Home Dept, Political, file no. 14/12, 1931. Colonel F. A. Barker, *The Modern Prison System* (London: Macmillan and Co. Ltd, 1944).

[38] *Administration Report of the Jails of the North West Frontier Province, 1928* (Calcutta: Central Publication Branch, 1928), p. 1.

[39] Mohit Sen, *An Autobiography* (New Delhi: National Book Trust, 2007, abridged edition), p. 30.

Deoli Camp was the special prison of the Central Government. Into it were brought only those thought to be the most dangerous opponents of British Rule. The security arrangements were also exceptionally severe. The entire prison was surrounded by iron barbed wire. In places, current had also been passed through this wire, so that those attempting escape would die on just touching it. Inside the camp itself, at the distance of every two or three hundred steps were tall wooden watch towers (observation platforms) on which armed soldiers used to be present twenty four hours, keeping a strict vigil on all the happenings in the jail. In addition to this, numerous armed soldiers used to be alert inside and outside the prison. In totality, to break the prison's security system and escape was impossible.[40]

The Camp housed 66 'A' class communists, 3 socialists, 11 prisoners from the Revolutionary Socialist Party (RSP), and 5 from the Hindustani Socialist Republican Army. Similarly, it had 90 'B' class prisoners, of which 72 were fellow-travellers. In this manner, they dominated both categories to become a full-fledged communist prison in 1938. Later, they organized themselves into two camps. In one of them S. A. Dange (1899–1991) and B. T. Ranadive (1904–1990) lectured on Marxism. They were among the founders of the Communist Party of India (CPI). As a result of their initiative, the communist inmates were better informed in the grammar of Marxian politics, and their example attracted others to the party. The jail became the veritable centre of Marxist education.[41]

If the initiation of people into the communist or socialist ways of life was a headache for the government, the increase in the numbers of political prisoners was a bigger headache. The answer UP came up with was to classify security prisoners into grades I, II, and III; their Punjabi counterparts classified them into two grades. This system of classification of prisoners in UP and Punjab included 'state prisoners' from after May 1918. The X types were 'more dangerous'; the Y's, mostly undertrials, were less so.[42] Often, these categories led

[40] Z. A. Ahmed, *Mere Jiwan ki Kutch Yadain*, in Hindi (New Delhi: National Book Trust, 2010).

[41] Gargi Chakravarty, *P. C. Joshi: A Biography* (New Delhi: National Book Trust, 2007), p. 9.

[42] Home Dept, Political, Proceedings, file no. 5, May 1907.

enumerators and ethnographers to view the subcontinent through the prism of caste, community, language, and tribe, and conclude that the 'political' category diverged with notions of criminal jurisprudence.[43] There is no denying 'offences of a political character' which the Extradition Act of 1870 itself made mention of, and the fact that Winston Churchill (1874–1965), Home Secretary, introduced a new rule to mitigate the more degrading conditions of prison for offenders whose crimes did not imply moral turpitude. But Delhi expressed no enthusiasm for it. It even dilly-dallied in letting the Secretary of State know the precise figures of those imprisoned or detained for political offences. This was despite George Nathaniel Curzon, the Viceroy (1899–1905), describing the Government of India as a subordinate branch of the Secretary of State.

The Sedition Committee Report exemplified the government's reluctance to initiate reforms that everybody expected during the War and for which the Congress and the Muslim League had submitted their petitions.[44] Also, the government refused to enter into dialogue, notably with the Congress, thereby showing its paranoia over 'revolutionary activities'. Hence, when somebody in Bihar's Hazaribagh Jail asked for a college textbook of economics entitled *Textbook of Political Economy*, his request was turned down because the word 'political' figured in the title. A far more serious instance is that of Fazl-e Ilahi of Lahore who faced rigorous imprisonment in August 1926 because J. H. Thompson, Peshawar's Additional District Magistrate, found on him books and pamphlets of an 'advanced description' of Political Science and Economics.[45] In other cases, political news items were cut out with scissors or inked out heavily. When asked why the ordinary prisoners were not subjected to the same 'raids', the reply was, 'You guys covertly get political literature. We want to confiscate that.'[46] In many more cases, visitors to the jail were not allowed to discuss politics. They sat in jail exchanging pleasantries while an official listened in.

[43] Home Dept, Political, Jails, file no. 80, 1930; Home Dept, Political, Jails, file no. 22/70, 1945.

[44] Mushirul Hasan, *Nationalism and Communal Politics in India, 1885–1930* (Delhi: Manohar, 1985).

[45] Home Dept, Foreign & Political, file no. 668-F, 1927.

[46] Home Dept, Political, April 1921, file nos 322–40.

Whenever a political movement erupted, the superintendent dealt with the inmates sternly.

The government turned down demands for preferential treatment of political prisoners, though it accepted an intermediate form of retribution without the benefit of the milder form of sentence being confined exclusively to the convicted. As a result, simple imprisonment was split into two classes, one without labour and the other with a liability to light labour. Ibrahim Rahimtoola (1912–1991), a Bombay legislator who had chaired Gandhi's lecture on 'Indentured Indian Labour' on 30 October 1917, contended that persons actuated by patriotic feelings were a class by themselves and could not be subjected to the same form of penalty. Rahimtoola advised caution and discretion in the light of Mahomed Fakir's and Hamid Ahmed's refusal to either furnish security or commit that they would not make speeches on the Khilafat.[47] Newspapers celebrated their patriotism, and published angry comments when their 'heroes' were put in jail for another term.[48]

Such sentences varied according to the circumstances and nature of an offence, and the offender's status.[49] So did the ambiguities in grading prisoners. The accused in the Lahore Conspiracy Case were pigeonholed into two classes: (a) persons previously convicted and serving a sentence under the Indian Penal Code, and (b) persons accused but not under sentence. The latter were undertrials; they could ask for food from outside or settle for the everyday jail diet, that is, boiled rice. They were given only an earthen pot, which was passed on to the next prisoner.[50] Convicts not labelled special

[47] Among Sunni Muslims, who formed an overwhelming majority of the Muslim population, the Sultan of Turkey was the *Amir al-Mu'minin* (Commander of the Faithful) and the protector of the Holy Places. The *Khilafat*, which in 1517 was transferred to Salim I of the House of Ottoman, was the viceroyalty of the Prophet of Islam, ordained by divine law for the perpetuation of Islam and the continued observance of its *sharia* (Islamic law). The *khalifa*, derived from the word *khalafa* (to leave behind), was both the religious head of the Sunnis as well as the ruler of an independent kingdom.

[48] Home Dept, Political, April 1921, file nos 322–40.

[49] Home Dept, Political, file no. 333, 1930.

[50] Ayub Mirza, *A Legendary Communist: Amir Haider Khan* (Azamabad: Prajasaki Book House, 2012), p. 208.

prisoners were entitled only to the run-of-the-mill diet.[51] Instead of attending to widespread graft and corruption, overcrowded jails, insanitary conditions, and the atrocious food,[52] a superintendent built a mosque and a temple in Jabalpur's Central Jail, assigned a *maulvi* and a *pundit* to minister to the religious requirements of the inmates, and declared holidays on religious occasions.[53] In this way, the prison was turned, in the words of Geffray Mynshul, into a grave to bury men alive. It was a microcosmos, a little world of woe, a map of misery.[54]

It had to be so. The gaols of the state system were similar to those of the previous decades and from one region to the other, but there was no consensus on either the outward appearance or direction of the Centre's involvement. As a result, the Centre could not overcome, in the dialectic between resistance and authoritarianism, its own contradictions. Whenever the provinces stepped in to adopt correc- tive measures, they found their proposals hanging in mid-air. A civil servant pointed out: 'Ceteris paribus, a bureaucratic administration, however efficient, does not appeal to the hearts of men—it is far too impersonal.'[55] Aurobindo Ghose and others made much of the govern- ment's indecision, lack of pragmatism, and perplexity. We see evidence

---

[51] The Delhi district jail was operated for administrative convenience as a unit of the Punjab prison system. Its prisoners were not sent to UP.

[52] *Report*, Bengal, week ending 22 June 1889. One of them in Madras made 40,000 rupees in thirteen years by unfair means. *Report*, Bengal, week ending 20 April 1899; *Sanjivani*, 28 June 1890; *Report*, Bengal, week ending 5 July 1890; 8 August 1908, *Selections from the Native Newspapers*, published in the United Provinces (hereafter *Selections*, UP), 1908; *Rehbar* (Moradabad), *Selections*, UP, week ending 24 September 1909; *Hindustani* (Lucknow), 1 March 1909; *Selections*, UP, week ending 6 March 1909; *Mashriq* (Gorakhpur), 4 October 1910, week ending 7 October 1910; *Rehbar* (Moradabad), *Selections*, UP, week ending 24 September 1909; *Naiyar-e Azad*, 12 September 1906, *Selections*, week ending 15 September 1906; *Advocate*, 15 August 1906, *Selections*, week ending 17 August 1906.

[53] *Akhbar-e Imamia* (Lucknow), 20 August 1910, *Selections*, UP, week ending 2 September 1910.

[54] 20 August 1942, Vijaya Lakshmi Pandit, *Prison Days* (Calcutta: The Signet Press, 1945), p. 30.

[55] Noronha, *A Tale Told by an Idiot*, p. 8.

of this in what the inmates were offered to eat and wear. Dress and food were instruments of subjugation, and they were not to be negotiated with anyone. What they had was what they deserved.

Dress and Diet

Bernard Cohn has offered a perspective on various ways in which clothes have been part of the history of colonialism. Specialists have turned to clothing as a bodily marker for constructing social, cultural, and racial identities, and for separating Indians from free Europeans.[56] When a group of Congressmen, socialists, and communists were brought to Deoli in early 1940 and told to take off their 'political uniform', including the Gandhi cap, Z. A. Ahmed stepped forward and said, 'If we deposit our caps in the office, what will we wear?' The authorities offered small turbans. To this, Ahmed replied, 'We are political workers, and if we are not to wear our uniform, how can we wear your turbans? This is not acceptable to us; we shall continue to wear our own caps.' A compromise was reached; accordingly, prisoners were given white caps but were allowed to wear the Gandhi cap, the symbolic focus of the British–Indian conflict and hence offensive to British sensibilities.[57] The Chief Justice of the Bombay High Court directed all judges under his jurisdiction to bar pleaders from wearing the Gandhi cap; defying his order was construed as contempt of court.[58] In Guntur (a part of present-day Andhra Pradesh which was then part of the Madras Presidency), many people were sent to jail for defying the magisterial ban on the Gandhi cap. But they continued to adhere to the conviction that the Gandhi cap was a symbol of the fight against caste and untouchability; it signified, moreover, comradeship of men and women and, above all, non-violence as a way of life.[59]

This settled, a standardized prison uniform, crudely cut, untidy and ill-fitting, separated the convicts along racial lines, with four distinct

[56] Bernard S. Cohn, *Colonialism and Its Forms of Knowledge: The British in India* (Delhi: Oxford University Press, 1997).
[57] Z. A. Ahmed, *Mere Jiwan ki Kutch Yadain*.
[58] Cohn, *Colonialism and Its Forms of Knowledge*, p. 149.
[59] C. Mehta, *Freedom's Child*, p. xxii.

colours—blue, white, red, and yellow—assigned to each class.[60] In Great Britain, the colour of the clothing depended on the prisoner's classification. For the ordinary male it was red; for the second division, brown; for debtors and 'remand', blue; and for those facing court martial, dark grey. The dress made of coarse cloth was uncomfortable in both summer and winter.

> The dress which is at present worn by prisoners in the jails is unsuited to the people of this country. The *jangyas*, while they do not afford sufficient protection in the cold weather, are positively disagreeable and painful in summer. Instead of *jangyas*, the prisoners should be allowed to put on dhotis made of long cloth. The prisoners now have iron collars round their necks, showing the dates of their imprisonment. This collar should be abolished, and the dates of imprisonment should be shown on small tin tickets to be worn round the arms.[61]

'Today only', reported M. N. Roy on 16 February 1932, 'I got my new uniform (jail clothes).... You could hardly imagine me in it. I feel like being in a monastery—mortifying the sinful flesh. It should have some early Christian influence on me. You can imagine how favourable these conditions are to encourage the weakness. It is unfair to be mortifying the flesh with coarse woollen textures and not have Benedictine and Chartreuse Verte to drink as the jolly old monks used to. I suspect they used to put on silken underwear.'[62]

In 1863, a Committee of the House of Lords declared that 'a diet may be made a just and useful element of penal discipline'. England followed this principle until 1918. That year the diet improved.[63] In India, on the other hand, diet remained an instrument of punishment. As for the diet scales, they were not only strictly regulated but applied to all, regardless of their very different food habits.[64] In 1881,

---

[60] Home Dept, Jails, Proceedings, July 1893, Part B, file no. 9; Anderson, *Legible Bodies* pp. 102, 126; *Rules for the Superintendence and Management of Jails in the Lower Provinces of the Bengal Presidency* (Calcutta: Bengal Secretariat Office, 1864), pp. 18–19.

[61] *Report*, Bengal, week ending July–December 1889.

[62] 16 February 1932, M. N. Roy, *Fragments*, p. 16.

[63] Stephen Hobhouse and Archibald Fenner Brockway, *English Prisons To-day: Being the Report of the Prison System Enquiry Committee*, 1922, pp. 126–7.

[64] *Rules for the Superintendence and Management*, pp. 34–6.

Surgeon-Major T. R. Lewis's new diet scale corresponded to Class II security prisoners in Punjab and Assam, and to Class C convicts.[65] All in all, the diet for prisoners led to a fairly large number of deaths.[66] With life reduced to searching for scraps of food, the obsession with food replaced all feelings and desires.[67] Class C prisoners were served foul-smelling *lapsi*, black rice; *bajra* or *jowar rotis*; pumpkin or radish or often rotten spinach; *dal* every alternate day plus a quarter pound of jaggery or *gur* on Sundays. Aurobindo Ghose's solitary cell was nine feet by five feet; it had no windows, in front stood strong iron bars. He could bear this appointed abode, but not the appalling food that was served day in and day out. Trailokya Nath Chakraborty or Maharaj ate *kali* dal or pulses all the 6 days of a week. The poet in him burst out: *Jelar beta boro khachwar; Khete daye dhan ar pathhar* (The jailor is very wicked. He serves us paddy and stones to eat).[68] Food in Dacca Jail consisted of coarse rice and minute quantities of oil and salt. The curry was made of jute leaves, *pnui sak*, and stalks of pot-herb called *dengo*.[69] The fare in Visapur Jail was a bowl of jowar gruel; at 12 noon, 2 *chapattis* and a cup of thick dal; at 3.30 p.m., 2 chapattis, which were full of dirt and grit, and a cupful of vegetables. Both the dal and vegetables were heavily spiced with chillies and garlic. Invariably, they caused stomach

[65] Captain D. McKay, *Scientific Memoirs by Officers of the Medical and Sanitary Department: Bengal Jail Dietaries* (Calcutta, 1910), p. 3.

[66] *Samachar*, 28 August 1889, *Report*, Bengal, week ending 7 September 1889.

[67] A Bengali newspaper remarked: 'If scarcity can do such mischief, does it not behove the Government to take proper measures for its relief where it prevails? If people, despairing of getting a mouthful of rice by honest means, commit crimes with the object of being admitted into a jail, and die there in numbers for want of proper care on the part of the jail authorities, certainly the blame rests with the Government, and Government is answerable to man and God alike for its indulgence' (*Saraswat Patra*, 12 July 1890, *Report*, Bengal, week ending 19 July 1890).

[68] Trailokya Nath Chakraborty, *Thirty Years in Prison: Sensational Confessions of a Revolutionary* (Calcutta: Alpha-Beta Publications, 1963), p. 111.

[69] *Dacca Prakash*, 29 September 1889, *Report*, Bengal, week ending 5 October 1889.

ailments.[70] In 1934, the authorities worked out on the following scale: rice 12 *chatak*; salt 1/2 *chatak*; dal 2/2 *chatak*; vegetables 4; mustard oil 5/16; condiments 1/8; *dahi* 2½ once weekly; tamarind 1/8; *gur* 1/4; onions and potatoes 2½; fish 2½, thrice weekly, whenever available.[71] The diet reflected the otherwise palpably false belief that Indians of all classes thrived equally on the same kind of food. So Rivers Thompson, Bengal's Lieutenant-Governor, shrugged off the criticism that 'respectable' castes and classes were often starved for want of suitable food.[72] But George Campbell (1824–1892), a civil servant, discerned the connection between the ill-health of the Bengali prisoners and the high mortality rate: 'the prisoners were far from healthy; the mortality was far too great, in some jails most excessive.'[73]

Torture and Whip

Two Calcutta newspapers, *Hitavada* and *Dainik Basumati*, took serious note of the public infliction of pain, and of 'stripes' being inflicted on the newly awakened sense of self-respect of the Bengali race.[74] Does this suggest that the Bengalis were cowards? No, they refused to submit to pride and arrogance.[75] The fact is that nobody could hide from the public eye illegal detentions, police firing, whipping, and torture. With the Indian Whipping Act (1864) in place, compassion or remedy for rehabilitation was foreign to official thinking.[76] Thus Surendranath Sinha, Panchanan Chakravarti, and Ram Sunder Singh of Garbeta village in Midnapore were flogged 15 times.[77] Bengal led the way with 364 such cases; UP and Bombay came close behind during Civil

[70] Congress bulletin, 5 August 1930, file no. G 30, AICC Papers, NMML.
[71] Home Dept, Political (Jails), file no. 7/7/62, 1932.
[72] *Report*, Bengal, week ending 11 May 1889.
[73] George Campbell, *Memoirs of My Indian Career*, 2 vols (London: Macmillan and Co., 1893), vol. 2, p. 268.
[74] 6 January 1922, *Anand Bazar Patrika*, 15 April, *Report*, Bengal, weeks ending 14 January and 22 April 1922.
[75] *Katha*, 24 March 1922, *Report*, Bengal, week ending 1 April 1922.
[76] Singha, *A Despotism of Law*, p. 230; Anand Yang, 'Disciplining "Natives": Prisons and Prisoners in Early Nineteenth-Century India', *South Asia*, vol. x, no. 2 (December 1987).
[77] *Dainik Basumati*, 4 January 1922, *Report*, Bengal, week ending 14 January 1922; Home Dept, Political, file no. 489, 1922.

Disobedience.[78] The victims were flogged for various 'crimes'; even for writing'Mahatma Gandhi ki Jai'.[79] The government refused to surrender the weapon of the'strong' to exercise authority and restore'law and order'. In Allahabad's Naini Central Prison, which was across the river Yamuna, despite the protests of Jawaharlal Nehru and his associates,[80] the officials went ahead with the flogging of Chandrashekhar Azad (1906–1931) of the Hindustan Republic Association. A pupil of Gandhi's Kashi Vidyapeeth, he repeated the same cry—'Mahatma Gandhi ki Jai'— for every lash that fell on his body. In all, flogging was prevalent in 541 prisons; the number dropped to 85 by June 1933.[81] Sixty A class, 100 B class, and 1,600 C class prisoners were, likewise, flogged in Punjab. Elsewhere, C class prisoners far outnumbered those of the other two classes.[82] Henry Cotton, Assam's Commissioner in 1876, recalled:

> The way of flogging is to tie a man up by his hands and legs to a wooden triangle so that he cannot move and then to inflict the punishment on his bare buttocks with a rattan. I do not like to dwell on the subject for it is exceedingly horrible, and I simply loathe this form of judicial punishment. It is impossible to conceive of a more brutalizing procedure, and it is with shame and sorrow I record that I was addicted to it. I can only plead that the scales very soon fell away from my eyes and that ever after in my service, in whatever office I held, I did my utmost to discourage it.
> (Indian & Home Memories, London: T. Fisher Unwin, 1910)

Handcuffing symbolized another, and wider, application of the coercive methods. Husain Ahmad Madani, the Deoband scholar, was handcuffed for protesting against the practice of *jharhti* (a word applied for physical checking of prisoners before they entered the prison compound after work in the field). Afterwards, his legs were fettered with an iron chain for a month. They were removed after this bit of news appeared in *Young India*.[83] Aurobindo was handcuffed,

---

[78] Home Dept, Political, file no. 362, 1930.

[79] *Advocate*, 2 June, *Selections*, week ending 10 June 1910.

[80] Home Dept, Political (Jails), file no. 36, 1936.

[81] Home Dept, Political, file no. 22/86, 1933.

[82] J. Crerar, 2 August 1930, Home Dept, Political, file no. 362, 1930.

[83] Maulana Syed Mohammad Mian, *The Prisoners of Malta: The Heart-rending Tale of Muslim Freedom Fighters in British Period (Asira'n-e Malta)*, translated by Mohammad Anwer Hussain and Hasan Imam (New Delhi: Jamiat Ulama-i-Hind, Manak, 2005), p. 130.

and a rope tied around his waist. Abinash Bhattacharya and Sailen Bose met with the same fate.[84] In Faridpur Jail, Kiran Chandra Das and his eight partners were brought to the magistrate's court chained together.[85] Similar stories revealed a degree of severity exceeding that in German jails. The *Dainik Basumati* wondered how a government could call itself civilized, if it kept hundreds in a place unfit for human habitation and starved them for three or four days.[86] It brutalized prisoners without paying heed to Edmund Burke's plea that justice is itself the great standing policy of civil society.[87] As a state prisoner at Giddapahar, Kurseong, Subhas Chandra Bose, better known as Netaji, was told:

I.   You shall reside at Mr. Sarat Bose's house at Giddaphar, Kurseong, and shall not proceed outside the boundaries given below without the previous sanction of Government.
     Boundaries:
     You are permitted to take walks within a radius of one mile from the residence.
II. You shall hold no communication written or oral with any person
     (a) Connected in any way to your knowledge with any movement subversive of Government authority;
     (b) Resident in or visiting Kurseong except as approved by the Superintendent of Police, Darjeeling.
III. You shall not concern yourself directly or indirectly with the affairs of any public body or engage directly or indirectly in any public activity or political movement.
IV. You shall not contribute to the Press nor will you cause to be contributed to, or expressed in, the Press by any other person, your views on political or public matters.
V.   Letters written and received by you shall be censored by the Superintendent of Police, Darjeeling, or by a gazetted officer duly authorized by him. You shall limit your correspondence to seven letters a week.

[84] Sri Aurobindo, *Tales of Prison Life*, p. 3.
[85] Home Dept., Political, file no. 137, 1930.
[86] *Report*, Bengal, week ending 7 January 1922.
[87] U. K. Singh, *Political Prisoners in India*, p. 201.

VI. You shall not entertain, receive visits from or allow to reside in the
house any guests, either resident or non-resident, at Kurseong, or
any relatives except with the permission of the superintendent of
police, Darjeeling.[88]

This was a far cry from the great utilitarian principles dominating
England's intellectual landscape. The prison's main purpose was to
destroy whatever was left of the morale of its inmates. On the eve
of the second Round Table Conference (RTC) in London, Gandhi
remarked sagely, 'You cannot have undiluted repression today and
responsible government tomorrow.'[89]

Fetters and Martyrdom

Fazl-e Haq Khairabadi saw other prisoners, besides himself, 'heavily
fettered and afflicted with diseases, being dragged in chains and fetters'.
They were link-fetters not exceeding three pounds in weight, including
ankle rings, and were suspended to the waist not by a string or rope
but by a strip of leather. In 1914, Trailokya Nath Chakraborty and
his comrades were transferred to Calcutta's Presidency Jail handcuffed,
ankles chained, and the waist bound with ropes. Two young men of
the Gandhi Ashram in Banaras were kept in fetters, night and day.
Jawaharlal Nehru suggested that their tormentors learn a few modern
and humane lessons from the Soviet Union.[90]

In 1928, in the North-West Frontier Province (NWFP), 2,484
convicts were fettered, as compared with 2,427 the previous year.[91]
The UP Jail Manual added insult to injury by instructing that
'prisoners on whom fetters have been imposed shall keep their fetters
bright and polished, and shall be provided with leather gaiters'. Here
the fetters consisted of two round iron bars half an inch in diameter,
each bar twenty inches in length, connected at one end by a ring and

---

[88] Home Dept, Political, file no. 22/92, 1936.

[89] Suhash Chakravarty, *V. K. Krishna Menon and the India League* (New
Delhi: Har-Anand Publications, 1997), p. 181.

[90] Letter to the Editor, 21 January 1928, *SWJN*, vol. 3, p. 403.

[91] *Administration Report of the Jails of the North West Frontier Province,*
1928, pp. 6–7.

with ankle rings at the other for fastening them to the legs.[92] M. N. Roy protested:

> A prisoner on transfer is put in bar fetters—heavy iron things, not at all nice to have on your ankles. Then, to be paraded in public in such an out-fit is outrageous. I don't know why these precautions are necessary in case of prisoners who walked into captivity, and would be free today if they wanted to avoid imprisonment. Well, it is all routine, I suppose. Anyhow, I don't like it, and am glad that I shall not have to repeat the experience.[93]

Iron fetters were put on the neck and feet of Muzaffar Ahmad and three other communists who were arrested in the Kanpur Bolshevik Conspiracy Case.[94] On 7 June 1940, Ram Manohar Lohia was hand-cuffed en route to the Allahabad court. Heavy fetters were put on him after the judge gave his verdict and he was taken to Bareilly Prison. 'The sentences passed against Lohia and other Congressmen,' declared Gandhi, 'are strong hammer blows on the chains that hold India in slavery.'[95]

Ali Sardar Jafri (b. 1913), a leading light in the Progressive Writers' Movement (PWM), learnt that the beautiful word 'creeper' could also be used for fetters. He imagined green delicate creepers of jasmine in which thousands of lamps of tiny red flowers were lit. Fetters reminded him of Zainab, the surviving sister of Imam Husain (626–680), and his son Zainul Abidin, the fourth Shia Imam.[96] Millions remember them for unmasking and eliminating evil and

[92] *United Provinces Manual, Containing the Rules for the Superintendence and Management of Jails in the United Provinces of Agra and Oudh* (Allahabad: Government Press, 1927), pp. 130–1.

[93] 22 September 1935, M. N. Roy, *Fragments*, p. 136.

[94] S. Chattopadhyay, *Muzaffar Ahmad*, p. 17.

[95] Indumati Kelkar, *Ram Manohar Lohia*, translated by Desh Raj Goyal (New Delhi: National Book Trust, 2010), pp. 42–3.

[96] The list of the twelve Shia Imams begins with Ali and ends with the Imam Mahdi, who has for the present withdrawn from the world but will appear again on the Day of Judgement. The religious life of the adherents of Shi'ism centres on a body of traditions, beliefs, and observances that have their source in Ali, Fatima, and their sons Hasan and Husain, who, with the Prophet, make up the *Panjatan Pak*, the Five Holy Ones.

not compromising with it. Mir Anis (1802–1874), the great elegist, summed up their strong emotions:

Anis aasan nahin aabad karna ghar mohabbat ka,
Yeh un ka kaam hai jo zindagi barbaad karte hain.

Anis, it is not easy to rehabilitate a house of love,
This is done by only those who sacrifice their own lives.

With the ideology of lamentation and grief gaining strength over the centuries, death has become a great and noble cause (*Jehad-e Akbar*), and a sublime, highly positive experience of altruism.

Ali ibn-e Abi Talib (d. 661), the Prophet's cousin and son-in-law, wanted his elder son, Imam Hasan (625–670), to protect himself from being a target of adversity and a victim of pain and death. Affliction is bestowed (only) on the Friends of God; oppression befalls the chosen men, and pain and suffering are proportionate to the degree of dignity and pre-eminence (while conversely) exemption from calamity and hardships is the trait of ill fate and wretchedness. Husain has been exalted for his piety and his deeds, and the ordeals he endured in the battle fought out on the plains of Karbala (in Iraq on the River Euphrates) on 10 October 680 are commemorated as examples of his *mazlumiyat*, or victimhood. Mohamed Ali and others utilized the same symbolism to convey their sense of violence, injustice, oppression, inhumanity, and grief—all embodied in the word *zulm* as a rhetorical instrument of mobilization.[97] Rampur, the city of his birth and a princely state in Rohilkhand, had a predominantly Muslim population. Its Nawab, a convert to Shi'ism, observed Muharram with utmost solemnity. Mohamed Ali could not have escaped its influences. From Paris, he reminded Shaukat Ali how Husain gave to the Islamic world the greatest tradition of 'No surrender.'[98] Hussain's adversary, Yazid, might have been the victor at Karbala, but it is Husain who will reign over the hearts of the faithful until dooms-day. Addressing the jury at the Karachi Trial in 1921, Mohamed Ali pointed out that for fourteen hundred years every Muslim has mourned

[97] R. V. Thadani (ed.), *The Historic State Trial*, introduced by Mushirul Hasan (Delhi, forthcoming), p. 321.
[98] Mohamed Ali to Shaukat Ali, 16 July 1930, in *Mohamed Ali in Indian Politics: Select Writings, 1920–23*, vol. 3, edited by Mushirul Hasan (Atlantic Publishers, 1988), p. 139.

for Husain, the victim, while Yazid, the victor, has been eclipsed into obscurity—many Muslim cities have a quarter just outside known as Karbala, whereas no traces of Yazid's grave can be found anywhere. Drawing an analogy from his own sufferings in jail, which he tended to magnify, he said, 'So, gentlemen, do not think of the consequences of your verdict today or tomorrow, but of its ultimate consequences here to human freedom and thereafter, in another world ...' [99]

Progressive writers spurned religion, but Shabbir Hasan Khan (1898–1982), popularly known as Josh Malihabadi, employed the Karbala catastrophe in mystical, lyrical, and emotional terms. Unique and inimitable, Husain's heroism was over and above the capacity of the common run of human beings. Combining his passionate love for him and his family with the grandeur and poetry of his own, Josh stands out as one of the greatest literary figures in the twentieth century.

> The blood of Muhammad's family,
>   the Hashmi blood is turning into hurricanes and floods
> How does it matter if the house of Abu Sufian (Yazid's grandfather)
>   is bright with dazzling lights?
> The flames of fire are rushing towards Lanka
> How does it matter if the courtyard of Ravan is the prison of Sita?[100]

To Sarojini Naidu, then in jail, Husain was a poignant figure, and a forerunner of the doctrine of Satyagraha that Gandhi perfected.[101]

> Over the sunlit grass,
> Slow in a mad possession
> The shadowy pageants pass...
> Hark, from the brooding silence
> Breaks the wild cry of pain
> Wrung from the heart of the ages
> Ali! Hasan! Husain![102]

[99]   Mohamed Ali to Shaukat Ali, 16 July 1930, in *Mohamed Ali in Indian Politics*, vol. 3, p. 277. The Karachi Trial speech is reported at length in Afzal Iqbal (ed.), *Selected Writings and Speeches of Maulana Mohamed Ali*, 2 vols (Lahore, 1963), pp. 207–44.

[100]   Available at http://www.urdupoetry.com/articles/art9.html.

[101]   To Padmaja and Leilamani, 15 May 1932, in *Sarojini Naidu*, edited by Marakand Paranjape (New Delhi: Kali for Women, 1996), p. 273.

[102]   V. S. Naravane, *Sarojini Naidu: Her Life, Work and Poetry* (Delhi: Orient Longman, 1980), p. 87.

She experienced the elaborate mourning in the princely state of Hyderabad.

> With ideals such as ours and a faith specially selected and approved for us by Allah and sent to us as the Last Word in morals through the last of His Messengers, we should show a disregard of all suffering in the cause as great as your illustrious and great ancestor, Husain, showed on the 10th of this month on the banks of the Euphrates when he saw all those he loved and held so near to his heart die one after another, even unto little Ali Asghar, before his eyes, and finally fought and died himself after having undergone hunger and thirst and much other physical suffering, besides the mental torture that must have been a hundredfold greater. And yet he could have avoided all this and lived and enjoyed his life if only he had acknowledged the succession to the Khilafat of the Prophet of one who defied the Law of God and rejected the example of His Apostle. But could all the suffering of those ten days, brimful of misery as they were, have been even a drop to the vast ocean compared with the soul torture of righteousness surrendering to iniquity and virtue [by] arranging a compromise with vice?

The martyr's blood became the source of patriotism in all religious traditions, Sikhism included. Following the murder of Pandit Lekh Ram (d. 1897) and Swami Shraddhanand (1856–1926), a section of Punjabi Hindus, mostly Arya Samajist, invoked martyrdom to galvanize their Hindu identity in their province. They constructed the Kanya Gurukul in Khanpur, Haryana, as the land of the blood of Bhagat Phool Singh (1885–1942), also murdered. It became a place of pilgrimage for the Arya Jats.[103]

Martyrdom, by its very nature, is a subversive discourse that provides examples of resistance to the oppressor.[104] Exemplified by the excitement attributable to Jatindranath Das' death, the martyr's blood is a major force and a sentiment in the secular domain as well. Bose paid for the carriage of the body to Calcutta, whereas Gopi Chand Bhargava and Mohammad Alam, the two Punjabi councillors, attended

---

[103] Nonica Datta, *Violence, Martyrdom and Partition: A Daughter's Testimony* (New Delhi: Oxford University Press, 2009), pp. 28–9.

[104] Joyce Pettigrew, 'Martyrdom and Guerilla Organization in Punjab', *Journal of Commonwealth and Comparative Politics*, vol. xxx, no. 3 (1992): 387–406.

his funeral in Lahore. The Calcutta procession was enormous.[105] One can visualize Maulana Azad citing Mir Taqi Mir (1723–1810) on the occasion:

> Many tasks were there in the path of love, but Mir!
> I accomplished all rather fast.

Dissent and Defiance

'God proclaims His will by the voice of the public.' (Sada-e khalq ko Naqqara-e Khuda samjho). Aurobindo Ghose alluded to nationalism as 'a force which has shaken the whole of India, trampled the traditions of a century into a refuse of irrecoverable fragments, and set the mightiest of modern empires groping in a panic for weapons strong enough to meet a new and surprising danger.'[106] No wonder, the vernacular press highlighted not just the sufferings, but also the individual and collective protests of political prisoners that were dispersed across the regions. For example, the inmates staged a 'mutiny' in Darjeeling Jail in July 1889, and in Fatehgarh (UP) in 1910 and 1916.[107] In May 1922, a special meeting in Lucknow Jail mourned the death of Pandit Ram Rakha and of Maulvi Bunyad Husain. Convicted to life imprisonment in the Burma Conspiracy Case (refers to conspiracies to overthrow the government between 1914 and 1917), the Pandit, who the warden offended by removing his sacred thread from his body, died in Port Blair Jail.[108] He believed that, 'when order is injustice, disorder is the beginning of justice.'[109]

Let me illustrate further: in 1921, seven Sikhs in Coimbatore's Central Jail protested. Next year, violence flared up in several Bengal jails. Satindra Nath Sen, a household word in East Bengal, took the route of hunger strike. Anaku Naha of Munshiganj (Dacca), in Hooghly Jail,

---

[105] Home Dept, Political, file no. 21/63, 1929.

[106] Sri Aurobindo, Bande Mataram, p. 908.

[107] Zul Qarnain (Budaun), 28 June 1910, Selections, UP, week ending 8 July 1910; Leader (Allahabad), 6 February 1916; Selections, week ending 12 February 1916.

[108] 'The Second Trip', SWJN, vol. 1, p. 263.

[109] Hoche in Romain Rolland's 'Fourteenth of July', SWJN, vol. 1, p. 314.

and Ram Chandra Gupta in Presidency Jail, followed. Both had links with revolutionary organizations. Likewise, Arun Chandra Gupta, Satya Bhushan, Manoranjan Gupta, and Bhupendra Kumar Datta went on strike in Yervada Central Prison.[110] In July 1936, Jawaharlal set up a civil liberties union. Rabindranath Tagore (1861–1941), in the quietude of Shantiniketan, served as honorary president; Sarojini Naidu, lent colour and dignity to the Chair.[111] The Union highlighted the death of J. M. Adhikari, brother of G. M. Adhikari of the Meerut Conspiracy Case, and Rajni Kanta Pramanick, a pleader.[112] Around this time, the country observed 'Political Prisoners' Day' to prevent the government from sending prisoners to the Andaman Islands without their consent. The beleaguered prisoners too, went on hunger strike. They evoked much sympathy. Bengal anxiously awaited their fate, and Tagore was in anguish. At Deoli, the government took recourse to force-feeding when, on 2 October 1941, hunger strikers asked for a survival allowance for their dependants, and an end to their isolation. The hunger strike lasted 19 days. Political parties rallied around the Deoli Camp inmates.

Another form of protest is illustrated by Krishna Nair, who headed Narela's Gandhi Ashram and took part in the Badli Railway Station attack on 6 November and on the Gheora Railway Station on 12 November 1942. Involved also in the Palam Bomb Case and the burning of the Narela Notified Area Committee office, he was detained by the police in mid-November 1942. Officials enunciated the guiding principle in dealing with him. Wrote the chief commissioner: 'From a political point of view it would be advantageous to the administration if the complicity of a man of the type of Krishna Nair, a personal follower of M. K. Gandhi, in crime of violence could be proved in court, and for this reason it has been thought worthwhile to proceed with the further cases against him though he is already subject to a sentence which will keep him in jail for two years to come.'[113]

[110] Home Dept, Political, file no. 44/22, 1934.
[111] On the Indian Civil Liberties Union, *SWJN*, vol. 7, pp. 425–9.
[112] Bi-weekly bulletin, 4 May 1937, file no. G 8, AICC Papers.
[113] Home Dept, Political, file no. 3/32, 1943; Home Dept, Political (Internal), file no. 22/11, 1943.

The last major hunger strike took place in Bhagalpur a couple of years before Independence.[114] It aroused sympathy from ninety-nine well-known British women who appealed to the Prime Minister, Winston Churchill, the Secretary of State, Stafford Cripps, and the Viceroy Wavell to open the door for negotiations with the country's statesmen so that, in the words of the All-India Women's Conference (AIWC), they 'take their rightful place in national and international affairs'.[115] Azad urged that this process be completed so that the past was buried.[116]

How does the present-day historian explain the hunger strikes? What are the lessons drawn from them, and what assessment can be made with hindsight? The memoir literature of participants, combined with academic writings, shows the way. What was once hidden in official records is now out in the open.

Nelson Mandela's well-thought-out strategy was 'a more active, militant style of protest ... actions that punished the authorities'. He and his brave partners on Robben Island questioned the rationale behind hunger strikes, especially when people outside remained unaware of them. In India, the communists agreed that jail struggles meant defying orders, even if it meant physical clashes with the warders. They reckoned that if one did this, it might galvanize the workers. In retrospect, Jyoti Basu (1914–2010), who moved from home and party office to his prison cell, unsurprised and without regret, rejected the 'Party Line'.

Sometimes it happens that if people are shot down and attacked, people get angry. But this is not the organized movement of any kind; it does not last long. In jail Bhagat Singh went on strike for—I do not know— two months or something. Others who were in jail for the Chittagong Armoury Raid also went on strike and I too went on strike later on. After five days we had to withdraw it as they conceded our demands. At that time four of our women activists were killed in Bow Bazaar

[114] Bimal Prasad (ed.), *Towards Freedom: Documents on the Movement for Independence in India*, 1945 (New Delhi: ICHR and Oxford University Press, 2008), pp. 205–7.

[115] B. Prasad, *Towards Freedom*, p. 230.

[116] B. Prasad, *Towards Freedom*, p. 397.

Street. They were defying orders 144 and raising their demands and so on and so forth and they were fired upon and four of them died.[117]

Gandhi had no doubt that his traditionally accepted form of protest had forced the government to ease its control.[118] He regarded fasting as 'a fiery weapon' and claimed that all public fasts were gifts from God. Besides maintaining that abstention from food led to the cleansing of body and soul, he made the case that when every means of justice failed, there was no alternative except to fast. Not all agreed with this view. C. Rajagopalachari (1879–1972), Congress General Secretary in 1921–2 and Congress Working Committee (CWC) member, thought that jail protest was inconsistent with non-violent non-cooperation.[119]

Meanwhile, families waited in breathless suspense for the policeman, the schoolmaster, or the postman to bring news of the whereabouts of their near and dear ones. 'The post is the consolation of life,' Voltaire had written, and some one else added: 'As long as there are postmen life will have zest.' Mothers, wives and sisters despaired over the long wait, and their freedom seemed a reproach to them when their loved ones were behind bars.[120] They yearned for the post to bring the one letter they wanted most—news of a child far away or just a love letter.[121] Even with stray bits of information, they wondered: 'What will he eat? I hear a good food is not even for animals. Can we not send him something? *Ai-hai*, and how will he sleep? He was fastidious about so many things. Tears melted her austere face as she thought of Hamid's predicament. In her deep concern, Masuma Begum forgot her anger against him for going away to join the stir.'[122] This extract

[117] Jyoti Basu, Oral History Transcript (781), Nehru Memorial Museum and Library (NMML); Gopalkrishna Gandhi, *Of a Certain Age: Twenty Life Sketches* (New Delhi: Penguin Books, 2011), p. 140.

[118] Nelson Mandela, *Long Walk to Freedom: The Autobiography of Nelson Mandela* (Boston: Little, Brown & Co., 2008), p. 502.

[119] C. Rajagopalachari, *Jail Diary: A Day-to-Day Record of Life in Vellore Jail in 1921* (Bombay: Bharatiya Vidya Bhavan, 1922), p. 59.

[120] Norman, *Nehru*, vol. 1, p. 84.

[121] 16 August 1942, Vijaya Lakshmi Pandit, *Prison Days*, p. 13.

[122] Zeenuth Futehally, *Zohra: A Novel*, edited by Rummana Futehally (New Delhi: Oxford University Press, 2004), p. 213.

from a contemporary novel eloquently highlights the stoicism with which the politically active accepted their fate, while that from another depicts the protagonist thinking only of the naked, the hungry, the sick, the defenceless, and the handicapped:

> 'I ask nothing for myself, but I extend my hands in supplication to you on behalf of your neglected children – the poor.'

> 'Z' felt tears well up in his eyes. He moved away from the bars which he had been resting his head against.

> He sat down on the floor. He wanted to move his lips but words would not come to them.

> Suddenly, his voice rose, 'The people come first. The people come first. The rest is vanity.'[123]

Escape from Captivity

Many Indian cities were seething with excitement in December 1921 in protest against the visit of the Prince of Wales. Arrests followed. From January to May 1922, between 20,000 and 25,000 educated persons filled up jails.[124] They had shed the fear of the jail establishment, of the 'dishonour of jail life' and of bullets and shells, and looked upon forbearance and the art of getting on with others as signifiers of success in public activism.

Were prisoners 'docile bodies', as Foucault had maintained? No, they were not. The weight of empirical evidence produced two kinds of responses—resistance to domination, and sanctifying jailgoing as a sacred *duty*. Thus, in most trial accounts, prisoners were calm and serene and willing to die. 'A great honour,' said Madan Lal Dhingra (1883–1909) in a British court.[125] Note, too, the following account for the year 1921:

> One Mahomed Baksh was arrested on the 4th instant in Hyderabad and sent up for trial ... for distributing copies of the Ulama fatwa ...

---

[123] Fakhar Zaman, *The Prisoner*, p. 146.

[124] *Nayak*, 27 April 1922, *Report*, Bengal, week ending 6 May 1922.

[125] He assassinated William Curzon Wyllie, Political Aide-de-Camp to the Secretary of State for India. V. N. Datta, *Madan Lal Dhingra and the Revolutionary Movement* (New Delhi: Vikas Publishing House, 1978); Keer, *Veer Savarkar*, p. 55.

to military sepoys. Interviewed in jail by the Superintendent of Police, Sind C.I.D, he asked to be pardoned, but at the same time stated that he would rather die than give evidence against anyone else in court ... He had formerly served in the Police as a constable. He believed in the pronouncements of the Ulama that it was Haram to serve in the Police and the army, and the orders of distributing them were binding on the Mussalmans, and he regarded this as an article of religious faith.[126]

This is one part of the story; the other is of Indulal Yagnik (1892–1972). His friends bid him farewell in the court itself on the morning of 7 April 1923, while he felt humbled entering a hermitage for about a year of quiet study and religious meditation.[127] Elsewhere, families put the traditional red mark (*tika*) on foreheads with which warriors of old were sent to battle. Followed by cheering crowds to the prison gates, the patriot hurled his Urdu couplets or Hindi or Sanskrit *shloka*s at the rulers. Margaret E. Cousins (1878–1954), founder of the All-India Women's Conference in 1927, offers a dramatic representation of how women fared.

> I knew a family group in which the grandmother was in prison at the same time as her three great granddaughters in their teens. The girls had to serve a ten-year sentence each but had the advantage of 'B' Class, while the old lady had to endure 'C', the lowest class, for one year. Women who had never been out of *purdah* faced the barefacedness of walking unveiled in public processions and all that was afterwards involved in prison life; mothers who were already in the family way braved the dangers of childbirth in prison and thought it no indignity to the coming babe, but an honour; the *Devadasi* or dancing girl heard the call of the Mahatma and left her vocation braving the treatment she might be given by her 'respectable' fellow-prisoners....[128]

---

[126] Weekly Bulletin on the Non-cooperation Movement for the week ending 15 October 1921, in *Regionalizing Pan-Islamism: Documents on the Khilafat Movement*, edited by Mushirul Hasan and Margrit Pernau (Delhi: Manohar, 2005), p. 295.

[127] Indulal Yagnik, *The Autobiography*, translated into English from the original Gujarati by Devavrat N. Pathak, Howard Spodek, and John R. Wood (New Delhi: Manohar, 2011), vol. 2, pp. 82, 103, 109–10.

[128] Margaret E. Cousins, *Indian Womanhood Today* (Allahabad: Kitabistan, 1941), pp. 69–70.

In Muslim families, the mother, sister or daughter acquiesced in the struggle by tying an amulet around the arm of the patriot—*Imam Zamin* (May the last Shia Imam be the protector!), or reciting a *nauha* to evoke the bravery of Ali Akbar, the son of Imam Husain, and of Abbas, his uncle. Then there is this account by Maulana Shahid Fakhiri:

> Next morning when the Maulana was going to court, antimony was put in his eyes, his hair was dressed and he was properly perfumed. All this was done by his stepmother herself. The old lady after grooming and dressing him carefully sent him to court. Maulana Sahib's wife sent him word from inside (the *Zenana*) that while he was going to carry out the example of Hazrat Zainul Abidin (the last survivor of Prophet Mohammad's family who was taken in captivity after the battle of Karbala), he must be prepared for the example of Hazrat Imam Husain himself (the grandson of the Prophet and principal martyr of Karbala). She prayed to God to steep her husband firmly in the faith. Twenty thousand people followed the carriage to court where he read out his statement in a clear, firm voice, refused to furnish security, obtained his sentence of one year and proceeded in his carriage to jail followed by the crowd.[129]

Escape from prison filled prisoners in Moradabad with joy.[130] The adventurous men in Hazaribagh or eighteen of the 40 involved in the First Supplementary Lahore Conspiracy Case felt likewise.[131] In April 1921, Bagga Singh and Hari Singh of Amritsar, once watchmen in Shanghai, turned fugitive. The former linked up with the Ghadar Party (started abroad in 1913), and took part in a raid in Kapurthala State.

Breakouts occurred in the Presidency Jail and Buxar Fort on 31 July 1934, in Bellary on 8 May, and in Vellore on 25 September 1941.[132] Two 'terrorist prisoners' escaped from Banaras with the help of a prison warden and an iron rod smuggled into the barracks. Two

---

[129] A. J. Kidwai, 'Conflict and Consensus', in *Communal and Pan-Islamic Trends in Colonial India*, edited by Mushirul Hasan (New Delhi, 1985), p. 148.

[130] *Selections*, UP, the week ending 8 September 1906.

[131] Home Dept, Political (A), Proceedings, November 1918, file nos 130–41.

[132] Home Dept, Political, file no. 3/9, 1942.

communists in Kanpur secured freedom as well.[133] However, neither
escape nor release ended their anguish and woes. Stricken by poverty
or ill health, they were turned into hewers of wood and drawers of
water and petitioned Gandhi and Jawaharlal on these lines.[134] Besides
denying employment to a civil resister,[135] the district authorities took
their own time scrutinizing the papers of 'B' and 'C' class prisoners.[136]
Bose talked of their plight: 'Have we no duty to those who have given
of their best in the service of their country and have received nothing
but poverty and sorrow in return?'[137]

Prisoners were restless souls, subject to moodiness. They chafed
and fretted at their surroundings, felt helpless at the many pinpricks
but ultimately settled down in resignation to taking things as they
came.[138] They lived up to the ideals of self-rule that were constantly on
their lips, hoping that their sacrifices would help rewrite the chronicle
of defeat, indifference, and dishonour.[139] They performed on the arena
of life another chapter in the history of justice and good deeds. Azad
smiled when M. D. Swinner sentenced him to rigorous imprisonment
on 9 February 1922, and said, 'It is much less than I had expected.' His
wife complained of the 'mild' punishment awarded to her husband.[140]
For her, as indeed for her husband, jail became the gateway to freedom.

Meanwhile, a blind man with a small tambourine in hand, walked
along singing this song:

Brother, why turn your face from the battle away?
    He who's a hero must fight and bring to his name worldly light.
Brother, why has your dignity vanished today?
    Brother, why turn your face from the battle away?

---

[133] Home Dept, Political, file no. 7/1, 1941.

[134] Home Dept, Political, file no. 87/1931.

[135] Marie Seton, *Panditji: A Portrait of Jawaharlal Nehru* (New York: Taplinger, 1967), p. 73.

[136] Seton, *Panditji*, p. 73.

[137] Sisir Kumar Bose and Sugata Bose (eds), *Subhas Chandra Bose: Congress President, Speeches, Articles and Letters, January 1938–May 1939* (New Delhi: Permanent Black, 2004, paperback), p. 29.

[138] Vijaya Lakshmi Pandit, *Prison Days*, p. 93.

[139] Rajagopalachari, *Jail Diary*, p. iv.

[140] Vishwa Nath Datta, *Maulana Azad* (Delhi: Manohar, 1990) p. 121.

Why do you wish to be a victor?
   Why do you fear to be a lover?
Brother, why do you hold on to sorrow and why?
   Brother, why turn your face from the battle away?
You're in the arena of life to show your compassion in strife
   Brother, why from the law of what's right go astray?
Brother, why turn your face from the battle away?[141]

Where does a historian situate Indian jails? They were metaphors for broader social practices in the construction of colonial knowledge, and sites of medical experimentation and observation. But they also administered rapid retribution: public executions, public flogging and labour in fetters aimed at the bodies of Indian subjects were preferred over calling upon troops or law courts.[142] The bureaucratic machine 'grinds slow or grinds fast, but grinding is its object.'[143]

To conclude, we need to place prisoners in a fluid category, formed at the intersection of the local/regional/pan-Islamic/pan-Indian and the explicitly/implicitly colonial. If a prisoner had to give up home, he did more than change his residence. He had to cut himself off from the outside world; had to learn to adjust to 'new' persons; had, in short, to create a totally new life in the barracks. It was not the loss of a profession, of status—that alone and by itself was painful—but rather another way of living that required readjustment. As Felix Edmundovich Dzerzhinsky (1877–1926), Lenin's comrade-in-arms, remarked: 'I am calm enough, yet the strange tranquility is utterly at variance with these walls and with the things from which they have separated me. The point is that everyday life has been replaced by a vegetative existence, activity by introspection.'[144]

---

[141] Premchand, *Rangbhumi*, p. 234.

[142] Premchand, *Rangbhumi*, p. 27.

[143] *Bande Mataram*, 18 June 1907, Sri Aurobindo, *Bande Mataram*, p. 223.

[144] 30 April 1908, Felix Dzerzhinsky, *Prison Diary and Letters* (Moscow: Foreign Languages Publishing House, 1959), p. 19.

3. Jail—'The Gateway to Freedom'

The depth of oppression in South Africa created Nelson Mandela, a revolutionary *par excellence*, the Oliver Tambos, the Walter Sisulus, the Chief Luthulis, the Yusuf Dadoos, and the Robert Sobukwes—all men of courage, wisdom, and generosity.[1] In India, thousands were jailed or made to kiss the gallows for freedom from enslavement. Trailokya Nath Chakraborty, a revolutionary in the Anushilan Samity, spent six terms in jail. His first test lay in quitting home, the second in organizing work in villages; the third lay in undertaking perilous tasks, and the fourth in courting imprisonment, suffering the torments of the police and the tyranny of jail. Having endured the many obstacles and perils, he earned laurels for keeping intact his personal and political integrity in trying times.[2]

[1] Nelson Mandela, *Long Walk to Freedom* (UK: Abacus, illustrated reprinted, 1995), p. 748.
[2] T. N. Chakraborty, *Thirty Years in Prison*, p. 344.

There was no lack of aspirants for the honour of entering jail.[3] B. C. Pal, the 'Prophet of Nationalism', did so in early twentieth century. Bengal celebrated; it also exulted over his release in March 1908. 'He came to us,' commented Aurobindo Ghose, 'purified by an act of self-immolation, with a soul deepened by long hours of solitude and self-communion to repeat the word of hope and inspiration, to call us once more to the task of national self-realisation. Welcome to him and thrice welcome!'[4] With the air thick with such legends, the young and old heard or read stories of Bal Gangadhar Tilak's (1856–1920) imprisonment on 14 September 1897. Shudha Mazumdar, daughter of an official, trembled with excitement when she heard of Annie Besant's (1847–1933) internment in June 1917. She was seized with a great longing to behold such leading figures in the flesh.[5] Brij Narain 'Chakbast' (1882–1926), the Faizabad-born Urdu poet, eulogized: 'You are more to us than our mothers/ The whiteness of your hair is the dawn of our nation.' Each one of them felt his limbs fettered and body bound with iron chains, and yet each one moved in, glittering like the morning star, full of life, splendour, and joy.

General R. E. H. Dyer's 'Crawling Order' and the murder of innocent civilians at the Jallianwala Bagh caused fury across the country. Tagore renounced his knighthood. 'This glimpse of his flaming spirit', and the beauty of his noble gesture completely captivated the young Mazumdar and she longed to set her eyes on him.[6] Poets and writers sanctified Jallianwala Bagh as a monument to those martyred for Mother India, and reimagined the sufferings of the victims as the nation's suffering.[7] Sardar Bhagat Singh earned nationwide adulation

---

[3] 'On the Dal', August 1928, *SWJN*, vol. 3, p. 171.

[4] Sri Aurobindo, *Bande Mataram*, 10 March 1908, p. 743.

[5] Savarkar's release was conditional on residence within Ratnagari district and on his not engaging in political activities for a period of five years. He also gave a public recantation of his political creed.

[6] S. Mazumdar, *Memoirs of an Indian Woman*, p. 134.

[7] Sherman, *State Violence and Punishment in India*, p. 35; V. N. Datta and S. Settar (eds), *Jallianwala Bagh Massacre* (Delhi: Manohar Publishers, ICHR Monograph Series 4, 2000).

and became a great inspirational force.[8] The Bengal revolutionaries and the Maharashtrian 'extremists' stimulated a new breed of publicists and journalists who felt drawn towards the weak and the oppressed, not towards the strong and the triumphant. They disregarded personal pride when it conflicted with the higher interests of the nation (*desh* or *watan*) and survival in the face of colonial exploitation. They asked searching questions about young men and women being put behind bars, challenged the idea behind 'disciplining', and exposed corrupt practices.[9]

Gandhi knew about Savarkar, Madan Lal Dhingra, the Chapekar brothers, as well as of the terrorist activities that led to the death of 82 persons between 1906 and 1917. He even commended their courage and bravery. At the same time, he did not want them to be presented before the nation as role models. He refused to secure clemency for Bhagat Singh and his comrades. Gandhi encouraged a nationwide consensus on principles and mechanisms to make possible self-expression and equal access to the levers of power; he gave the non-Congress legislators the go-ahead to espouse democratic ideals as corollaries to the goals of national independence and unity.[10] Alarmed at the fate of undertrials, the mistreatment of the 'political' detainees most of the time, and of other inmates routinely, the poor amenities, and the high death rate, he supported demands seeking a review of the Criminal Law Amendment Act.

Stimulated by Gandhi's stand, a UP legislator bemoaned the incarceration of nearly twenty thousand of 'the best sons of Mother India.'[11] In March 1923, he and others set out to secure the release of the

---

[8] B. N. Pande (ed.), *A Centenary History of the Indian National Congress* (New Delhi: Vikas Publishing House, 1985), vol. 2, p. 614.

[9] *Urdu-e-Moalla* (Aligarh), 5 February 1911, *Selections*, UP, week ending 11 February 1911.

[10] Home Dept, Political, file no. 37/III/1924 & K. W.

[11] He asked, 'Is there another greater, more magnanimous, and more statesmanlike act to be done than the setting at liberty of all the political prisoners … and making His Royal Highness's visit always remembered and blessed by all …?' (Home Dept, file no. 155, part 4, Serial no. 1 & K.W., 1922)

Guru-ka-Bagh, Kirpan, and Gurdwara prisoners. Lajpat Rai pleaded the case of the Bengal detenues.[12] Gandhi wondered why they were detained, and that too indefinitely. He was indignant when 'barbarities' were committed in Chittagong in October 1931, following the death of two detenues in police firing in Hijli. The two incidents beckoned him to hurry to India from the Round Table Conference in London.[13] But he was not prepared to leave abruptly in anger. On another occasion, he secured the release of Prithvi Singh Azad (b. 1892), 'the legendary crusader'.[14] His meeting with Bengal's Governor in November 1937 led to the liberation of eleven detenues. The thought uppermost in his mind was twofold: to ensure that the public did not regard such releases as capitulation, and, second, that administrative clemency should not weaken respect for law and order.[15]

Regional and local actors also entered the prisoners' arena to secure as many concessions as they could to improve their living conditions. Ganesh Shankar Vidyarthi (1890–1931), editor of the Hindi newspaper *Pratap* and UP legislator, visited the Central and Borstal jails to meet Bhagat Singh and Batukeshwar Dutt (1910–1965), along with Gopi Chand, Srimati Parvati Devi, and Sardar Kishan Singh. Meanwhile, the Congress protested against the detention of Bhai Santa Singh, Bhai Gajjan Singh, and Bhai Daswandha Singh, and the death of six prisoners in Bengal. With the observance of 'Andaman Day' on 14 August 1929, these events called for a nationwide restructuring of the jail system.[16]

Shibban Lal Saxena, a UP legislator, voiced his anxiety over legal exemptions and immunities to the white Briton, the misuse of prisoners for pulling the *punkha* (fan) for Westerners, and the supply to them of socks, boots or shoes, spoons, combs and brushes, and mattresses

[12] V. C. Joshi (ed.), *Lala Lajpat Rai: Writings and Speeches* (Delhi: University Publishers, 1966), pp. 258–68, 327.

[13] 'Speech at Meeting of the Commonwealth of India League', 30 October 1931, *CWMG*, vol. XLVIII, p. 249.

[14] He was convicted for life in the Lahore Conspiracy Case (1915).

[15] Linlithgow to Provincial Governors, 11 December 1937, in *Towards Freedom: 1937–47*, Vol. I, Experiment with Provincial Autonomy 1st January–31st December 1937, edited by P. N. Chopra (Delhi: ICHR, 1986), p. 1242.

[16] 18 January 1929, file no. G 35, 1928–9, AICC Papers.

and pillow. Furthermore, he also noted that for offences that brought down heavy penalties on others, the Westerners received light ones.[17] Day after day, month after month, year after year, council and assembly members urged officials to heed the voice of reason and release political prisoners or give them a fair trial.[18] In Bihar, they succeeded in having many crude forms of severe punishment curbed.

The Civil Disobedience Enquiry Committee, which the All-India Congress Committee (AICC) appointed in 1922, identified 55 non-cooperators who were tried under the Criminal Law Amendment Act. One of them succumbed to an attack of fever in Lucknow Jail.[19] The Congress in 1925 demanded the transfer of Jogesh Chunder Ghose, Samarendra Sen, and Santosh Kumar Dutt from Berhampore to Hazaribagh. Their transfer without proper clothing caused a furore.[20] On 2 January 1926, Pandit Madan Mohan Malaviya (1861–1946) took up the cause of Sardar Kharak Singh of the Shiromani Gurdwara Prabandhak Committee (SGPC),[21] and demanded recognition of political prisoners as a separate category. But he was informed that 'there is no definition of what is and what is not a political prisoner'.[22] Thereafter, the Punjab Enquiry Committee Report (1928) proposed

[17] Home Dept, Political, Proceedings, May 1907, file no. 5; Home Dept (Jails), file no. 7/7/62, 1932, and file nos 201, 192; Home Dept, file no. 28/V, 1925; Home Dept, file no. 119/36 (Jails), 1936.

[18] S. Chattopadhyay, *Muzaffar Ahmad*, p. 4; Hari Dev Sharma (ed.), *Selected Works of Acharya Narendra Deva, 1928–1940* (New Delhi: Radiant Publishers, 1998), p. 139. Home and Political Dept (Frontier), file No. 656-F, 1931. Speech on 24 March 1925, in *Selected Works of Govind Ballabh Pant (SWGBP)*, edited by B. R. Nanda, vol. 2, p. 232; Basudev Chatterjee (ed.), *Towards Freedom*, 1938 (Delhi: ICHR and Oxford University Press, 1999), part 2, p. 1507.

[19] *Selected Works of Motilal Nehru (SWMN)*, vol. 3, edited by Ravinder Kumar and D. N. Panigrahi (Delhi: Vikas, 1984), p. 22.

[20] H. N. Mitra (ed.), *Indian Annual Register*, July–December 1925, vol. 2 (Calcutta: Annual Register Office), pp. 302–3.

[21] Home Dept, Political, file no. 28 IV/26, 1926. During his absence, Mehtab Singh acted as President. Kharak Singh was in and out of jail for making what the government held to be seditious speeches.

[22] Home Dept, (Jails), file no. 80, 1930; 25 December 1927, Foreign & Political Dept, file no. 668/F, 1927. Fazl-e Ilahi of Lahore was arrested in Bombay on 5 April 1927. As a *mujahir* in 1920, he crossed over to the

creating the 'First Division' to which Europeans, Americans, other foreigners or Indians (who had adopted Western ways) were to be admitted. But Chaudhri Afzal Haq (1891–1942) of the Majlis-e Ahrar considered preferential treatment to be against common sense, against the spirit of religion, against the spirit of the times, and against jail discipline itself.[23]

As part of the Congress' drive to highlight cases of repression Motilal Nehru headed the defence committee in the Meerut Conspiracy case. In July 1930, the CWC looked into the goings-on at the Visapur Jail, situated 27 miles from Ahmadnagar city, and deplored the invidious distinctions between political prisoners.[24] A more publicized form of protest assumed other dimensions: the UP Provincial Congress Committee (PCC) observed the seventh anniversary of Jatindranath Das' martyrdom on 13 September 1936. Besides, the Congress persuaded Jogesh Chandra Chatterjee to give up his hunger strike on the assurance that every effort would be made to mobilize public opinion in his favour.[25]

Penal and prison reforms figured in the CWC resolution on 28 February 1937, and in the reforms envisaged by Rajendra Prasad (1884–1963), Congress President.[26] A sense of exhilaration filled the air when the Congress assumed power in several provinces in 1937, and the communists observed 'Prisoners' Day' in UP. Yet, the impression gained ground that Govind Ballabh Pant (1887–1961), Chief Minister, and Kailash Nath Katju (1887–1968), Minister of Justice, had blazed no new trails as far as civil liberties were concerned. It was said that they and their counterparts in other provinces had bitten off

---

Frontier and joined M. N. Roy who arranged for his education in Moscow. Mohammad Shafiq was let off relatively lightly. As in the case of Fazl-e Ilahi, he was charged with conspiracy in the course of the years 1920–1 at Tashkent and at Moscow. He had links with Ubaidullah Sindhi, Raja Mahendra Pratap, and Abdul Rab (Home Dept, Political, file no. 268, 1924). For Sindhi, see Ayesha Jalal, *Partisans of Allah*, pp. 217–24.

[23] *Report of the Punjab Enquiry Committee, 1928*, p. 19.

[24] Congress bulletin, file no. G 30, 1930, AICC Papers.

[25] May 1936, file no. G 66/1936, AICC Papers.

[26] Valmiki Choudhry (ed.), *Dr. Rajendra Prasad: Correspondence and Select Documents* (New Delhi: Allied Publishers, 1984), vol. 2, pp. 13, 305.

more than they could chew.[27] Jawaharlal Nehru and Subhas Chandra Bose agreed and wondered whether it was not a matter of shame that the Congress did not have power enough to get the young political prisoners released.' If the Governor's special powers on 'law and order' imposed constraints, why did the ministers hold the reins of office? At the Haripura Congress in February 1938, Bose demanded the abandonment of the basic tenets of imperial governance.

G. D. Birla (1894–1943) told Mahadev Desai (1892–1942) that 'it does not enhance our prestige to say that we are merely puppets of the Governors and we have no power, we cannot do much'.[28] True, the party rallied round Gandhi's *jail bharo* and 'no return' projects,[29] but the ministers adapted themselves far too much to the old order.[30] Jawaharlal Nehru modified his own stand on hunger strikers in the Andamans.[31] He knew that the Prisoners Release Committee had organized a procession in Lahore on 24 January 1938, and that Amulya Charan Choudhry's suicide in Chittagong had led to a tumult, but he did not take any bold step to set matters right. On the other hand, Gandhi attempted to resolve the ministerial crisis in UP and

[27] 21 December 1923, in *SWGBP*, vol. 3, pp. 304–5; Haig to Linlithgow, 22 January 1938, in *Towards Freedom*, 1938, part 2, p. 1145. Indian Civil Liberties Union, 4 May 1937, file no. G 8, AICC Papers; Home Dept, Political, file no. 31/85, 1932. Jawaharlal Nehru, 'The Agitation for the Release of the Detenus', 28 October 1937, *SWJN*, vol. 8, p. 271. To N. B. Khare, 22 December 1937, *SWJN*, vol. 8, p. 372.

[28] Birla to Mahadev Desai, 26 January 1938, in *Towards Freedom*, 1938, part 2, p. 1145.

[29] 'Those people who come back from jail must remember that a great deal depends on their readiness to return. For if it appears to government and the people that such persons are not prepared to return to jail then government wins. Only when it sees that there is terrible determination will it realise that it must own defeat. Government itself has been laying stress on the fact that in many places people who have returned from jail keep at a safe distance from it. This kind of thing has a bad psychological effect ...' (To Gandhi, 28 April 1938, *SWJN*, vol. 8, pp. 387–9).

[30] To Gandhi, 28 April 1938, *SWJN*, vol. 8, pp. 387–9.

[31] Jawaharlal Nehru, 'The Hunger Strike of the Prisoners in the Punjab', 20 January 1938, *SWJN*, vol. 8, p. 275.

Bihar with the following suggestions: (*a*) cases should be individually examined, (*b*) that the right and duty of such examination must rest with ministers, and (*c*) that before releasing prisoners ministers should make sure that they had renounced violence.[32] In mid-January 1938, Sarat Chandra Bose (1899–1950) interviewed prisoners repatriated from the Andamans to the Alipore Jail and forestalled the possibility of their hunger-strike.

In November 1939, the Congress ministers resigned. To remain in office after the discovery of their impotence would have been to court ignominy. 'To remain in office for the protection of civil liberty would have been to mistake the wood for the tree,' Gandhi said to M. N. Roy, once 'the symbol of revolution in the East'.[33] The news that Europe was at war produced an extraordinary quickening in the wheel of life. P. C. Joshi who had been elected General Secretary of the CPI in June 1936 continued to remain so until 1948. Hungry for new forces of energy, the internal quarrels which had been so resonant earlier were now much muted.

Meanwhile, the freedom-loving enthusiasts were locked up.[34] The UP government detained Bishambhar Dayal Tripathi, MLA of Unnao district and Secretary of the Forward Bloc in UP, and Manmatha Nath Gupta, a former Kakori prisoner.[35] In a province where the average total population in jails had been steadily increasing, the numbers swelled to 28,700 ordinary prisoners and 13,354 *satyagrahis*. In this way, they totalled 42,000 in June 1941. Sajjad Zaheer, the communist, hoped that the long, dark night of subjugation and poverty would come to a close.[36] He was strong, dedicated, painstaking, and efficient.

[32]   Linlithgow to Brabourne, 3 March 1938, *SWJN*, vol. 8, p. 1205.

[33]   To M. N. Roy, 18 November 1939, in *Towards Freedom*, 1939, part 1, edited by Mushirul Hasan (New Delhi: Oxford University Press and ICHR, 2008), p. 215.

[34]   Y. A. Godbole to all District Officers, November 1939, in *Towards Freedom* 1939, part 1, pp. 462–3.

[35]   Chandrashekhar Azad, Ramprasad Bismil, and Ashfaqullah Khan (1900–1927) and some others were involved in the robbery of treasure money in a train. This took place between the Kakori station and Alamnagar, within 40 miles of Lucknow, on 9 August 1925.

[36]   The writings on Sajjad Zaheer are fairly extensive. The history of the Progressive Writers' Movement cannot be written without a discussion of his

Prison foisted a 'second adolescence' on Faiz Ahmed Faiz, 'a period in which his sensitivities and sensibilities were sharpened once again to the point that he was acutely aware of his environment ... [and] brought to the fore his emotions and affections towards his loved ones, but also towards his activist political causes'.[37] Prison enabled him to write a considerable number of poems in which his ideals took on strength by being alloyed with harsh experience, and which were eagerly devoured by the public.[38]

During the hunger strike at the Deoli Camp, many others discussed their isolation from society and family, and warned the Home Secretary that they, too, might resort to a hunger strike. After much dilly-dallying, they were transferred to the district jails. The morale of the young prisoners belonging to the RSP, the Forward Bloc and the Revolutionary Communist Party was very high indeed. None of them felt homesick and most were confident of the victory of the Indian National Army (INA).[39]

The Kozhikode-born V. K. Krishna Menon (1896–1974), 'an indefatigable worker on the Congress line',[40] headed London's India League. He prevailed upon the 'Release the Prisoners Committee', whose campaign brought independence to the Irish political prisoners, to condemn British imperialism.[41] Thus Dublin's Women's Prisoners' Defence League enlarged its brief to include Indian cases as well. Led by Madam Gonne MacBride, a public meeting held on 18 January 1931, took a strong stand on execution, torture, and the government's savagery.[42] While suppression could not crush the people's moral fibre,

---

initiatives and vision. In Urdu, the most recent work is by Ali Ahmad Fatimi, *Sajjad Zaheer: Ek Tarikh, Ek Tehrik* (Allahabad: Josh and Firaq Literary Society, 2006).

[37] Yasmeen Hameed, (ed.), *Daybreak: Writings on Faiz* (Karachi: Oxford University Press, 2013), p. 98.

[38] V. G. Kiernan (ed. and trans.), *Poems by Faiz* (London: George Allen and Unwin, 1971), p. 25.

[39] Ansar Harvani, *Before Freedom and After* (New Delhi: Gian Publishing House, 1989), p. 45.

[40] Amery to Linlithgow, 29 April 1942, in *Transfer of Power*, Nicholas Mansergh (UK: H.M. Stationery Office, 1983), p. 867.

[41] S. Chakravarty, *Krishna Menon and the India League*, p. 23.

[42] S. Chakravarty, *Krishna Menon and the India League*, p. 96.

it left behind a trail of sorrow and grief.[43] A German firm produced musical boxes for sale, with the inscription 'The Great Heroes of India' on the upper side, and two-colour portraits of Gandhi and Tilak.[44]

In early March 1930, Fenner Brockway, the Labour parliamentarian, demanded the unconditional and immediate release of the Meerut prisoners and the Garhwali Riflesemen who had refused to fire on an unarmed gathering of fellow-countrymen and, as a consequence, had been sentenced to life imprisonment. Political beliefs and commitments cannot be quantified, and yet each one of the prisoners left behind them the memory of their talents and, above all, their deep devotion to the duties of their sacred calling. As a result, their commemoration has become a tradition passed on from generation to generation.

Kamaladevi Chattopadhyay (1903–1988) had heard the story of the British officer presenting before Bahadur Shah Zafar his son's head. The emperor smiled before declining the offer. 'Why smile?' asked the courtiers. The emperor replied that he did not want the the officer to feel triumphant over this cruel mockery. By smiling, he had thwarted the officer's aim. The moral is that of such stuff should patriots be made.[45]

[43] *SWMN*, vol. 3, p. 30.

[44] Home Dept, Political, file no. 427, 1924.

[45] Kamaladevi Chattopadhyay, *Inner Recesses, Outer Spaces: Memoirs* (Delhi: Navrang, 1986), p. 165.

4. The Karachi Trial

A trifle for children is creation to me
Night and Day at the races; existence to me
By my lights, Solomon's throne is deception.
The healing breath of Jesus is just diction to me.

—Ghalib[1]

Mohamed Ali, for one, depicted the many vicissitudes of Islam and
of Indian Muslims in history to prove that they have always stood
together.[2] During his long wartime imprisonment, his correspondence
became his sole emotional and intellectual outlet. The essential point
of this chapter is to understand, rather than endorse, his passion and
commitment.

---

[1] Translated. by Andrew McCord, *Caravan* (Delhi), 1 February 2014.
[2] *My Life—A Fragment* is an important source for understanding the
early life and career of Mohamed Ali. So are his letters and speeches that
I have edited. Recently, I have analysed Gandhi's relationships in *Faith and
Freedom: Gandhi in History* (New Delhi: Niyogi Books, 2012).

As the War progressed in the Balkans, educated Indian Muslims could not help noticing the change in European politics from the time when Great Britain had fought side by side with Turkey against Russia half a century ago. Two newspapers of the time, *Al-Hilal and Comrade*, publicized widely the view that Britain had acquiesced in the Italian attack on Tripoli and concluded treaties with Russia and France to disintegrate the Ottoman Empire. The independence and safety of the Holy Places were, indeed, the driving force behind the pan-Islamic upsurge; however this notion is contradicted, as a little reflection will show, by the prominent part played by the Turks themselves in destroying the *Khilafat*.

The ulama and the Western-educated linked up with each other in pursuit of a common goal. So did Gandhi who brought into being an extraordinary convergence of interests. Abul Bari, the theologian at the seminary in Lucknow, emerged as his principal ally. Their meeting produced astonishing results. One of them was the alliance with the Ali brothers (Mohamed and Shaukat). As powerful spokesmen of north India's Muslim intelligentsia, they came close to Gandhi and acted at his behest on political matters of common interest to them. During Gandhi's fast in 1924, people from all walks of life flocked for a *darshan* to Poona. So did Shaukat Ali, Mohamed Ali's younger brother; he fumbled about the Mahatma's bed to touch his feet, and upon finding them with some difficulty, he uncovered the sheet and kissed them.[3]

Urdu biographers laud Mohamed Ali for his lightning flash of genius, and his ability to mingle old beliefs with new ones.[4] They make much of his fortitude in pain and adversity, exalt his years in prison as 'years of illumination, the rediscovery of self, (and) the emergence of perspectives', and attribute his large following to his simplicity, humility, and inexhaustible energy. They lionize him as the *Mujahid-e Azam* or the *Ahrar-ul Islam*.[5] At gatherings, he held their attention and that

[3] Mahadev H. Desai, *Day-to-Day with Gandhi* (Varanasi: Sarva Seva Sangh Prakashan, 1969), p. 3.

[4] 'Rehlat', in *Kulliyat-e Josh Malihabadi*, in Urdu, edited by Ismat Malihabadi (Delhi: Farid Book Depot, 2007), p. 379.

[5] Farooq Argali (ed.), *Mujahid-e Azam Maulana Mohamed Ali Jauhar*, in Urdu (New Delhi: Farid Book Depot, n.d.).

of others for hours making them laugh or burst into tears. Women in *purdah* stood listening and responded by donating their jewels or small incomes to the Khilafat Fund.

Mohamed Ali borrowed heavily from a radical past to argue that the days were gone when the government could base its political beliefs upon the clamour of the imperialists or upon the uninformed beliefs of the conservative lobby. He would privately say that he could count on the greater part of the Indian Army and the railway staff to take his side when the time came, and that volunteers would undertake civil disobedience from 1 August.[6] He also said that if he survived this cataclysm, he could erect the great Islamic fabric and justify the ways of God to men.[7] These remarks were general topics of conversation.[8] Individuals and groups often asked each other when the British would quit.

The All-India Khilafat Conference held at Karachi between 8 and 10 July 1921 threatened Gandhi's vision of a non-violent movement. One of its resolutions forbade 'every Muslim to serve or enlist himself in the British Army or to raise recruits for it ... it [became]... incumbent on all Muslims in general and all ulama in particular to carry their religious commandment to every soldier in the British Indian Army'. Mohamed Ali also raised the spectre of an Afghaninvasion of British India, to which several Congress leaders took serious exception. His pronouncement placed the Hindu–Muslim alliance in jeopardy.

Life in Fragments

Fatherless at a young age, depending on nobody but his mother, Mohamed Ali threw himself into the whirlpool of college life at Aligarh. He

[6] Weekly Bulletin on the Non-cooperation Movement for the week ending 16 July 1921, in *Regionalizing Pan-Islamism*, p. 274.

[7] *Muhammad Ali: His Life and Services to the Country*, with a foreword by C. P. Ramaswami Aiyer, (Madras: Ganesh & Co., 1918), p. 96.

[8] Mohamed Ali to Gandhi, 20 February 1918, in *Mohamed Ali in Indian Politics*, vol. 2, p. 240.

lingered on within its walls until it became necessary to choose a profession. Shaukat Ali raised funds for his younger brother to study Modern History at Lincoln College, Oxford, but Mohamed Ali's thoughts were all wrapped up in the pleasure and the prospects of a life at home. He did go to Oxford and, after his matriculation in 1902, returned to India and took a crack at a teaching position at Aligarh. But his 'radical' past as a student stood in his way. He made an effort to develop his personality by focusing his attention in other directions, like seeking a government job, but the officials, after having led him up the garden path, turned him down. He then took up a job at the Opium Department in Baroda. Gaekwad Sayaji Rao (1875–1936) of Baroda was a good master, but the opium department could hardly offer solace to Mohamed Ali's exuberant spirit.

Groping about in an intellectual daze in search of a 'cause', Mohamed Ali left Baroda in 1910 with no clear plan for the future. In essentials he followed the line of the 'Aligarh Movement', but shared the ideal, so characteristic of the middle classes, of a representative government. He did not take long to express his thoughts, emotions, and aspirations regarding the European conspiracy to break up the Ottoman Empire. The Turco-Italian War made him criticize the existing regime, and the desperate situation in which Turkey found itself after the War filled him with a zeal for martyrdom. 'Such sufferings and privations as ours,' Mohamed Ali wrote from his internment in Chhindwara, 'have only too often been the lot of mankind, in all ages and climes.'[9] He put it in another way in jail:

> Grieve not over imprisonment in the cage, but
> Do not forget the action of the plucker of the rose.
> Oh foolish nightingale! When free in the garden.
> When did you ever find repose? [10]

The Kanpur mosque incident in 1913[11] heightened anti-government sentiments. Mohamed Ali himself boasted that this city of textile

---

[9] Mohamed Ali to James DuBoulay, 18 February 1919, in *Mohamed Ali in Indian Politics*, vol. 2, p. 190.

[10] Gail Minault, *The Khilafat Movement: Religious Symbolism and Political Mobilization in India* (New York: Columbia University Press, 1982), p. 160.

[11] In July 1913, the Kanpur municipality decided to demolish a part of a mosque to build a new road. This was condemned as an act of desecration

industries had become the battleground of Muslim self-realization, and the result of the movement signalled a victory for Muslim solidarity.[12] This was an exaggerated claim, but modesty was not one of Mohamed Ali's virtues. Nonetheless, his writings left the most lasting memory upon the readers of *Comrade* and *Hamdard*. Likewise, his writings on the Aligarh Muslim University (AMU) Movement enthused the Western-educated Muslims in north India. They dreamt of a 'Muslim Oxford'. But the government showed poor judgement by turning down a perfectly legitimate demand.[13] It led to serious discontent and disillusionment. In the eyes of the intelligentsia, which Mohamed Ali led from the front, the Muslim cause would best be served in alliance with the Congress. In some circles, of course, the Muslim League (founded in December 1906) was regarded as a catalyst for change. Mohamed Ali had some part in its making, though he was left out of the Simla deputation[14] by the landowners and government servants. His reputation for being daring, impetuous and fiercely independent-minded did not go down well with them.

Nationalism in the Islamic Mode

Ordinarily, Mohamed Ali's career would have taken a predictable course—a degree followed by a teaching position or a place in the legal profession. Instead, he defied his mentor, Syed Ahmad, to become a front-rank publicist. The article 'The Choice of the Turks' earned him and his brother a stint in British jails as it was viewed as an incitement to Turkey to go to war . Interned on 15 May 1915 in Mehrauli, they lived in the shadow of the world-famous Qutub Minar before moving

---

of a sacred place of worship and as a threat to Islam. Violence broke out at a meeting on 3 August, where the police fired at the mob; several Muslims were killed and many arrested.

[12] To Hardinge, 24 April 1919, in *Mohamed Ali in Indian Politics*, vol. 2

[13] In addition to a 'Muslim Oxford', this 'demand' refers to the restoration of the demolished section of the mosque.

[14] On 1 October 1906, a deputation of 70 representatives led by Aga Khan presented to Lord Minto, the Viceroy of India, a plan for separate electorates for the community.

on 25 November 1915 to Chhindwara, a small town in the Central Provinces. 'Places changed,' writes their recent biographer, 'but not the vexations and corrosive cares of an unfair treatment.'[15] The Ali brothers claimed that they were punished for their allegiance to Islam, a religion that compelled them to do certain acts, and that no law could restrain them from doing so.

'Who does not love to recall his youth and years as a child without worry and without any thought of the morrow,' Dzerzhinsky had written. This was nothing new for the Ali brothers, who fretted in that sorrow-laden world of the prison, effectively played cat-and-mouse with officials, and reminded them that they had the passport of Heaven to honour. Stricken by bouts of acute depression, they sulked. They embraced all they came in contact with, but advised others to bear with equanimity the calamity which had befallen them.[16] Their burqa-clad mother, Abadi Bano Begum (1852–1924), waxed lyrical:

Boli Amma Mohamed Ali ki
Jaan beta Khilafat pe de do

Said the mother of Mohamed Ali,
give your life for the Khilafat.

'Every day belongs to loneliness, every night to solitude; every morning has become a reunion with isolation,' wrote Mohamed Ali.[17] With his heart too full and his emotions too intense, he called up imaginary companions to converse with in solitude, and in loneliness. In his free time, he read the Quran which he had not done before. That is when Tauhid grew upon him as a personal reality—man in the dignity of his 'service' as vicegerent of God, and himself as part of this great strength. He read the Sihah-e Sitah, a compilation of the Prophet's traditions (hadis), as also the works of Imam Ghazzali (1058–1111), theologian, jurist and mystic; T. W. Arnold (1864–1930), professor of philosophy at Aligarh since 1888 and the author of Preaching of Islam, and of

[15] Khalid Ali, Ali Brothers: The Life and Times of Maulana Mohamed Ali and Shaukat Ali (Karachi: Royal Book Company, 2012), p. 371.

[16] Muhammad Ali, pp. 89–90.

[17] Sabauddin Abdur Rahman, Maulana Mohamed Ali ki Yaad Me, in Urdu (Azamgarh: Shibli Academy, n.d.), pp. 129, 131; G. Minault, The Khilafat Movement, pp. 160–1.

Shibli Nomani (1857–1914), the historian and biographer who made the symbols of Islam a living reality for Aligarh students. He experienced 'an exquisite thrill of delight' reading *Asrar-e Khudi* (*Secrets of the Self*) by Mohammad Iqbal (1875–1938). Mohamed Ali had, in fact, immersed himself Iqbal's poetry from college days.

The time spent in prison enabled Mohamed Ali to steep himself afresh in his Islamic heritage and turn to the study of Islam and its great figures. At Chhindwara and Lansdowne, he had the undisturbed peace and quiet to read the *Quran*, the 'perennial fountain of truth'.[18] Faith in Allah, clear conscience, and loyal friends gave life meaning and value, and provided solace during tragedies and calamities.[19] 'Our only talisman in all such tests,' he told the Viceroy, 'is a combination of patience and prayer.' He shared his feelings with Gandhi, who shared his religiosity:

> Whatever else my internment may or may not have done, it has I believe set the soul free, and that compensates me for so many items on the wrong side of the account. What I could dimly perceive before I now realize with distinctness, and it is this that the whole aim and end of life is to serve God and obey His commandments ... I confess I had never before grasped this truth in all its fullness. Internment made us seek refuge in the Holy Quran, and for the first time, I have to confess it, I read it through and with new eyes. It was then that this truth dawned upon me and gave me coherence and a unity to a thousand vague aspirations to do good to my people, my country and men and women in general.[20]

In jail, Mohamed Ali set out to write the Prophet's biography. But, unlike Azad, he could not carry through all his writing projects. But he did write poetry; the *ghazals* traceable to his prison years are reasonable both in quality and quantity. As a poet, he treats us to a good many historical particulars.

---

[18] Mohamed Ali, *My Life*, p. 111.

[19] Mohammad Fadhel Jamali, *Letters on Islam: Written by a Father in Prison to His Son* (London: Oxford University Press, 1965), p. viii. He was arrested on 14 July 1958 when the Revolution broke out in Iraq. The Military Tribunal condemned him to death, and to 55 years' imprisonment.

[20] To Gandhi, 20 February 1918, Mohamed Ali Papers, Jamia Millia Islamia [JMI].

Ye nazar-bandi to nikli rad-e sehar
Deeda hai hosh ab ja kar khule
Ab kahin toota hai batil ka talism
Haq ke uqde ab kahin mujh par khule
Ab hua ma-sewa ka purda faash
Maarifat ke ab kahin daftar khule
Faiz se tere hi ai qaid-e Firang
Baal-o-par nikle qafas ke dar khule.[21]

This incarceration's turned out to be
A foil to magic and sorcery.
It's opened my mind's eyes at last,
The enemy's spell has broken finally.
The truth is out, the mystery unravelled.
At long last the secrets stand exposed,
The ledgers of wisdom've been revealed to me.

If I've grown wings and can defy the dungeon,
It's only through thy courtesy, O British prison.

(Translated from the Urdu by Nishat Zaidi)

Mohamed Ali was freed on 28 December 1919 under the terms of an amnesty. The road was open to Amritsar where, in keeping with the wartime practice, the Congress and the League held simultaneous meetings. Flushed with 'victory', he spoke of the omnipotence of Allah, both in Heaven and on earth, and said he was determined to give away everything he had, including his life, for the sake of Allah and Islam. Muslims were subjects of Allah, he said, and not of Great Britain. Consequently, he exhorted his audience to defend the Kaaba at all cost. One of them, Mohammad Mujeeb, then a student at Oxford, did not approve of Mohamed Ali's appearance—'his waxed moustaches and immaculate dress'—and also reacted sharply to what he considered his theatrical behaviour. 'I have not been able to overcome that impression,' Mujeeb remarked, adding, 'and the closer I have studied Maulana Mohamed Ali's writings, the more confirmed have I become in my initial impression of his personality and character. He was much too selfish and self-centred, and such a person to my mind was the least entitled to lead a people.'[22]

---

[21] Farooq Argali, *Mujahid-e Azam*, p. 97.
[22] Oral History Transcript (407), NMML.

The Trial

J. Crerar, an official, complained on 31 August 1921 that Mohamed Ali and five others had adopted a specific resolution at the Karachi Khilafat Conference on 8–10 July 1921. Accordingly, the police arrested them. Following this, S. M. Talati, Karachi's City Magistrate, committed them to trial. B. C. Kennedy, Sindh's Judicial Commissioner, presided over the court and T. G. Elphinstone led the presentation. The trial began on 26 October 1921 and continued until 1 November that year.

Trials in colonial India exposed the racial arrogance of British judges, and their unabashed contempt for the idea of a free India. On the other hand, the men and women on trial exemplified courage and sacrifice and their fate and fortune was a matter of deep public attention and care. Ordinary people assembled at the site of a trial, and newspaper reports turned the judicial proceedings into a trial of Pax Britannica itself. At the end of the day, the people and not the jury sat in judgement on the legitimacy of laws that were decreed to stifle the free expression of opinion through *hartals*, boycotts, non-cooperation, and *satyagraha*.

In the light of previous histories of hartal, the 'Karachi Trial' bears salience for three reasons. First, noted public figures asserted their inherent right to express an opinion without restraint, and endorsed their right to offer services to, or remain in the employ of, the civil or military departments. Accordingly, Jawaharlal urged the 30,000 peasants in Gorakhpur district to follow Mohamed Ali. The ulama of Deoband extended this appeal to other classes as well. Writes Gail Minault, biographer of the Khilafat Movement: 'The campaign to proclaim the Karachi resolutions and the fatwa from every soapbox was more prudent than civil disobedience.'[23]

Mohamed Ali's arrest and trial imparted strength to the people's anti-colonial sentiments. The British were now seen as enemies of religion in general, and not just of Islam. Sections of the ulama revisited the nineteenth-century discourses on whether India was a *dar al-Islam* (house of Islam) or a *dar al-harb* (house of War) to determine the strategy for 'Muslim India', but their efforts yielded no worthwhile result. Apart from the differences in the phalanx of orthodoxy, community leaders knew that they could do nothing to sap the foundations of the

---

[23] G. Minault, *The Khilafat Movement*, pp. 171–2.

powerful British Empire. Yet, it became almost customary to reiterate either the Khilafat resolution or the proscribed *fatwa* at public meetings. The agitators resolved to fill the jails.[24]

If doubting and questioning are taken to be the quintessence of the intelligentsia, then the Karachi trial offered Mohamed Ali and his partners the platform to explain the basic rudiments of Islam, the essential features of South Asian Islam, and its place in Indian history. Although the rhetoric was overwhelming, they attempted to define their community's place in the colonial system. Moreover, with the Ottoman Empire and other Muslim countries in disarray, they regarded pan-Islamism as a means of attaining their liberation as well as that of India. This attempt to connect the global with the local was part of the grand design of Jamaluddin Afghani (1838–1897), the ideologue of these radical ideas in the 19th century.

Trial and Error

The accused men on trial in the 1921 Karachi case were the Ali brothers; Bharti Krishna Tirathji, an odd man out in the company of avowed pan-Islamists; Saifuddin Kitchlew (1884–1963), the fiery orator from Punjab who considered military service to be 'unlawful'; Pir Ghulam Mujadid (1881–1958), a Sindhi follower of Abdul Bari; Maulana Nisar Ahmad of the Jamiyat al-Ulama-e Hind, founded in 1919 as a platform for the Deobandi ulama; and the learned Husain Ahmad Madani (1879–1957) from the same theological seminary. Interned in Malta from 1917 to 1920,[25] he was one among the *Aseeran-e Malta*. Drums were sounded from the minarets of Saharanpur's Juma Masjid (UP) to announce his arrest. The police eventually caught up with him after a show of opposition by volunteers armed with spears, who assaulted a police inspector.[26]

---

[24] Mushirul Hasan and Margrit Pernau, 'Khilafat Movement in the United Provinces', in *Regionalizing Pan-Islamism*, p. 75.

[25] D. R. Goyal, *Maulana Husain Ahmad Madani, A Biographical Study* (New Delhi: Published for Maulana Abul Kalam Institute of Studies, Kolkata, by Anamika Publishers and Distributors, 2004).

[26] 'Khilafat Movement in the United Provinces', in *Regionalizing Pan-Islamism*, p. 75.

The popular chant of the time was, *Keh rahe hain Karachi ke qaidi;
hum to jaate hain do do bars ko* (the prisoners of Karachi put it so/for
two years away we go).[27] The rumours going round were that a family
of Syeds in Karachi was engaged in inciting the Mekranes of the 'lowest
classes' to press for the release of the Ali brothers or to enter the jail
themselves,[28] and also that Pir Imamshah, son of the Jhandewalla Pir, and
Pir Mahbubshah of Hyderabad had collected revolvers to harm the wit-
nesses. The local government moved in to protect the Jhandewalla family
until their return to their village.[29] According to an intelligence report

> [t]he Khilafat Movement [was] ... becoming more intense and more
> general. While the trial of the Ali Brothers among other things caused
> the idea to crystallise that the Ali Brothers were endeavouring to give a
> political agitation a cloak of religion, general feeling in sympathy with
> the religious view of the Khilafat question [was] ... very widespread....
> Moderate opinion among the educated classes ... [was] ... chiefly
> centred in Hyderabad and Karachi. In these circles, 'repressive' action
> taken against the minor agitators in cases where there [had]... been no
> incitement to violence [was] ... viewed with great dislike; the results of
> Gandhi's civil disobedience and of the possible reply of Government
> [were] ... viewed with serious apprehension; and the danger of the
> spread of fanaticism among Mahomedans [was] ... also regarded as
> real. The general feeling among Mahomedans [was] ... reflected in
> increased activity to collect money for the Angora Relief Fund. (Hasan
> and Pernau, *Regionalizing Pan-Islamism*, p. 305)

Given the intensity of feelings, the local administration stationed
soldiers and policemen to guard the road from the venue of the trial
to Khaliqdina Hall, and to gird the wall facing the Bunder Road
with barbed wire. Elsewhere, thousands were busy protesting.[30]

---

[27] Rahman, *Maulana Mohamed Ali ki Yaad Me*, p. 129.

[28] 'Weekly Bulletin on the Non-cooperation Movement for the week
ending 12 November 1921', in *Regionalizing Pan-Islamism*, p. 304.

[29] 'Weekly Bulletin on the Non-cooperation Movement for the week
ending 29 October 1921', in *Regionalizing Pan-Islamism*, p. 298.

[30] Afzal Iqbal, *Life and Times of Mohamed Ali: An Analysis of the Hopes,
Fears, and Aspirations of Muslim India from 1878 to 1931* (Lahore: Institute
of Islamic Culture, 1974). pp. 274–80.

Rijhumal Kundanlal Lahori in rural Sind spread the word that volunteers would be called upon to undertake civil disobedience from 1 August 1921.[31] Overall, sympathy grew among Sindhi Muslims.[32] As general topics of conversation, Mohamed Ali's statements became known even among the rural folk. People asked each other when the English would leave the country.[33]

Women expressed affection, concern, and goodwill. The 73-year-old Abadi Bano Begum cast off the veil. She travelled widely,[34] and her appeal for financial help brought hundreds of thousands of rupees to the Khilafat Fund.[35] Presenting the image of dignity for all that she had endured, she asked questions and gave opinions. 'The three women (Abadi Bano, Annie Besant, and Sarojini Naidu),' Gretta Cousins noted, 'were deeply significant of the new era in Indian social and political history. Womanhood had come out of its seclusion to share with manhood the struggle for gaining freedom for Bharat Mata—the Motherland.'[36]

Friends of the accused turned up at the hearing on 24 October 1921. Jamnalal Bajaj (1889–1942) wore a worried look in court. By 2 p.m., two hundred cloth merchants had joined him,[37] along with plainclothes police officers who mingled with the crowd. The prosecution began:

> That you all the seven accused at some time or times between the months of February 1920 and September 1921 both inclusive at Karachi and other places in British India were (with others) parties to a criminal conspiracy to seduce Mohamedan officers and soldiers in the Army of his Majesty the King Emperor from their duty and thereby

---

[31] 'Sind, CID. Report for 1921', in *Regionalizing Pan-Islamism*, p. 274.

[32] 'Sind, CID. Report for 1921', in *Regionalizing Pan-Islamism*, p. 305.

[33] For the Khilafat Movement in Sind, see Shabnum Tejani, *Indian Secularism: A Social and Intellectual History, 1890–1950* (Bloomington: Indiana University Press, 2008).

[34] Hasan and Pernau, *Regionalizing Pan-Islamism*, p. 82.

[35] Shan Muhammad, *Freedom Movement in India: The Role of Ali Brothers* (New Delhi: Associated Publishing House, 1979), pp. 160–1.

[36] Cousins, *Indian Womanhood Today*, p. 63.

[37] Cousins, *Indian Womanhood Today*, p. 301.

committed an offence punishable under section 120 B/115 read with section 131 of the Indian Penal Code and within the cognizance of this sessions court....

And further that you Mohamed Ali on or about the 9th day of July 1921 at Karachi made a statement to wit that 'It is in every way religiously unlawful for a Mussalman at the present moment to continue in the British army or to enter the army or to induce others to join the army' with intent to cause or which is likely to cause Mussalman officers and soldiers in the army of His Majesty to disregard or fail in their duty as such, and thereby committed an offence punishable under Section 505 of the Indian Penal Code and within the cognizance of this sessions court ...

And further that you Mohamed Ali on or about the 9th day of July 1921 at Karachi abetted the commission of an offence punishable under Section 505 and or Section 131 of the Indian Penal Code by more than ten persons, in that, you stated in the All-India Khilafat Conference that 'it is the duty of all Mussalmans in general and the *ulema* in particular to see that these religious commandments (referring to the words quoted above) are brought home to every Mussalman in the army' and thereby committed an offence under Section 117 of the IPC and within the cognizance of this sessions court.[38]

There is no doubting the broadness of Mohamed Ali's interests, his instinctive reactions, and his freedom from the sort of prejudices that many evinced. He displayed a theatrical exhibition of militarism, but his principal distinction lay in his talent to tell the story of his entire life. He expounded the notion of free opinion and intellectual autonomy, and acted out his role and read out his lines unhesitatingly. He talked of the superiority of God's law to any man-made law. It followed, then, that 'the trial [was] not "Mohamed Ali and six others *versus* God", but "*God versus man*"'. The whole question was, 'Shall God dominate over man or shall man dominate over God?' Mohamed Ali declared:

So far as I am concerned, the Quran is my law, giants or no giants, and I shall fight when my God demands it of me and shall not rest, and not

[38] Thadani, *The Historic State Trial*, p. 268.

ask him to fight the giants himself. And if I am to be hanged for it—for it is not sec. 120-A or B then, but 232, (waging war against the king, gentlemen) I will still say that this is my law and that it is right and even my carcass hanging from the gibbet will I trust say the same. Do not therefore think of saving me, gentlemen, from transportation for life. But if you have a God and if you have a soul to save and if you have faith you will decide according to your conscience....[39]

A Muslim's faith consisted in believing in a set of doctrines, living up to them, and exerting oneself to the fullest extent. A Mussalman could not say 'I am not my brother's keeper', for in a sense his or her own salvation cannot be assured without exhorting others to avoid evil and to do good. If compelled to wage war against the *Mujahid* (warrior) of Islam, a Muslim had to persuade his brethren to defend the faith. This represented Mohamed Ali's belief.[40] His face drew up in a grimace of pain and anger, but he stood immobile for a moment. The jury (one European, two Christians from Goa, and two Hindus) listened.

Shaukat Ali, who too had belched fire and passion in what he said, now stood by his brother, arms crossed in confidence over his chest. As the judge read his judgement, Husain Ahmad Madani controlled rising emotions.[41] On the charge of seducing troops from their allegiance, the jury had a unanimous verdict of 'not guilty' for the other co-accused. But, on the minor charge of publishing a statement *likely* to have that effect, the judge sentenced six of the accused to two years' rigorous imprisonment. He discharged the Shankaracharya.[42] He tried

[39] Thadani, *The Historic State Trial*, p. 268.
[40] Thadani, *The Historic State Trial*, pp. 288–9.
[41] Home Dept, Political, file no. 155, 1922.
[42] W. C. Smart, District Magistrate, Karachi, reported to the Secretary, Home Dept:

In the case of the Hindu accused No. 6 his story is that he was totally unaware of the nature of the resolution to be moved. He does not know, he says (as is very probably the case), Hindustani. He was not a member of the subjects committee and merely came to the conference to give the weight of his 'pontifical authority'" to any resolutions that may be passed, without troubling to examine their nature. If this is true he is an almost intolerably frivolous and irresponsible person, but he is not to be punished for that. His speeches were no doubt highly noncommittal and of course the subject was one of which he had no authority to speak. On the other

to make amends for his acquittal to his Muslim friends by reaffirming his support to them. As a matter of fact, the *fatwa* campaign did not run out of steam but gained more adherents. The man on the street revered the *'fatwa* prisoner' as a champion of a noble mission.[43]

With his head held high, Mohamed Ali returned to the Congress platform as its head. In his first public address after attaining his freedom, he spoke of the gloom of finding on his shoulders the burden of freeing India and Islam. The whole social structure that Gandhi had so assiduously built quaked, as if it were built upon shifting sands. Mohamed Ali said that he had come out 'from a smaller prison to a large one', and exhorted every Congressman to sacrifice his life for independence. Non-cooperation was still the main plank of politics, and he criticized, for this reason, the Swaraj Party for letting some of its stalwarts take up legal practice. The nationalist press hoped that he would infuse fresh life into the people's drooping hearts. 'A powerful figure with a massive intellect and a commanding personality,' stated Lucknow's *Indian Daily Telegraph*, adding, 'Mohamed Ali walks the past scenes of his "larger jail" as he calls India bereft of Gandhi.'[44]

Some commentators questioned Mohamed Ali's belief that religion and politics must go hand in hand, that the mixing of the two did not trigger the most violent and protracted conflicts of the time, and that Gandhi's earnest direct-action type of protest (*hartal*) was not responsible for the 'rise' of communalism. They also contested his argument that the Congress had not done enough to safeguard minority interests, and that some like Lajpat Rai and Madan Mohan Malaviya represented the Hindu Mahasabha, *shuddhi*, and *sangathan*. How, then, could the Congress inspire confidence in the minorities? This

---

hand he is no doubt a Khilafat sympathizer and prepared to further the cause of the Khilafatists to the best of his ability. You must consider his case on its own merits very carefully. (Home Dept, Political, file no. 155, 1922.)

[43] G. Minault, *The Khilafat Movement*, p. 174.

[44] The *Hamdam* remarked that at a time when the Hindu–Muslim disturbances had intensified, the patriots looked up to Mohamed Ali to restore the happy relations between them. The confidence which the people had in him had been practically proved by his election as President of the next Congress (*Selections*, UP, week ending 1 September 1923).

76   ROADS TO FREEDOM

was a fair question, but the Congress leadership failed to offer a satisfactory explanation. With the political horizon changing dramatically, the old shibboleths collapsed. Sarojini Naidu, the only female member of a Congress delegation to Punjab in 1923, wanted to go on 'churning the ocean' till 'some supreme gift of harmony' was evolved,[45] but there were not many statesmen who shared her optimism. Mohamed Ali was, for example, in too much of a hurry to secure rapid solutions to complex problems of secularism and communitarian representation. After every conference or meeting, he felt that time was running out and that the Hindu communal party would bring no justice to the religious minorities.

The poetry of the Khilafat was ultimately defeated by the prose of political and military events in Turkey itself.[46] Its self-styled custodians, acting as arbiters of the Khilafat destiny, lived in a world of make-believe even after the abolition of the Khilafat by Mustafa Kemal Pasha (1881–1938), the first president of Turkey. Azad, for his part pictured pan-Islamism as an ideal, not a reality, and he began to feel his way towards new political impulses. He could thus build bridges of retreat which Mohamed Ali could not. After 1924–5, every speech was a battle-cry, and Delhi rang with the sound of conflict. He allowed his emotions to guide him.

Mohamed Ali had the oratorical skills to stir the masses to a high pitch of religious enthusiasm, but he seldom addressed their actual grievances, or provided remedies for them. In many situations, he demonstrated poor judgement. Of this, a striking example is the *hijrat* fiasco, the migration of Muslims that took place in July 1920 from British India to the *dar-us-Islam* (land of Islam) in Afghanistan. The tribesmen, aided by their Amir, rose in thousands; disasters followed in quick succession, redeemed by incidents of courage and devotion. But Mohamed Ali, Azad, and Abdul Bari must be called to account for their serious error of judgement. By hitching their wagon to the Khilafat crescent, they had led innocent Muslims 'up the garden path.'[47]

[45] Jawaharlal Nehru (ed.), *A Bunch of Old Letters*, Centenary edition (Delhi: Oxford University Press, 1989), p. 25.
[46] Peter Hardy, *The Muslims of British India* (Cambridge: Cambridge University Press, 1974), p. 197.
[47] Hardy, *The Muslims of British India*, p. 198.

Although Gandhi broke with the colonial past to restore to them the absolute values of self-government, integrity, and dignity,[48] he had to engage with men like Mohamed Ali, who, in the quest for success, turned increasingly 'mobbish'. Joseph Conrad (1857–1924)—born and bred in Poland—wrote in his preface to *A Personal Record* (1912): 'Those who read me, know me, know my conviction that the world, the temporal world, rests on a few very simple ideas; so simple that they may be as old as the hills. It rests notably, among others, on the idea of Fidelity.' This governing idea of fidelity, of keeping faith between man and man, was not the mainspring of Mohamed Ali's life. The power of evocation remained, but his faculty of self-criticism and self-introspection had diminished by the time he delivered his 'Last Word' at the Round Table Conference in London where he died in 1931 and was buried in the Al-Aqsa Mosque in Palestine.

Mohamed Ali's own trajectory led him from liberalism to conservatism. Starting from positions inevitably determined by his social background and his education, he ended up fulfilling his obligations to those who had pledged themselves to weaken the liberal foundations of nationalism. This was the spirit that brought him close to the reactionary and politically conservative leaders who were fighting hard to defend their rights in the Nehru Report of 1928. He preferred to perish politically rather than reflect on the report with care. Had he shown patience and understanding, he might have agreed with the Nehrus and Sapru on its fundamentals. But he did not. 'Alas,' wrote Syed Sulaiman Nadwi in his obituary, 'the last soldier of the defeated army who was fighting alone amidst the surrounding enemy forces fell down with numerous wounds, never to rise again.'[49]

Mohamed Ali is deserving of a biographer who will unravel his complex role as a Muslim interlocutor. Going by the experience of so many decades, probably no serious and engaging biographer will be

---

[48] Syed Mahmud, recalled in *1921 Movement: Reminiscences* (New Delhi: Publications Division, Ministry of Information and Broadcasting, Government of India, 1971), pp. 144–5.

[49] Muhammad Khalid Masud, 'Sayyid Sulayman Nadwi's Yad-i Raftagan', in *Muslim Voices: Communities and the Self in South Asia*, edited by Usha Sanyal, David Gilmartin, and Sandria B. Freitag (Delhi: Yoda Press, 2013), p. 142.

found. Is he then, like Neville Chamberlain, fated to go on being the man of no luck?[50] Perhaps, yes. Or, Muslim institutions will continue to do what they have done in the Jamia Millia Islamia—eschew critical scholarship on Mohamed Ali. Institutional memory, if any, will remain divided between two outstanding individuals of the twentieth century. What are the main components of the divide? We follow Azad's jail life to answer these questions.

[50] A. J. P. Taylor, *Essays in English History* (London: Hamish Hamilton, 1976), p. 295.

5. Calcutta's Maulana*

Colonialism on Trial

Height about 5' 5"; exceptionally thin; noticeably fair; age about 33 years; has practically no hair on his face though he does not shave; long sharp face with prominent nose. This is the 'official' description of Maulana Abul Kalam Azad, the golden boy of the Independence struggle.

---

* Elsewhere, I refer to the wilful scholarly neglect of Azad (Mushirul Hasan, ed., *Islam and Nationalism: Reflections on Abul Kalam Azad*, Delhi: Manohar Publications 1992). All that has appeared in Urdu gives but a blurred, and at times seriously distorted, picture of Azad's career. Writings in Pakistan have resulted in a deplorable one-sidedness. The earlier works by Ian Henderson Douglas (*Abul Kalam Azad: An Intellectual and Religious Biography*, edited by Gail Minault and Christian W. Troll, New Delhi: Oxford University Press, 1988), V. N. Datta, and Kenneth Cragg are instructive. To Francis Robinson, a British historian, the relative neglect of the tombs of Azad and Ansari

What is the city but the people?
The citizens at once shouted their assent:
True,
The people are the city.

—William Shakespeare, *Coriolanus*

Azad lived in a city associated with reformers like Raja Rammohun
Roy (1772–1833), founder of the Brahmo Samaj. His family
belonged to a strong tradition of learning; his ancestors had come
from Herat under Babur's rule (1526–1530). Maulana Shaikh
Mohammad Khairuddin (1831–1908), his father, studied under
Fazl-i Haq Khairabadi, the man exiled to the Andaman Islands. He
belonged to the Qadiri and Naqshbandi orders. The family carried
forward the Sufi traditions. They were devoted to the Chishti saints.
Azad, from his college days, was inspired by the high values upheld
by them. He did not give up. On 16 October 1942, Azad wrote from
the Ahmadnagar Fort Prison:

> This entire commerce of existence, its every mode and form is gathered
> into one single question: 'What is all this?' 'Why all this?' 'What for all
> this?' We take the support of reason, and in the light of what we have
> named learning, we keep moving along whichever path becomes visible.
> But we do not find any solution which can slake the thirst for discovering
> the ends of the tangle.... As we turn towards the old solution ... that
> 'an embodiment of knowledge and strength is the Presence behind
> the veil' ... we suddenly emerge into the light. Now radiance floods in.
> Every question finds its answer, every demand finds its fulfilment, every
> thirst is slaked—as if this perplexity was a vice-like grip which opened
> at the gentle touch of a key.[1]

Azad read the Quran, under the supervision of his tutors and of his
aunt, the elder sister of his wife Aliya and daughter of his teacher,

---

suggests that Indians may have lost interest in keeping their memories alive
(*Separatism among Indian Muslims: The Politics of the United Provinces' Muslims
1860–1923*). It also suggests that India may no longer value, as before, and
perhaps may not even know the principles for which they stood.

[1] Quoted in *Contemporary Relevance of Sufism* (Delhi: Indian Council for
Cultural Relations, 1993), p. 1

Shaikh Ahmad Zahir Vatri. Azad showed signs of brilliance even before completing the standard Islamic syllabus in 1903. He published his first *ghazal* in January 1899. Enjoying a free run of his father's library, he read widely and picked up some books in English, including the Bible. He also could not escape the influence of the writers connected with the 'Bengal Renaissance'.

At the age of 15, Azad launched *Lisan al-Sidq*, a literary journal. Over the years his journalistic ventures continued with *Al-Nadwa*, a journal of the Nadwat al-ulama, *Vakil*, and the *Rifah-e Am* Press in Lahore. His political links were with the revolutionaries in Bengal, which he revived with their counterparts in Punjab. His essay on Sarmad (c. 1590–1660), a seventeenth-century Persian Jew-turned-mystic, is a guide to his early disposition. On 9 July 1910, he wrote:

> In his search for the goal, (Sarmad) discarded the distinction between temple and mosque. Just as he bowed his head in humble respect before Muslim *dervishes*, so he showed faith in Hindu ascetics. Which person of genuine mystical experience would quarrel with this principle? If, in this realm too, we insist on maintaining the distinction between unbelief and Islam, what difference will remain between the blind and the clear-sighted? After all, it is the candle (as such) which the moth has to find. If the moth is in love only with the candle of the sacred precincts of Mecca, then its quest to be burned up is imperfect. Here he quoted the Persian couplet: The lover is scalded both by Islam and *Kufr*. The moth does not discriminate between the lamp of the mosque and of the temple ... (and) of whatever kind it may be, love (*ishq*) is always the first step towards the station of truth and reality (*haqiqat*) ... Or, better, love is the door to be passed though before man can become man. Whoever's heart is not wounded, and whoever's eyes are not wet with tears, how can he fathom the meaning of humanity?[2]

In Azad's young days, Aligarh's MAO College emerged as the nerve centre of debates on reforms, interpretation, and innovation. Hence he turned to Syed Ahmad Khan, a vocal protagonist of interpretation, *mujtahid-e mutlaq*. Shibli Nomani (1857–1914), the erudite scholar, opened his eyes to, among other things, new vistas of life in Iran and

---

[2] Tariq Wali, 'Maulana Azad's Views on Learning about Religions as Part of the National Education System', *Indian Horizons*, vol. 44, no. 3 (1995): 84–5.

Turkey.[3] During his travels in the Middle East in 1908, Azad met young Turks in Cairo and kept up his correspondence with them for years after returning to India.[4] His contacts with the followers of Shaikh Mohammad Abduh (1849–1905), the Egyptian jurist at Al-Azhar, enabled him to learn way beyond the eighteenth–century curriculum, which was heavily laden with medieval classicism, and acquaint himself with other reformist clusters.[5] When the unfettered Azad moved into his own sphere, he found it easy to identify himself with the urge for national liberation stirring the Turks, the Arabs, the Iranians, and the people back home. He wanted them to be united with each other in their struggle to secure liberation. Accordingly, he began the *Al-Hilal* on 13 July 1912 to engage with the Arab world and its religio-ethical complications.[6] No other paper in the early twentieth-century obtained such resounding success or led to so much controversy. It was then that Azad reached the apex of his renown. Not long afterwards, he was at war with authority and social conventions and, like Gandhi whom he venerated, he was as deeply moved by injustice and tyranny.

Azad had paid a security of Rs 2,000 under the Press Act. Soon, he lost both the deposit and the Press.[7] At the site of his internment in Ranchi, he prayed in a village mosque, lectured on the *Quran* after Friday prayers, and established a *madarsa* and an Anjuman-i Islam. The authorities showed no mercy even after Azad completed the term of his externment. Fearing his 'secret' contacts with the Angora nationalists,[8] they invalidated his passport on 19 September 1923 and

[3]   Speech at Calcutta, 27 October 1914, *Khutbat-i Azad* (Delhi, 1974), p. 30; *Masla-i Khilafat wa Jazirat al-Arab* (Calcutta, 1920), pp. 26, 119.

[4]   Maulana Abul Kalam Azad, *India Wins Freedom: An Autobiographical Narrative* (Calcutta: Orient Longman, 1959), pp. 6–7; Rajat Ray, 'Revolutionaries, Pan-Islamists and Bolsheviks: Maulana Abul Kalam Azad and the Political Underworld in Calcutta, 1905–1925', in *Communal and Pan-Islamic Trends in Colonial India*, p. 105.

[5]   Azad, *India Wins Freedom*, pp. 6–7; Rajat Ray, 'Revolutionaries, Pan-Islamists and Bolsheviks', p. 105.

[6]   Azad, *Intikhab-e Al-Hilal* (Lahore: Adabistan, n.d.).

[7]   Azad, *India Wins Freedom*, p. 8.

[8]   Note by S. C. Majumdar, 13 June 1924, Home Dept, Political (B), file no. 10/xxx1, 1924.

jettisoned his travel plans to France and London.[9] Azad has written about this stern coercion in *Ghubar-e Khatir*.

> The country is caught up in a situation in which there are only two options open to its people: either to be insensitive or to be sensitive. A life of insensitivity is possible anywhere and everywhere but for the other option there is no place other than the prison house. I had both the options before me; the former did not agree with my temperament; so I had no choice but to opt for the latter course.[10]

Doubts and Scepticism

The curtain was drawn on *Lisan al-Sidq* in May 1905.[11] This coincided with Azad's quest for a new path, a search for a new trajectory to answer his searching doubts. One has only to cast a glance at some of his early writings to realize that he had entered the valley of doubts and uncertainties to demolish the suppositions guiding theologians and to free minds from the shackles of religion. His opposition to Syed Ahmad and Shibli became the springboard of his intellectual activity.[12] Azad rejected the 'scripturalists' or the 'literalists' and their literal interpretation of the *Quran* and the *Sunna*. Soon, his interest in the externals of religion diminished, but not in his authentic inward piety. Azad comprehended the *Quran* within the verses of the first *Surah*, and conceived and pursued the politics of Islam within the dimension of *taqwa* (piety) and *tawakkul*.[13] He studied the Quran from within itself, in its own right, and not in response to an extraneous pressure, for self-sufficient understanding and not for explanations or endorsement or rejections, nor for extraneous pressures, motives or criteria.[14]

---

[9] Home Dept, Political (B), file no. 99, VI, 1925.

[10] 11 August 1942, Azad, *Sallies of Mind: English Translation of* Ghubar-e-khatir (Kolkata: Maulana Abul Kalam Azad Institute of Asian Studies, 2003), p. 45.

[11] Only ten issues of this literary journal came out between November 1903 and May 1905.

[12] Ahmad, *Islamic Modernism*, p. 176.

[13] Kenneth Cragg, *The Pen and the Faith: Eight Modern Muslim Writers and the Quran* (Delhi: Indian Society for Promoting Christian Knowledge, 1988), p. 30; Ahmad, *Islamic Modernism*, pp. 177–8.

[14] Ahmad, *Islamic Modernism*, p. 177.

He wrote the *Tazkira* and the *Tarjuman al-Quran* to produce philosophic truth or artistic beauty of universal value and appeal. In this respect, he had a much closer affinity with Gandhi who regarded Truth as the cornerstone of his life. It came first, last, and always. And, like Gandhi, his moral order was based not on a materialistic way of life, which he regarded as the stagnation and retardation of religion, but on *rahmat* (benevolence) and *adalat* (justice).

Gandhi and Jawaharlal expressed the two dominant perspectives on the place of religion in public life—one stood for unity between politics and religion, and the other for separating the two. Azad adhered to the view, which was strictly speaking the Islamic view, that religion and politics are intertwined. He highlighted Islam's moral and ethical dimensions and not just its external manifestations. According to him, 'if all the curtains due to external forms and terminologies could be removed and Reality were to appear before us unveiled, all the (religious) differences of the world would suddenly vanish and all quarrelsome people would see that their object was the same, though it had different names'.[15] Rammohun Roy and Swami Vivekananda, who had founded the Ramakrishna Mission, had argued on these lines. The available evidence seems to suggest that long before Azad came under Gandhi's influence, he had felt his way towards a pluralistic religious coexistence.[16]

From his perspective on religion, Azad discussed the motivating logic beneath pan-Islamism. He made a case for the Khilafat as a God-sent institution to secure obedience to Him and believed that the political Khilafat, which passed from the Abbasids in Egypt to the Ottoman Empire in 1517, outwardly expressed man's acceptance of *tauhid* (unity) as the centre of Muslim life. Mindful of the Khalifa's symbolic value for bolstering Muslim solidarity and anti-colonial sentiment,[17] he turned it into a vehicle for articulating political aspirations and religious sensibilities. But, by the end of 1922, the same issue appeared hollow. Impressed by the Muslims, Christians, and Druzes uniting in Syria for their

[15] Mushir U. Haq, *Muslim Politics in Modern India, 1857–1957* (Meerut: Meenakshi Prakashan, 1970), p. 63.

[16] Ahmad, *Islamic Modernism*, p. 184.

[17] G. Minault, *The Khilafat Movement*, p. 176.

country's liberation under the slogan 'Religion is for God and the homeland is for everyone', Azad decided to strive for the development of a similar nationalism in India.[18] He felt duty-bound to justify Hindu–Muslim cooperation by taking the juristic view that the Quran draws a distinction between those who commit aggression against Muslims and those who do not. He cited the Prophet's covenant with the Jews in AD 622 as a historical precedent to justify Hindu–Muslim cooperation. Azad worked out a system of beliefs and sentiments to establish a common bond transcending conflicts, and stressed upon the development of a secular personality within a democratic framework. He expected no new heaven or new earth to be attained immediately, but he had faith in the immanent revelation of man's reason applying itself to the changing circumstances of man's social existence.[19] Inspired by the Bhakti and Sufi saints, he envisaged an Islam not of sectarian belligerence but of confident partnership in a cultural and spiritual diversity where a strident divisiveness would be its betrayal.[20] Azad saw the essential unity behind all that diversity, and realized that only in unity was there hope for India as a whole. In the opinion of one of his followers:

> The greatest service which the Maulana did was to teach people of every religion that there are two aspects of religion. One separates and creates hatred. This is the false aspect. The other, the true spirit of religion, brings people together; it creates understanding. It lies in the spirit of the service, in sacrificing self for others. It implies belief in unity, in the essential unity of things.[21]

The *Tarjuman-al Quran* enjoined on the Muslims to discover a new world of religious thought to redress the balance of the old.[22] Azad postulated an equation between Islam and Indian nationalism on the one hand, and between Islam and universal principles, on the

[18] Donald Eugene Smith, *India as a Secular State* (Princeton, N.J.: Princeton University Press, 1963), p. 144.

[19] Hardy, *Muslims of British India*, p. 100.

[20] Cragg, *The Pen and the Faith*, p. 29.

[21] Quoted in Douglas, *Abul Kalam Azad*, p. 276.

[22] Mohammad Mujeeb, *The Indian Muslims* (Delhi: Munshiram Manoharlal, 1985), pp. 460, 463.

other, to enlarge conceptions of what was possible, enrich intellectual imagination, and diminish dogmatism. With his integrated, harmonious, and creative Islam, he adumbrated the position of a religious humanist, very much along the lines of the humanism embodied in the classical Persian Sufi poetical tradition. In this way, he brought an element of stability in his own life which was otherwise full of vicissitudes, difficulties, and disasters. Overwhelmed with Allah's blessings and gifts and exhilarated with the greatness and beauty of His creation, he made earthly life a reality, and that is where he belonged. For this sober, practical, and forward-looking person, a new order emerged like—to use the imagery of Ghalib— 'dispersed light in the mirror, a speck of dust; caught in the sunlight in the window'. For him a new message came from ordinary quarters—from Mahatma Gandhi and Jawaharlal Nehru. He adapted himself, as best as he could, to their ways. From this standpoint it appears that there is too much emphasis on 'jihad' in Ayesha Jalal's narrative, and too little on love, mercy, and religion and piety being the source of Azad's drive for doing good.[23]

India's Muslims were divided by the geographical distance, by differences of dialect and custom and, in some cases, by the deeper chasm of sectarianism. Taking these factors into account, Azad explored the rich treasures of Indo-Islamic thought to become a torchbearer of synthesis. He cultivated a look of venerable age to lend heft to his learning, and exuded an air of gravity and seriousness.[24] Azad's genius and method were too individualistic to found a school, but his patient learning introduced a breath of fresh air in contemporary political discourses and captivated whosoever came in close contact to him. In his discovery of 'a new world of religious thought to redress the balance of the old', he shared in the effort to give the lie to the steady charge, or implication, that living without benefit of statehood would inevitably entail a slow assimilation of Muslims into the dominant ethos of Hinduism. He proved well beyond doubt that Islam could be lived in harmony and not in conflict with the followers of other religions.

[23] Jalal, *Partisans of Allah*, pp. 194–202.
[24] Nehru, *An Autobiography*, p. 193; G. N. S. Raghavan, *Aruna Asaf Ali* (New Delhi: National Book Trust, 2005 reprint), p. 20.

The Wilful Illusion

Azad was set free on 1 January 1920. He and the Mahatma were supposed to meet some days later, but the government prevented this. Nonetheless, they knew each other well enough to form the same opinion on the most important issue of the day—the future of the Khilafat and the safety of the Holy Places. When Azad landed up in jail on 10 December 1921 and accepted the sentence with his characteristic poise and dignity, Gandhi commented in *Young India* on 23 February 1922: 'What a change between 1919 and 1922—nervous fear of sentences and all kinds of defences in 1919, utter disregard of sentences and no defence in 1922.' A year later, at the age of 35, Azad became the youngest person to become the Congress President. 'The caravan of my hopes,' he remarked in *Tazkira*, 'is seeing now the signs of a new goal.'

Azad sought legitimacy from the ulama as well. But the solid phalanx of orthodoxy thwarted his ambition to be the *Imam-ul-Hind*. It is difficult to exaggerate the loss of prestige he suffered through the melancholy failure of his enterprise, but it is quite clear that he miscalculated the temper and outrage of the Muslim divines. Having realized his error of judgement, he led a life of sublime simplicity in the Congress or in jails, mediated on how best to wrest freedom from the British, and swallowed his personal grief, prejudices, and vanities in search of a national consensus. At another level, he bore the emotional and mental strain caused by Jinnah's two-nation theory. He knew that the enterprise of forging a Muslim nation was costly in terms of violence, death, and other forms of human suffering, hence he did not ever abandon the idea of composite nationalism. Azad declared himself 'a part of the indivisible unity that is Indian nationality', and 'indispensable to this noble edifice'. Without him, the 'splendid structure of India' was incomplete. He stood on the burning deck, while a great body of his compatriots clamoured for a Muslim nation. He opposed Partition heart and soul. And indeed he made his opponents feel it. He could not conceal the contempt he felt for his adversaries, and at no stage did he stoop to compromise. Instead, he reminded them of Indians working out a new way of life and boldly defying the accumulated prejudices and animus of the past. Without looking around to find a mirror that might reflect radical faces, he identified pluralism as the weapon of both the strong and the weak against the British. He preferred the conviction of Dara Shikoh (1615–1659), the eldest Mughal prince and a victim of Aurangzeb's conspiracy, and put forth the idea that in the search for the ultimate truth mosques as well as temples validly mediate the one candle's light.[25] As Minister of Education in free India and sponsor of an 'official' history of the 1857 Rebellion, he referred to the two communities standing 'shoulder to shoulder' to liberate themselves from the British yoke. Why did Azad and others think that it was worth their while to make this point? Probably, to record the regret that 'the British swept away and rooted out the late Mughals' pluralistic and philosophically composite nationalism',[26] and to bemoan that they ensured that common action by Hindus and Muslims would in future not be brought to fruition that easily.

Azad had not sought the tumult of political life; political life sought him out. Even though he preferred solitude and could not bear the crowds that exhilarated others, he reminded his readers of his message in *Al-Hilal*, which called for changing lazy habits and reorienting political attitudes.

Jihad for Freedom

Meet one who is a man and keep his company
Who does not pride himself on knowledge and ability;
When eloquent, a world may flock to hear him speak,
When silent, in himself the whole world he should be.

—Mir Taqi Mir

Overwhelmed by the morning sunlight and the evening darkness, Azad was thrown into a new world whose geography did not extend beyond a hundred yards and where the population was no more than fifteen faces.[27] Like Antonio Gramsci, he conceived of writing something that might absorb him and give a focus to his inner life. For this he

[25] Christian W. Troll, 'Abul Kalam Azad's *Sarmad the Martyr*', in *Urdu and Muslim South Asia: Studies in Honour of Ralph Russell*, edited by Christopher Shackle (New Delhi: Oxford University Press, 1991), p. 114.

[26] Mushirul Hasan, 'The Musketeers of Hind: 1857—A Time That's Become a Place in Our Minds', *Outlook*, 17 March 2008.

[27] Azad, *Sallies of Mind*, p. 75.

drew inspiration from the scriptures.[28] It is important to realize—and important particularly for the full knowledge and comprehension of times past—that internment kindled his Islam into warmth and fervour. Like Aurobindo Ghose who found God as a result of the wrath of the government, he too felt comforted and serene. And like the future sage of Pondicherry, he found it impossible to explain the love for his motherland or sacrifice to the thick-skinned Britons in India.

Azad looked for excuses to be alone in jail. When he heard that so and so had been sentenced to solitary confinement, he wondered how solitude could be punishment for a person. Even if worldly things were denied to him, solitary imprisonment was welcome, as was the twilight in which day and night so gently caressed one another. He remarked:

> The prison house where the morning smiles every day, where evening goes behind the veil every night, whose nights are lit up now by the torches of stars and then with the beauty of moonlight; where noon shines daily and so does the twilight, why consider it bereft of the means of pleasure just because it is a prison house. There is no dearth here of the means; the only problem is that our heart and mind gets lost. We look for everything outside and never look for our lost heart though if we find it all means of epicurean delights would be available in it.[29]

Azad wanted all patriots to fill up jails so that no worldly power could pronounce judgement on their self-sacrificing spirit. So, when the Karachi verdicts were pronounced against the Ali brothers and five others, he urged Muslims to continue the work for which the brothers had gone to jail. He recalled being interned for nine months in 1915, and was sorry that the Ali brothers had stolen a march over him. 'Today also,' he added, 'instead of sorrowing, we give them congratulations and shall again say that they have outdone us all.'[30] According to Azad, when the gates of another Court would be flung open, it would be no other than the Court of Law of God and its verdict would be final in all respects.[31]

---

[28] Cragg, *The Pen and the Faith*, p. 15.

[29] 27 August 1942, Azad, *Sallies of Mind*, p. 80.

[30] G. Minault, *The Khilafat Movement*, p. 175.

[31] K. L. Gauba, *Famous and Historic Trials* (Lahore: Lion Press, 1946), p. 250.

The iniquities of courts of law constitute an endless list and history has not yet finished singing the elegy of such miscarriages of justice. In that list we observe a holy personage like Jesus who had to stand in his time before a foreign court, convicted even, as the worst of criminals. We see also in the same list Socrates who was sentenced to be poisoned for no other crime than that of being the most truthful person of his age. We meet also the name of that great Florentine martyr to truth, the inventor Galileo, who refused to belie his observations and researches merely because their avowal was a crime in the eyes of constituted authority.... When I ponder on the great and significant history of the convicts dock and find that the honour of standing in that place belongs to me today, my soul, becomes steeped in thankfulness and praise of God.

Azad cogitated on his past and future in prison. He stated at one of his trials: 'For four years I have suffered internment; but during my internment I have never desisted from pursuing my work and inviting my people to this national goal. This is the mission of my life, and if I live at all, I elect to live only for this single purpose.'[32] As the pseudo-judicial proceedings against him moved toward the inexorable outcome, he stated: 'At all events, how strange and glorious a place is this prisoner's dock where both the greatest and the best of men are made to stand!'[33] He further stated:

This is an interesting and also illuminating chapter of history in the writing of which both of us are equal participants. You have for yourself the Magisterial chair over there while we have the docks here. I do admit that for the completion of the task that chair is as essential as these docks here. Let us complete this memorable chapter soon, which will assume historic importance. The historian is waiting for us and so is the future. Let us come here quickly one followed by the other and you in your turn continue to pass judgments with the same rapidity. For some days this will go on, and then the time will come when another and a higher Court will be guided by the Laws of God. Time will be its Judge. The Judge will write a judgment and it is this judgment which will be final.[34]

---

[32] Douglas, *Abul Kalam Azad*, p. 162; Gauba, *Famous and Historic Trials*, p. 244.

[33] Douglas, *Abul Kalam Azad*, p. 180.

[34] Gauba, *Famous and Historic Trials*, p. 21.

The rhetorical flourish reaches its climax with the following words:

> Give me the maximum punishment that can be awarded without hesitation. I assure you that the pain that your heart will feel while writing the order, not a hundredth part of it will be felt by me while hearing the judgment.[35]

As an intensely reserved man and a careful and deliberate writer, Azad tended to keep his public and private lives apart. A great believer in *tahmiz* (Arabic for *hors d'oeuvre* or appetizer or starter.), he enjoyed taking a break from serious thoughts at least twice or thrice daily for a few minutes when he busied himself with odd things like pruning creepers, or just talking at random for the sake of amusement. On such occasions it became a game of playing with words or ideas, parodying the well-known. All this being said, this was just a fragment of his passion; otherwise, 'the audacious nature of some', he wrote on 3 August 1942, 'would not tolerate the prison life's restrictions; they followed the old maxim: "Give me drink and declare it wine for here it is permitted"'.[36]

India's Maulana had to go through many trials from Ranchi to Ahmadnagar. Sind's Premier had to seek official permission for meeting him in Allahabad Jail.[37] Again, the authorities refused to let him travel to Calcutta to deliver a memorial lecture at the university.[38] They did not even let him nurse his ailing wife who was on her deathbed.[39] As the pain and agony of this tragedy heightened ('I had saved my body from the shock but could not save the heart'),[40] he committed to memory the joys and sorrows of living with her. But Azad was characteristically restrained in acknowledging that she shared his thoughts and beliefs and, despite being a *purdah-nashin* (behind the veil), she emerged as a comrade in practical life. Her mention invariably brought to his mind forgotten memories of several decades of togetherness. Jawaharlal Nehru, who had lost his wife, could gauge Azad's agony and reported:

[35] Gauba, *Famous and Historic Trials*, p. 250.
[36] *SWJN*, vol. 13, p. 39; *SWJN*, 18 September 1942, p. 29.
[37] Home Dept, Political (1), file no. 239, 1941.
[38] Home Dept, Political (1), file no. 163, 1942.
[39] Home Dept, Political (1), file no. 44, 1943.
[40] Azad, *Sallies of Mind*, p. 21.

'The death of the Maulana's wife has been a great blow to us all and we have lived for some days under the shadow of gloom. He has behaved wonderfully, as he always does, but he cannot hide the changes that have taken place in his face by just outward behaviour. He has grown thin and his face is all lined.'[41]

Shakespeare's view of life is that 'round the lonely great ones of this earth there is inevitably a conspiracy of envy and hatred, hatched by the base and common sort'. On 30 December 1941, the gates of Naini Prison were opened for Azad; on 9 August 1942, the new gate of the old Ahmadnagar Fort Prison closed behind him. The building in which he and some other prisoners were kept had earlier been used as residence for the cantonment officers. At times war prisoners had also been kept there. During the Boer War, a group of officers among the prisoners had been kept in this place. During World War I, the Germans had been housed, and during World War II, Italian prisoners had been brought from Egypt. Reflecting on the prison's history, Azad noted how, 'in this world of thousand caprices and moods, so many doors are opened to be closed and so many are closed to be later thrown open.'[42]

Azad penned a host of books during his time in jail. In Meerut Jail, besides the *Tazkira*, he toiled over writing the *Tarjuman al-Quran*,[43] which differs widely in spirit and aim from the former. This book suffers from exaggeration and effervescence, but its great merit lies in its accent on the transcendental oneness of all faiths and the theology of multi-religious cooperation. In this sense, the *Tarjuman al-Quran* is the most eloquent defence of the ideals of pluralism. According to Syed Sulaiman Nadwi (1884–1953), it 'is a significant product of the ages. No home should be without it; every Muslim library should have a copy of it, and every young Muslim should make it a point to study it carefully'.

---

[41] Jawaharlal Nehru to Krishna, 16 April 1943, in *Nehru's Letters to His Sister*, edited by Krishna Hutheesing (Faber and Faber: London, 1963), p. 116.

[42] Quoted in Mushirul Hasan, '"The Great Akbar" of Independence', 8 November 2013, *The Hindu*.

[43] On 20 March 1929, thirty-three prominent trade union leaders were arrested in Bombay, UP, Bengal and Punjab on charges of conspiracy; among them were fourteen communists. The legal process in Meerut went on for more than four years.

The Anguished Heart

When Azad and others were set free, Europe was in the midst of a struggle, one goal of which at any rate was a regrouping of men in ways which would fulfil national ideals and accord with national aspirations. Azad's writings closely follow this course of events: they are enlivened by constant glimpses at the wider world. He was too proud to think in terms of alliance, affiliation, or opposition.[44] One of his followers writes about his overweening pride, his aloofness from the public, and his disdain for those whom he considered undignified or beneath him in intellectual attainment.[45]

As an author, Azad hurried across large tracts of issues and lingered over the 'errors' of Gandhi and Jawaharlal Nehru. He thought they played fast and loose with their promise of keeping India united; some of his insinuations in *India Wins Freedom* breathed disenchantment. Some events were described with infinite detail, others, no less important, were scarcely noticed. He generalized from isolated facts, and traced great events to trivial causes.

Azad followed the Cripps Mission and the Cabinet mission, but failed to give us the insights expected of him.[46] In his negotiations with the British he showed firmness,[47] but he did not reveal his precarious position as a Congress Muslim. It seems that he had lost faith in those Muslims who were impregnated with the dogma of secular nationalism. In general, his assessment of character and his estimate of statesmanship were weak.

Azad's silence on the Mountbatten Plan in the CWC meeting on 2 June 1947 is a contentious issue. Maybe, he lived under the illusion that the plan would prevent class war and civil strife. Possibly, he distanced himself owing to the League's vilification campaign against him with Jinnah referring to Azad as 'the Muslim show-boy' of the

[44] Mujeeb, *The Indian Muslims*, p. 442.

[45] G. Minault, *The Khilafat Movement*, p. 38.

[46] For Azad's negotiations with Cripps, see Sarvepalli Gopal, *Jawaharlal Nehru—A Biography, Volume 1 (1889–1947)* (New Delhi: Oxford University Press, 1975), pp. 279–80, 283, 285.

[47] Linlithgow's telegram to Amery, 30 April 1942 in *Transfer of Power*, vol. 1, p. 876.

Congress. He was about to suggest to Gandhi that some tangible steps were required and not just idealistic preaching on communal amity, but the prospect of their success was already dimmed by the close of 1941.[48] The Viceroy thought: 'To talk of those two communities [Hindus and Muslims] as majority and minority is a dangerous misuse of terms, because it tends to imply that right of the numerically smaller community to have its individuality respected is less than that of the larger. It is, after all, in defence of that right that we are at war today.'[49]

Azad rushed from one problem to another, rarely finding the time or inclination to work any of them through to the end. In early March 1942, he organized the All-India Azad Muslim Conference to permeate all classes, from the top to the bottom, with a common opinion in favour of composite nationality. In this effort he worked as much with and through the Liberals as with and through the ulama representatives. But Jinnah beguiled the masses with unexpected and, for the most part, great success.[50] The street violence that erupted in Calcutta on 16 August 1946 broke down the springs of Azad's initiative. In his defence, however, it may be useful to remember the words of Rosa Luxemburg, who said that a system of ideas which is merely sketched in broad outline proves far more stimulating than a finished and symmetrical structure that offers no scope for the independent efforts of an active mind. In the end, Partition plunged Azad's spirits into depression. 'There is no more certain test of statesmanship,' wrote H. A. L. Fisher in his *History of Europe*, 'than the capacity to resist the political intoxication of victory.'[51]

Through the smoke and flames, Azad perceived the growth of a new India and converted every sad moment into a positive one. With his cool-headed and careful reasoning, he aspired to create a political and social order in which the values of the political class may possibly be multiculturalism and plurality. What is more, he carried his tribulations

[48] Penderel Moon, *Gandhi and Modern India* (London: The English Universities Press, 1968), p. 213.

[49] 'The Indian Political Situation', 28 January 1942, in *Transfer of Power*, p. 82.

[50] Linlithgow to Amery, 7 March 1942, in *Transfer of Power*, pp. 361–2.

[51] H. A. L. Fisher, *A History of Europe* (London: The Fontana Library, sixth impression, 1965), vol. 2, p. 1068.

with a stoical dignity, pursued his active role through stresses of inner disquiet,[52] and ultimately suffered for the sake of truth. In one of his many elegant passages, he remarked that 'the flowering trees whose off-spring once represented beauty and grace were now lying in a heap in a corner, like burnt-out bushes and trampled up grass'.[53] The story which opened with the bright colours of the *Al-Hilal* ended in deep shadow.

Yet, Azad personified the fact that adversity could be triumphantly overcome. He struggled with life after his own fashion, a purely personal struggle. Like the poet Mir Taqi Mir, he could either voice affirmation of the historical process or protest against the iniquities of time and the suffering it caused to the sensitive mind and soul. He had indeed no time for small talk or for little human foibles, but in his famous speech after Independence at Delhi's Red Fort, he lambasted those Muslims who threw themselves more and more deeply into the communal vortex. This was unfair criticism, though Azad made up by securing to them the comfort of peace and security in the turmoil raging around them. He insisted, as he had always done, on India's rich diversity of life. His exchanges with the League stalwarts reveal the contrast between a social and democratic ideal in which pride of place gives way to the interests of all sections of society; and an alternative ideal in which the state, apart from being a theocracy, excludes its non-Muslim citizens from the nation-building project.

Azad's legacy lives on in the *Ghubar-e Khatir*, a book that uncovers the extent to which the mystical and romantic elements lived on beneath his nationalism. His 'cosmopolitan morality', an expression Ernest Barker used long ago, transcended the function or functions allotted to his station in a particular community. His spirit was soured, but his political stance, far from being a spent force, survived the shock of Partition. His personal position was precarious, but he could not let go of the poetry of the past, of the dream, the fancy, and the fairy tales of freedom. As Minister of Education, we get a glimpse of his social and cultural commitments, some of which were intertwined with the nationalist struggle.[54] He founded the Indian Council for Cultural

---

[52] *SWJN*, vol. 13, p. 39; *SWJN*, 18 September 1942, *SWJN*, p. 29, p. 16.

[53] 14 June 1943, Azad, *Ghubar-e Khatir*, p. 233.

[54] Mahavir Tyagi (ed.), *Maulana Abul Kalam Azad: Profile of a Nationalist* (New Delhi: Anamika Publishers, 2013).

Relations (ICCR), the University Grants Commission (UGC), and the Sahitya Akademi. Based on the recognition that individuals live, and live with all their fullness just when and just so much as they cultivate their specific field, such institutions were designed to promote nationalist consciousness, humanism, and intellectual freedom. Hopefully, some day, Azad will earn his place in the gallery of serious-minded patriots. That is when his intense and passionate nobility will shine in our memory like a star, and we would make this light shine for others as well.[55] Many a young student could echo the words of Monod: 'I owe my vocation for history to him; I am not a disciple, but I am inspired by a deeper feeling, that of filial gratitude.'[56]

[55] I have paraphrased Bertrand Russell's comment on Joseph Conrad. Bertrand Russell, *The Autobiography of Bertrand Russell* (London: Routledge, [1967]1998), p. 219..

[56] G. P. Gooch, *History and Historians in the Nineteenth Century* (Boston: Beacon Press, 1959), p. 177.

6. Poets in Prisons

Wish to These Arrests Is Prohibited[1]

Let the efforts of the Nationalists spread like clouds of mercy.
In a short time the honour of the Government will sink.
There is no power greater than the power of forbearance.
How can the power of Government stand before this.
In the end the oppressed will score victory over the oppressor.
Your stringency and oppression is the sign of your defeat.
O Mushtaq, the law has received a legal defeat.
The glory of courts of the Government has been humbled into dust.
                              —Abdul Ghafur Saheb Mushtaq of Allahabad

A Song of Breaking Down[2]

Break down those iron gates of the prisons.

---

[1] *Daur-e Jadid*, 18 January 1922, *Report*, Bengal, week ending 28 January 1922.
[2] *Banglarkatha* (Calcutta), 20 January 1922, *Report*, Bengal, week ending 28 January 1922.

Who is that ruler who punished the free and emancipated truths?
Give a forcible shaking to the Mother's prison.
Give a kick and break down the padlocks;
Set fire to that prison house of the Mother;
Set fire to it and uproot it.

—Havaldar Kazi Nazrul-Islam

Mirza Ghalib wrote, 'Prisoner of thy tresses, why would I escape fetters?/A captive of sorrow, why would I fear the dungeon?/If the preacher has locked me, so be it/Shall we ever renounce these ways of love's passion?'[3] Cutting across regions and languages, fellow-prisoners mingled with each other, and wrote about their experiences. They combined distinct forms of expression and made pathways for new ideas.

In Urdu literature, *zindan* (prison), *qaidkhana* and *dar-o-rasan* (scaffold) are emblems of subjugation. The word *qaidi* or 'prisoner' conjures up the image of victimhood—*aseer-e zindan*. In other forms, prison became a metaphor for purdah, a common practice among Muslim women in urbanized spaces. A group of women had said to Margaret E. Cousins (1878–1954), founder of the AIWC, 'We are in prison.'[4] In Mohamed Ali's poetry, the patriot imprisoned is like the caged bird longing for the beauties of the garden of freedom.

In the colonial era, writing elegies or *marsiyas* was a powerful medium of public declarations of the past and present tyrannies and transgressions of the rulers. Mir Babar Ali Anis (1802–1874) and Mir Salamat Ali Dabir (1803–75) were its best exponents in Lucknow. They were followed by poets like Brij Narain Chakbast, who adopted the marsiya genre with relative ease. Poets of a later generation used the old symbols in a new context to lend contemporary meanings to the existing themes of repression and subjugation, and in a way they transformed political suffering through the imagery of resurgence that followed all kinds of oppression through an optimism rooted in conviction rather than emotion.[5] The 'executioner' in their works signified the British, a commanding and lasting image against authoritarianism and absolutism. Ram Prasad Bismil, a revolutionary,

---

[3] *Khanazad-e-zulf hain zanjeer se bhagengey kyun?/Hain giraftar-e-bala zindan se ghabrayenge kya?/Gar kiya naseh ne humko qaid achcha yun sahi/Yeh junoon-e-ishq ke andaz chhut jayenge kya?*

[4] Cousins, *Indian Womanhood Today*, p. 51.

[5] Ahmad, *Islamic Modernism*, p. 101.

threw his full weight behind the newest and most ardent protagonists of nationalism. Reciting the lines at the gallows, he immortalized the words of Bismil Azimabadi, a poet from Bihar:

> In our hearts is now the desire for sacrifice,
> We shall see how much strength is in the arms of the attacker,
> When the time comes, we will show thee o Heaven! In the heart of the wounded there exists just
> One desire, to achieve martyrdom.[6]

People sang this Urdu lyric with full-throated zest. The chords of every heart vibrated. There was no let up. Millions were thrilled by the idea of sacrificing one's head, symbolically prostrating oneself for Mother India. As for protests against tyranny in general, 'Jo kue yaar se nikle toh sue daar chale,'[7] wrote Faiz Ahmed Faiz (1912–85), whose poem 'Hum dekhenge' was sung by the melodious Iqbal Bano amid rapturous applause.[8] The poems 'Dastoor' (System) of Habib Jalib (1928–1993), and 'Hisar' of Ahmed Faraz are still enormously popular with the masses. It is impossible not to admire these and other dissenting voices and their tenacity.

Men and women in public life used the imagery of *qaidi* and *qaid-khana* either to evoke sympathy or to voice their defiance. Gandhi, of course, used them to critique British colonialism. Describing India as 'a vast prison-house', he stated that it was his sacred duty was to break the 'mournful monotony of compulsory peace choking the heart of the nation for the want of free vent....'[9]

'The Progressives'

From the 1860s to the 1930s, Parsi theatre was the dominant form of dramatic entertainment in urban India, and the impetus

---

[6] *Sarfaroshi ki tamanna ab hamare dil me hai*
Dekhna hai jor kitna bajue katil me hai
Vakt ane de tujhe bata denge ham asman
Sirf mit jane ki hasrat yak dil e bismil aye hai
Kya tamannae shahadat ki dil e Bismil me hai.

[7] Leaving the lane of the beloved, he headed for the gallows...

[8] Faiz was imprisoned during Ayub Khan's martial law regime.

[9] M.K. Gandhi, *Young India*, 12 March 1930, in CWMG, vol. XLIII, p. 52.

given to performance in Urdu by Dadabhai Sohrabji was especially noteworthy.[10] Then followed the era of the Indian People's Theatre Association (IPTA) that produced striking, highly cultivated and accomplished personalities like Zohra Sehgal (1912–2014), Habib Tanvir (1923–2009), Asrarul Haq 'Majaz' (1911–1955) and A. K. Hangal (1914–2012), and represented an awareness of the socialist ideal. They and many others opened the doors of the stage and let life in. With changes in verbal, emotional, and intellectual contents of the plays staged, they were much less concerned to make the theatre a refuge from reality.[11]

As for progressive writers and poets, they were part of the *avant garde* in Urdu literature, arguing that creative writing ought to be the servant of a cause, a beacon to poor humanity's afflicted will, and not a mere display of ornamental skill.[12] A wide group with diverse interests, they reflected the urge of a large number of intellectuals who began their assaults on social abuses, brutalities of officialdom, bogus education, law courts, and government departments. This meant, among other things, that Urdu poetry had at last sloughed off its middle-class skin.[13] With a broad-minded realism, they gave the impression of the prisoner and the prostitute being equals in their predicament. Josh Malihabadi, who returns to the subject of prison again and again in order to arouse us from our thoughtless indifference, treats the world of the prisoner with a lively and artistic interest. In *Zindan ka Geet* (A prison song), he expects the hour of victory to draw closer and closer so that the masses would breathe and partake of the intellectual and cultural life. *Shikast-e zindan ka khwab* ('A Dream of Prison-Break'), on the other hand, pictures the world coming to an end to be replaced by a better place to live in—thanks to the prisoners' answer for tyranny. In 'A Dream of Prison-Break' and 'Address to the Sons of the East India

---

[10] Kathryn Hansen, 'Languages on Stage: Linguistic Pluralism and Community Formation in the Nineteenth-Century Parsi Theatre', *Modern Asian Studies*, vol. 37, no. 2 (2003).

[11] Nandi Bhatia (ed.), *Modern Indian Theatre: A Reader* (New Delhi: Oxford University Press, 2013).

[12] *Josh Bani, Taraqqi Pasand Nazm* (5–6), Allahabad, July 2010–June 2011.

[13] Muhammad Sadiq, *A History of Urdu Literature* (New Delhi: Oxford University Press, 1964), p. 406.

Company',[14] he enunciates his theory of reconstruction. Some of his couplets powerfully capture his revolutionary optimism:

Behind the facade of the destruction of this fossilized man
The work of creating a new man is in progress.

* * *

How India's prison quivers as the slogans reverberate!
Some peeved prisoners perchance are breaking their chains!
How beneath the bulwarks, all the captives congregate!
The tumult of lightning in their hearts, their eyes burnished swords
The famished have fire in their gaze, the cannons have gone cold
Fate eloquently favours the prisoners, failing are the tactics to dominate
Eyes of the beggars are ruby red, the ruler's visage colourless
Wreckage has unfurled its flags, constructions have fallen prostrate
Did those who crushed the nation's soul ever in their dreams speculate?
That the earth will ooze out poisonous snakes, the sky would shower swords?
Did those who pilfered blood from human hearts, ever in their dreams anticipate?
That one day the same monochrome would churn out a million images?
Did those who fettered speech, ever in their dreams cogitate?
That one day the same silence would breed speeches that would resonate?
Watch out! The prison vibrates; Rush! The prisoners are at large
Rise! The walls are crumbling down; Run! The chains are breaking free.[15]

In 'A Prison Nightfall' and 'A Prison Daybreak', Faiz Ahmed Faiz captures the extraordinary optimism amidst war and tyranny and echoes sentiments that transcend time and space. He describes what the experience of imprisonment did for his development as a poet. He points out that the verse he wrote in jail continued the same strand in

---

[14] Josh Malihabadi, 'East India Company kay farzandon kay nam' in *Azadi ki Nazmein*, edited by Syed Sibte Hassan (Lucknow: Halqa-e-Adab, 1940), pp. 175–80.

[15] Josh Malihabadi, '*Shikast-e zindan ka khwab*' in Josh Malihabadi, *Shola-o-Shabnam*, (Delhi: Maktaba-e-Jamia Delhi, 1936), p. 51; translated from the Urdu by Nishat Zaidi.

his poetry that began with 'Love, Do Not Ask' (*mujh-se pahli-si muhab-bat meri mehbub na mang*). He also wrote 'Two Elegies' in memory of a young progressive who perished in jail. He is imagined to be speaking in his own person. *Mulaqat* (meeting) became jail jargon for time prisoners spent with visitors.[16]

> *Har ae din ye khudawandgan-e-mehr-o-jamal*
>   *Lahu men gharq mere gham-kade mein ate hain*
> *Aur ae din meri nazron ke samne unke*
>   *Shahid jism salamat utha e-jate hain.*

Each day that comes these deities of kindness and beauty
   Drowned in blood come into my house of grief,
And daily before my eyes their
   Martyred bodies are lifted up, healed.[17]

During the War, an anthology entitled *Azadi ki Nazmein* (Poems of freedom) came out and it contained some stirring poems. They were recited till late in the evening to the accompaniment of much wit and banter. Even the wardens could not help being moved by Sardar Jafri's poem that went: 'Dance, O spirit of freedom, for all life the universe is dancing/The universe is whirling on the axis of time'.[18]

Will These Ways of Impassioned Love Come to an End?
Yeh Junoon-e-ishq ke andaz chhut jayenge kya?[19]

'If the communist virus is born in Bombay it is largely bred in the UP, where steady pressure is keeping the contagion from spreading,' reported an intelligence officer.[20] Hundreds gathered in Lucknow in August 1937 to protest against the functioning of the Congress Ministry. Amongst them were the most wretched and abject who

---

[16] Kiernan, *Poems by Faiz*, pp. 37, 286.

[17] Kiernan, *Poems by Faiz*, p. 207.

[18] Ali Sardar Jafri, 'Jang aur Inqilab' in *Azadi ki Nazmein*, edited by Sibte Hasan (Lucknow: Halqa-e-Adab, 1940). Also published by Uttar Pradesh Urdu Academy Lucknow, 1985.

[19] Mirza Asadullah Ghalib, *Dewan-e-Ghalib*, Taj edition (Lahore: Taj Company, 1938) p. 19.

[20] Home Dept, Political, file no. 7/1, 1941.

had been united by the *kisan sabhas* and, when united, had acquired a great deal of political muscle. Already, the literature of the mid-1930s imagined and embodied the radical vision of anti-colonial nationalism, nurtured working-class and peasant struggles, fought it out with employers, landlords, and the police, and forged working-class and peasant solidarities. For this reason autobiographies bridge 'a particularist frame of mind and a universalist consciousness'.[21] They show the will of the revolutionary steeled by severe trials.

In the 1930s, a wonderful change came over Urdu literature and the change has ever since altered the tone and spirit, as well as the external form of Urdu writings. This change was, in part, reflected in *Angare* (Embers), a set of stories authored by Sajjad Zaheer, Ahmed Ali (1910–1994), Rashid Jahan (1905–1952), and Mahmuduzzafar Khan (1908–1956). Each one of them moved away from sentimental language, romantic situations, and upper-class characters towards addressing social inequity and life among the oppressed.[22] They exposed the hypocrisy and double standards of the conservative establishment, and acquired, for this reason, a large following at the first and second conferences of the Progressive Writers' Association. They abandoned many old words, considering them useless, and more or less modified the meanings of many others to meet the requirements of newly introduced conceptions and ideas, for which no expressions existed in the language as it formerly stood. 'In short,' writes Carlo Coppola, '*Angare* did not merely transition Urdu literature, and with it, Indo–Muslim culture, into a Marxist-shaded, twentieth-century modernity, challenging the validity of contemporary middle- and upper-class Indo-Muslim morality and mores, and even Islam itself. *Angare* jettisoned them there.'[23]

Sajjad Zaheer's *London ki Ek Raat* (A Night in London) was a great success. Becoming aware of the destructive aspects of British rule, he learnt, in the company of radicals in London—the charismatic Bloomsbury Group, to see through the machinations of colonialism,

[21] Igal Halfin, *Terror in My Soul: Communist Autobiographies on Trial* (Cambridge, Mass.: Harvard University Press, 2003), p. 28.

[22] Gail Minault, *Secluded Scholars: Women's Education and Muslim Social Reform in Colonial India* (Oxford: Oxford University Press, 1998), p. 275.

[23] Carlo Coppola, 'Zaheer v Ali: Dissenting Views on the Early Years of the Progressive Movement in Urdu Literature', in *Indo-Muslim Cultures in Transition*, edited by Alka Patel and Karen Leonard (Leiden: Brill, 2012), p. 208.

and conceived and translated the idea of a progressive writers' movement in November 1934. Giving up the career in law he had embarked
upon at Lincoln's Inn, he returned home convinced that the way ahead
lay in destroying the existing order and re-structuring the new one on
socialistic lines. For such pains, the government jailed him from 1936
to 1937, and again from 1940 to 1942. Harry Haig, UP's Lieutenant-
Governor, informed Linlithgow, the Viceroy, on 23 June 1937:

> We have also recently authorized several prosecutions under Section
> 124-A of the Indian Penal Code. These are I think in all cases against
> leftwing or communist Congressmen. Among these is Sajjad Zaheer,
> the young communist son of Sir Wazir Hasan, late Chief Judge of the
> Chief Court of Oudh. He has been, ever since his return from England
> a year or two ago, a very active communist worker. His prosecution for
> a seditious speech was sanctioned last cold weather; but at the urgent
> entreaty of his father, who gave a guarantee that the son would refrain
> in future from seditious speaking, the prosecution was withdrawn. The
> young man immediately repudiated the father's assurance and there can
> be no ground now for further leniency. Incidentally, Sir Wazir Hasan
> has now openly espoused the Congress cause.[24]

Sajjad Zaheer communicated with his wife Razia, a short-story
writer, through double talk, code words, evasion, and digressions.
Through essays published in *Roshnai* (*The Light*), Zaheer sought to cor-
relate criminal accusations with political falsifications, and predicted
the destruction of imperialism.[25] 'Lights may twinkle or they may
not, but life goes on,' wrote Zaheer, introducing progressive literature.
His memoirs, written in Central Jail (Macch, Baluchistan) from 1951
to 1955 and published in 1956, capture an era of great tumult, with
the global landscape changing at a rapid pace. It bares his unshakable
faith in the masses and their future triumph. Earlier, he reflected on
the communists making inroads in the landlord-dominated Awadh
countryside, and in Kanpur where unrest among the working classes
had spread rapidly to raise new levels of working-class consciousness.
Sajjad Zaheer encountered representatives with different backgrounds

---

[24] P. N. Chopra (ed.), *Towards Freedom*, p. 676.
[25] Sajjad Zaheer, *The Light: A History of the Movement for Progressive
Literature in the Indo-Pak Subcontinent, A Translation of Roshnai*. Translated
from Urdu by Amina Azfar (Karachi: Oxford University Press, 2005), p. xviii.

and ideologies—petit-bourgeois youngsters who put on revolutionary airs. Quite a few were educated at Sir Syed's College in Aligarh.

Ali Sardar Jafri

Syed Ahmad had warned the Aligarh students to eschew politics, but in the early twentieth century the pan-Islamic cry radicalized the campus. Gandhi provided the inspiration in one way, and the socialists in another. They were markedly different from each other, but they converged on the high ground of anti-colonialism. In the 1930s, worldwide currents against imperialism and the steady development of socialist ideas in India reinforced Marxian ideas in educational institutions. Some Aligarh graduates exposed the limitations of the so-called moderate ideology and stirred fellow-students into raising revolutionary slogans. The pro-government establishment turned to repression. Thus Sardar Jafri was rusticated even before completing his studies. K. M. Ashraf (1903–1962) writes: 'One of my "communist friends" ... was the poet Ali Sardar Jafri (his contemporary at Aligarh though a class junior).... It was about him that I once quipped, "The communists exploit every single platform—including the railway platform." He would often hold forth, explaining the current party line, while walking up and down the Aligarh railway station platform.' Jafri was expelled from Aligarh University for his communist views, and he later completed his course from Lucknow where he became friends with a Kashmiri student called Durga Prasad Dhar—DP for short. Sibte Hasan, also an expellee from Aligarh, had spent some years helping the famous Urdu writer, Qazi Abdul Ghaffar, who edited *Payaam*, a nationalist Urdu daily from Hyderabad. Both made a name for themselves in progressive Urdu literature—Sardar as a poet and Hasan as a critic. (Sibte Hasan and Sajjad Zaheer were both 'exiled' to Karachi when Pakistan was established and the Communist Party needed 'Muslim' communists to start the radical movement in Pakistan).

In Lucknow, Jafri was drawn to be part of the *Halqah-e arbab-e zauq* (informal circles of writers). Subsequently, he was put in jail for political activities. In the adjoining barracks was housed Sardar Chander Singh Garhwali who had refused to fire at the Pathans in Peshawar and was serving a life sentence, like many others imprisoned there. They roared from their barracks to greet Sardar Jafri. As Bhagat

Singh's companions, they had been brought back from *Kala Pani* after a protracted hunger strike. Jafri's first night in jail turned out to be cool and pleasant, like many nights of Lucknow's early winter.

In 1940, the year Jinnah laid the seeds of a Muslim nation, Jafri and his comrades took the erstwhile nawabi city by storm. These friends included Asrarul Haq 'Majaz', Sibte Hasan,[26] Shafeeq Ahmed Naqvi, an economist, Abdul Aleem, lecturer in Arabic in Aligarh in those days and later vice-chancellor of the university, Anwar Jamal Kidwai, then a student but later a senior civil servant, and Rashid Jahan, daughter of Shaikh Mohammad Abdullah (1887–1965), the chief protagonist of girls' education in Aligarh. Armed with degrees from Isabella Thorburn College in Lucknow and the Lady Hardinge Medical College in Delhi, Rashid Jahan married the Oxford-educated Mahmuduzzafar. Their home, 7 Bisheshwar Nath Road, became a centre of lively literary activity. She had stepped out of the *sharif* woman's expected role and trained as a doctor, devotedly using her energy and skills to help women who could never have afforded medical care.[27]

The PWM attracted Ismat Chughtai (1915–1991), who brought into the ambit of Urdu literature the complex and forbidden terrains of female sensibility and treated it with unusual openness. There were other homes where the socialists gathered: in Firangi Mahal, the citadel of Muslim orthodoxy; in the house built by Syed Wazir Hasan (1874–1947), a successful lawyer and Chief Justice of the Awadh Chief Court—the same house which is now the 'Cloud Nine' Luxury Apartments.

Lively, intelligent, witty and earnest, the young communists 'seemed to be drunk on the winds of revolution and patriotism that were blowing in at the time'.[28] Each one of them looked forward to the 'leap from

[26] Syed Sibte Hasan (1916–1986) belonged to Azamgarh, Uttar Pradesh. A graduate of AMU, he received his higher education from Columbia University, USA. A member of the Communist Party of India, Hasan migrated to Pakistan after Partition. He also served as editor of noted journals such as *Naya Adab* and *Lail-o-Nehar*.

[27] Ralph Russell, *Losses, Gains: Part II of Ralph Russell's Autobiography*, edited by Marion Molteno (New Delhi: Three Essays Collective, 2010), p. 214.

[28] Zaheer, *Progressive Literature in the Indo-Pak Subcontinent*, p. 158.

the kingdom of necessity to the kingdom of freedom' (Hegel).[29] They spoke for the poor and the hungry and painted pictures of a society that encouraged the young to envisage possibilities they otherwise would not have dreamt of. Invoking socialism as the new revelation, they sought to exorcize communal rancour by uniting the majority from all communities in a struggle against their common poverty, and to make independence a blessing to the poor as well as to the elite.

They made their presence felt by ensuring that the university would bustle with the sound of whistles at noon whenever a national figure went to jail. Students would be on their feet for five minutes. In November 1940, the university held its convocation. Maurice Gwyer, Vice-Chancellor of Delhi University (1938–50), was the guest of honour. Students went on strike with their litany of complaints. Majaz appeared from somewhere and recited a poem standing atop the boundary wall of the compound: *Musafir bhag waqt-e bekasi hai; terey sar par ajal andla rahi hain* (Run O traveller, these are vulnerable days; death hovers over your head!). That day turned out to be a contrast of light and shade, of humour and tragedy.

Jafri's postgraduate studies ended prematurely as he was imprisoned in Lucknow's District Jail. His C class barracks had ten or twelve large windows with thick iron bars in front of which were two rows of graves, each grave had a blanket laid out on it—these were beds for prisoners. A warder with a stout baton stood next to an unlit lantern. A couple of prisoners had iron chains and fetters on their legs, which clinked when they turned. Jafri was assigned one grave. Other than the blanket, his trophies were an iron vessel and a *tamlot* (a tin mug). But the warder offered him *bidi* against the rules of the C-class manual.

In 1940, the ominous clouds of communal conflict produced thunder and lightning in the form of the demand for Pakistan. Jafri, on the other hand, enunciated his vehement anti-imperialist views, gave voice to his ardour for social justice and his clear-cut preference for broad-mindedness.

[29] Friedrich Engels, *Socialism: Utopian and Scientific*, available at https://www.marxists.org/archive/marx/works/1880/soc-utop/ch03.htm, accessed September 2015.

Woh dekho maulsari ke darakht ke peechey
  Ufaq ki god mein rakhkha hua hain chand ka sar
Woh dekho raat ki aaghosh mein simat aayi
  Urus-e-shaam ki dosheezgi-o-ranaai
Lipat ke so gaya suraj zameen ke seene se

  Look there, behind the Maulsari tree
  The moon rests in the lap of the horizon
    Lo! The bride of eve in all her youthful charm
  Recoils in the arms of the night.
    The sun has slipped into slumber
  Holding the earth in close embrace.[30]

The Iranian mind, says the one-time poet-prisoner Reza Baraheni, beating to the rhythm of musical words, is a great reservoir of images strung to short and long lines of modern poetry. Urdu poetry has the same quality. Besides their soft and rhythmic effect, the words are imbued with collective fears and expectations, and they convey the pain behind torture and the exhilaration brought about by freedom.[31]

The Maverick and the Gadfly of the Independence Movement

With the huge gates of Sabarmati Jail closing on him, Indulal Yagnik was plunged into misery by the extreme rigidity and heartlessness of the officials, the food provided, and the jail regulations. He was a prisoner of a particular number and not one of justice.[32] Indeed, not everybody managed to get to the shore in the perilous journey to self-government; many drowned along the way. But many persisted with open eyes and intense will. Hasrat Mohani was one of them.[33] In jail, he worked grimly, straining every nerve to find refuge in poetry. His ghazals, written with the utmost finished elegance in words of the truest harmony, are imbued

[30] Ali Sardar Jafri, 'Lucknow ki Panch Raaten' in *Sarmayaa-Sukhan*, vol. 1 (Delhi: Maktab-e-Jamia, 2001) p. 44. Translated by Nishat Zaidi.

[31] Reza Baraheni, *God's Shadow: Prison Poems* (Bloomington: Indiana University Press, 1976), p. 232.

[32] Yagnik, *Autobiography*, p. 174.

[33] Atiq Siddiqi has provided a graphic description of his life. His essays are incisive and well-researched. I have also utilized the works of Abdul Shakoor and Khaliq Anjum. The *Kulliyat-e Hasrat* carries a useful introduction.

with a tone of sprightly gaiety. We need a great deal of cultural and intellectual maturity to evaluate them, but suffice it to say that he was a poet of
undiminshed stature—as much at home with the contemporary poets as
he had been with the old ones. In one of his couplets, he called his poetry
a beautiful confluence of the Delhi and Lucknow schools of literature:

The features of Delhi emerge in Lucknow style
Hasrat, you have brightened the art of poetry.[34]

What he wrote expresses his love for the working man and disgust
for his oppressor,[35] and his spirited outlook offered a ray of hope to
them (*Achha hai ahl-e jaur kiye jaen sakhtiyan; phaile gi yun hi shorish-
e hub-e watan tamam*).[36] Besides revealing his innermost personality,
his verses address contemporary situations, even as they endure as a
model of fine poetry. Thus he says, 'my opinions are free and so is my
spirit/It is useless to lock up Hasrat's body.'[37] And again, 'in vain you
frighten me with tyrannical imprisonment/my devoted spirit would
feel free there all the more.'[38]

Ghalib delighted in the enigmatic and the difficult, and subjected
everything to wit, passion, feeling, and thought.[39] He wrote, *Likhte
rahe junoon ki hikayat-e khoon chikaan; har chand is mein haath hame
qalam hue.*[40] Hasrat too, buttressed the claim: *Hai mashq-e sukhan jari
chakki ki mushaqqat bhi/ik turfah tamasha hai Hasrat ki tabeeyat bhi* [41]
(Hasrat continues writing poetry along with the labour of grinding

[34] Unless otherwise stated, the verses and translations are from C. M.
Naim's paper (see footnote 31).

[35] C. M. Naim, 'The Maulana Who Loved Krishna', *Economic and Political
Weekly* (*EPW*), 27 April 2013.

[36] It is good for the oppressors to continue with their oppression; this is
how the love of the country will spread far and wide. Hasrat Mohani, *Kulyat-
e-Hasrat*, (comp. Begum Hasrat Mohani), second edition (Karachi: Hasrat
Memorial Hall and Library, [1976] 1997), p.166.

[37] Mohani, *Kulyat-e-Hasrat*, p. 157.

[38] Mohani, *Kulyat-e-Hasrat*, p. 240.

[39] Ahmed Ali (ed.), *The Golden Tradition* (New York: Columbia
University Press, 1973), p. 223.

[40] Mirza Asadullah Ghalib, *Dewan-e-Ghalib*, [Nushkha-e-Arshee]
compiled and corrected by Imtiaz Ali Arshee (Aligarh: Anjuman Tarraqqi-e-
Urdu-e-Hind, 1958), p. 226.

[41] Mohani, *Kulyat-e-Hasrat*, p. 177.

wheat; with what an odd nature is Hasrat blessed!). This refers to his hand-grinding, jointly with another prisoner, one maund (37.3 kg) of corn every day. Instead of being downhearted by the other harsh aspects of life, he showed great powers of endurance. At times, he felt sore at heart, but never did he abandon his principles. On one occasion he spurned the suggestion to accept the house arrest order by citing the *Quran* to vindicate his case: *Fa ma wahanu lima asabahum fi sabili Allahi* ('And they did not act weak in the face of what befell them in the path of Allah'). He observed:

> You wrote that I should accept to be put under house arrest. It certainly appears to be a plausible thing. But when I sought guidance from the *Quran*, I first ended up reciting *Sura-al-Anfal*. After reciting this *Sura*, my heart received strength and I pledged that I would never bow my head meekly before oppression. Because doing this will be tantamount to supporting oppression, which by itself is a sin. At the end of this letter, I quote some verses from this *Sura*. You look them up in the *Quran* and go through the translation yourself. After reading this, *Insha'Allah*, you will also be relieved of this tension. There is nothing to worry, *Insha'Allah* we will finally prevail.[42]

At first, Hasrat did not give the slightest indication of being anti-British; on the contrary, he extolled Theodore Morison, Professor of English at MAO College (1889–99), and Theodore Beck, its Principal from 1884 to 1899.[43] Gradually, however, his thoughts travelled beyond the campus and, ending up in Tilak's camp,[44] he wrote the following:

> *Ta'at hai firangiyon ki jinka dustoor*
> *Kya khak unhen dadgari ka ho sha'oor*
> *Insaf ke dushmanon ka Dawar hai laqab*
> *Bar aks nihand name zangi kafoor*

> Those who have submitted to the British
> Justice can never be expected from them
> The unjust are given the title of *Dawar* (Lord of Justice)
> As if a Negro has been named Mr. White.

---

[42] Khaliq Anjum, *Hasrat Mohani* (Delhi: Publications Division, 1915), pp. 54–5.

[43] Anjum, Hasrat Mohani, pp. 30–1.

[44] *Kulliyat-e Hasrat Mohani* (Delhi: Farid Book Depot, 2007), p. 168.

Again,

Jab tak wo rahe dunyā men raha ham sab ke dilon par zor unkā
Ab rah ke bahisht men nizd-i-khudā hūroN pe karenge rāj Tilak

So long as he lived he ruled our hearts, and now in Paradise,
Nearer to God, Tilak shall rule over the Houris.

The young and the idealists presumed that big events would follow Tilak's release.[45] Working with redoubled energy on social problems, Hasrat set up a *swadeshi* store in Aligarh. Shibli put him in touch with the Bombay merchant and mill owner Fazulbhoy Currimbhoy (b. 1872), and the store had its sunny days on Meston Road for about five years. It prompted Shibli to comment, *Tum aadmi ho ya jin? Pehle shair thhe, phir politician bane aur ab bania ho gae* (Are you a man or a Djin? At first you were a poet, then you became a politician, and now you have become a *bania*).

Saikron azadian is qaid par Hasrat nisar
Jin ke baais kehte hain sab inka zindani mujhe

Let a thousand days of freedom be sacrificed to this imprisonment,
As a consequence of which people call me a prisoner.

Hasrat possessed Mohamed Ali's fighting spirit and passion for *azadi*,[46] and, for this reason, Gandhi said of him, 'When I have a talk with Hasrat, I cannot sleep in peace.'[47] At the Khilafat Conference on 23 November 1919, the poet wanted the Punjab wrong to be combined with the Khilafat grievance. But Gandhi overruled him. At the Khilafat Workers' Conference held between 18 and 19 March 1920, he sought the same as regards commercial boycott, en masse resignation from government service, and the boycott of law courts. He clashed with Gandhi yet again over the efficacy of non-violence, or when, in December 1921, he called for total Independence. Moreover,

---

[45] *1921 Movement: Reminiscences*, p. 57. He was imprisoned for sedition on 14 Sept. 1897 and in July 1908. He was sentenced to six years' imprisonment. He had already suffered seven and a half years of prison. D.V. Gokhale (ed.), *The Tilak Case 1916* (Poona City, n.d.).

[46] *1921 Movement: Reminiscences*, p. 251.

[47] Halide Edib, *Inside India*, with an Introduction and Notes by Mushirul Hasan (New Delhi: Oxford University Press, 2002), p. 83.

he fumed at the Bardoli programme; if religion enjoined violence, he said, non-violence could not be adopted at the bidding of a 'dictator'.

Hasrat's reasoned and deliberate exposition at the Ahmedabad Congress worried the Home Department: 'The serious consequences of such a speech at the time and in the circumstances it was delivered can hardly be exaggerated, and it was openly laying down a challenge which no self-respecting Govt. could overlook.'[48] Gandhi may not have thought so, but he hustled everybody to throw overboard Hasrat's resolution. But the poet fought back.[49] He gave figures of Muslims sacrifices without adequate rewards.[50] In Agra, he called not only for resignations from the police and the army, but declared total freedom from British rule as his ultimate goal.[51]

Time and life brought fresh sorrows and joys. Remarkable for the integrity of his character, the lucidity of his views, and the strength of his will, Hasrat was regarded by officials with vehement disapprobation for his anti-colonial stance. The most painful incident that occurred during his imprisonment was his father's death. Earlier, his father had been traumatized when his son was taken from Aligarh to the Naini Jail, bound in handcuffs and shackles.[52] Begum Hasrat Mohani wondered: 'Is he under house arrest or, God forbid, will he be charged under some case? Nothing is clear. I worry. There is no saviour but God.'[53] She read the 'Sura al-Anfal' (The Spoils of War)—the eighth chapter of the

[48] Note by C.W. Gwyne, 24 February 1924, Home Dept, Political, file no., 29, 1924.

[49] Indulal Yagnik, an eyewitness, mentioned that he was 'wonderstruck at his courage'. He further added,

His argument on the whole appeared to me logical. The point that Bipin Chandra Pal had raised at the time of the partition of Bengal now appeared completely self-evident at the time of the non-cooperation movement. Again, if we were to enter into a final battle against British rule how could we desire to attain *swaraj* under their protection? Yet, [the] Maulana's amendment was strongly opposed by Gandhiji in his typical manner and therefore it was disapproved. (*Autobiography*, vol. 2, pp. 124–5.)

[50] *Pioneer*, 15 March 1922, Home Dept, Political, file no. 439, 1922.

[51] G. Minault, *The Khilafat Movement*, p. 172.

[52] Hasrat was the pen-name he used in his poetry, and Mohan his birthplace.

[53] To Abdul Bari, 14 April 1916, in *Begam Hasrat Mohani aur Unke Khutoot* (The letters of Begam Hasrat Mohani), in Urdu, edited by Atiq Siddiqi (New Delhi: Jamal Printing Press, 1981).

Quran with 75 verses.[54] But his daughter, Naeemah, told her father, 'Be brave in facing the calamity that has befallen you. Do not worry about me or the household. Have courage and do not waver.'

Confined in a cell with a small opening for light, Hasrat had no access to books—not even the Quran—or to his friends and relatives.[55] Once his sentence was commuted, he canvassed for the Republic of Hejaz, a region in the west of present-day Saudi Arabia, against Ibn Saud (1876–1953). This annoyed the Ali brothers.[56] In 1925, he chaired the first CPI conference at Kanpur; he had reached the conclusion that communism was the final and the best form of politics.[57] A strange turnaround and a quixotic tenacity on the part of an individual with a traditional background! Inspired by the Bolshevik Revolution and conscious of the danger in which Indians lived under colonial rule, the revolution appeared to public intellectuals like him as a chiliastic deed, a transformation ending oppression and emancipating the individual. The bold approach of Lenin, whose authority towered above that of others, and his desire to help the disadvantaged and the poor, had not only brought hope where there had been despair, but significantly changed Russia.

Hasrat weighed up the merits of socialism. For the first time in world history, the outcry of the people had been expressed against the ruling elites for being hand in glove with the British. Looking at it from this angle, socialism represented not only the interests of the working classes but also the progressive aspirations, that is, for Independence. It saw in its success a victory of the Islamic doctrines as well. For Hasrat, Islam and socialism complemented each other, and they conflicted only when the men of politics or the men of religion trespassed the limits of their fields and methods. After the Great Depression (1929–39), it seemed that communism provided the only solution to the periodic booms and depressions which bedevilled the industrialized countries (the Soviet Union was an exception). On one occasion, Hasrat called himself a Sufi man of faith and a communist Muslim, whose chosen

[54] To Abdul Bari, 25 April 1916, in *Begam Hasrat Mohani aur Unke Khutoot*.
[55] A. Montgomerie to Secy., GOI, 6 March 1924, Home Dept, Political, file no. 229, 1924.
[56] Mitra, *Indian Annual Register*, July–December 1925, pp. 342–3.
[57] Khalid Hasan Qadri, *Hasrat Mohani* (New Delhi: Adara-i-Adabiyat-Delhi, 1985), p. 253.

path was revolution and unworldliness (*darweshī-o-inqilāb maslak hai merā Sūfī momin hūn, ishtirākī Muslim.*)

In July–August 1928, the All-Parties Conference set out on a programme of constitutional experimentation. It served to show the problem of combining castes and communities in a stable form. Hasrat neither accepted a half-hearted federalism nor centralization. Instead, he stuck to the demand for complete independence or 'Long Live Revolution',[58] and rejected the Nehru Report for recommending dominion status instead of *purna swaraj*. At this point, his estrangement from the Congress widened, and he also became a suspect in the eyes of radical Muslims. The CPI expelled him; it refused to approve of his links with the Congress and the League.[59] Hasrat, who had his identity spelt out, gravitated towards the venerable Sufis of Firangi Mahal (Shah Abdul Wahab, Shah Abdur Razzaq,[60] Shah Abdul Wali, and Maulana Anwar Ali). He performed Hajj on eleven occasions (including once overland), a remarkable feat at a time when travelling overland or by ship was quite hazardous, and visited the shrines in Basra, Baghdad, Kazmain, Karbala, and Najaf, the birthplace of Ali Ibn-e Abi Talib—the Prophet's son-in-law. He brought back a dying veneration for Arab philosophy and scholarship, and he loved to recall his debt.

> My eyes behold the mosque and the temple,
> And light up every time with the Beloved's Beauty.

And how he put that experience into practice in his life is expressed in another verse:

[58]   He once read his statement out to Muzaffar Ahmad, op. cit., p. 31.

[59]   G. Adhikari (ed.), *Documents of the History of the Communist Party of India*, vol. III c. 1928 (New Delhi: People's Publishing House, 1982), p. 454; S. Chattopadhyay, *Muzaffar Ahmad*, p. 21.

[60]   Shah Abdur Razzaq (1636–1724) of Bansa, not only won the recognition of his contemporaries but also exerted after his death one of the most powerful influences on Awadh's spiritual history. His shrine, a nucleus of ascetic pietism, shelters the devotee from disease and mental ailments, and offers a place where one seeks refuge from the pressures of everyday life. The Shah's twenty-three immediate successors included at least three members of the Kidwai, and six of the Firangi Mahal family. See Mushirul Hasan, *From Pluralism to Separatism: Qasbas in Colonial Awadh* (New Delhi: Oxford University Press, 2012).

Take to your heart no lesson but one:
Serve all life, and love Truth.

There is, then, the love for Lord Krishna whose birthplace Hasrat
visited for *darshan*. He watched the dance and drama festival, and fash-
ioned poems describing Him as head of the company of lovers. He
believed in Krishna being a complete 'Wali', who embodied love, and
found no real difference between Islam and the *Gita*. He referred to
him as one who inspired him in life. From Yervada, he wrote (probably
between 26 and 30 September 1923):

> The path of love is to worship Beauty,
> We know nothing of Reward or Punishment.

Starting with Amir Khusrau, Malik Mohammad Jaisi (b. 1498),
Raskhan (1533–1618), Abdur Rahim Khan-e Khana (1556–1627)
expressed their love and devotion for Hindu gods and goddesses. Love,
as some of them proclaimed, became the reason for every motion.
Hasrat followed this tradition. According to him, 'Regarding Hazrat Sri
Krishna (Peace Be upon Him) I am a follower of the path of love of my
pir and pir of pirs Hazrat Saiyyid Abdur Razzaq Bansvi (1636–1724).'

> When he cast at me his especially kind glance,
> My eyes lit up with a nameless unending vision.

> Revered Krishna, bestow something on me too,
> For at your feet lies the entire realm of Love.

> May that you accept Hasrat too at Mathura—
> I hear you are specially kind to lovers.

On the occasion of Janmashtami on 28 August 1928, he wrote the
following poem at Barsana, Radha's birthplace in Mathura district:

> I stand where Love's perfect knowledge is found.
> Whose is the flute whose melody fills me?
> 'Men of Heart' obtain in Mathura that fragrance of Unity
> Which eternally permeates all life.
> What good fortune, Hasrat, that your heart brims
> With a glowing love for that musk-hued Beauty!

These are not two parallel concurrent strands, but merely two
compatible phases in Hasrat's thinking. His devotion to Krishna was

in the true Sufi spirit. It was said of the Greeks that they were formed of three parts: their tongue spoke one thing, their mind mediated another, and their actions accorded with neither. Hasrat was made of very different stuff from the time-serving politicians. His faith gave him the strength to carry on in spite of adversities.

Hasrat Speaks

Hasrat's first major encounter with the police took place on 3 June 1908; he was sentenced to two years' imprisonment for criticizing the British colonial policy on public education in Egypt. He spent the greater part of his confinement in Naini Jail but was set free before his term; Hasrat attributed this to the miracle of Ahmad Abdul Haq, who had earned a place of honour in the Sabri-Chishti school of Islamic mysticism. After his release, he went to Rudauli, a *qasba* in Barabanki district, to attend the *urs*.[61]

In May 1922, the five jurors confirmed his innocence, and he escaped punishment on the following ground: 'He is not a political prisoner ... in the sense of the manifesto issued by the Independent Labour Party at home. He was willing to change the Congress creed so that all possible and proper means might be adopted to secure this goal ...' [62] Around this time, stories of valour and benevolence were woven around the man wearing meagre clothes—a shirt, knickers, a cap, a piece of jute cloth—and who had a rough blanket for his bed. When the wardens held him guilty of accumulating papers, coloured pencils, as well as a pen-knife in his cell,[63] Hasrat defiantly wrote:

Jo chaho sazaa de do tum aur bhi khul khalo
Par ham se qasam le lo ki ho jo shikayat bhi.

---

[61] Urs, literally 'wedding', refers to the death anniversary of a Sufi saint, usually held at the saint's dargah, that is, shrine or tomb.

[62] Note by C. W. Gwyne, 24 February 24, Home Dept, Political, file no. 29, 1924.

[63] He used to be punished for this, but soon enough the same sort of thing would get to the cell from unidentified sources. Yagnik, *Autobiography*, vol. 2, pp. 54–6.

The gist of Hasrat's defence was that punishing anyone without formally charging the person bolsters tyranny and a sin which religion forbids. It is on this basis that he refused to obey the government's command: 'Let the case come up. *Inshallah*, I will give them a befitting reply. After that, if I have to be arrested anyway, I have no hassles. *Wa ufawwidu amree ilalla, wallahu ala kulli shai-in qadeer* (I entrust my affairs to Allah. Whatever is on Earth and in the Heavens is Allah's)'. G. N. Atre, the intransigent Magistrate, sentenced him to two years' rigorous confinement. Having described him as 'an educated and intelligent man,' he remarked:

> It is common knowledge that in all service Departments corrupt practices do prevail among the law paid subordinates; and no law on earth can adequately prevent such practices wholly. It becomes therefore the duty of every person with authority to punish the offender with extreme punishment in order that this may serve as an example to deter others from taking this wrong path. If such offences even when detected go unpunished, the consequences will be disastrous. There will be no meaning in inflicting imprisonment on convicts if they can go on enjoying all the comforts and eating *halve* which they secure while at home, the intention of the law will be frustrated.[64]

In personal life, Hasrat and Nishatul-Nisa (1885–1937) were devoted to each other for better and for worse through many years of vicissitudes and successes, sorrows and aspirations. Very few women in the Awadh qasbas were as urbane as Nishat, daughter of Shabbir Hasan, a lawyer. And very few attended political meetings with unfailing regularity, or served on the CWC. At the time of Hasrat's arrest in 1908, she urged him to be firm and resolute.[65] At the time of his rearrest in April 1916,[66] she prayed for his long life. 'If he has been arrested in connection with [the] freedom struggle,' she persisted, 'then he should also be treated like others who have been arrested. But God

[64] Home Dept, Political, file no. 229, 1924. On 19 March, the Chief Justice and Justice Lalubhai Shah of the High Court's appellate side reduced the sentence from two and a half years to six months.

[65] Atiq Siddiqi, *Adabiyat: Mohammad Atiq Siddiqi ke Adabi Mazameen* (New Delhi: New Bismah Kitab Ghar, 2010), p. 19.

[66] A. Siddiqi, *Adabiyat*, p. 20.

only knows His plans.' In another letter, she talked of her husband's steely resolve and of his patience:

> May God shower His kindness and we have faith only in Him. May God give Hasrat courage! And help him succeed. *Amen*. Let's see what happens. God forbid, even if he is arrested, I should have patience and pray to God to give me strength to somehow take revenge on those who have gratuitously inflicted cruelty on Hasrat even if I am also put in jail or hanged. I will pray to God that He destroys these *kafirs*, and *Insha'Allah*, my prayers will certainly be answered. You also pray that may God keep Hasrat steadfast and safe.[67]

This is hardly a tribute, but more an acknowledgement that wives and daughters were partners in the struggle for freedom, and that Begum Hasrat Mohani encouraged her husband to fight for freedom.

Maulvi Zafar Ali Khan (1873–1956)

Phoonk dala hai meri atish nawai ne mujhe,
Aur meri zindagani ka yehi saman hai.

My fiery voice has reduced me to ashes,
But this is the very existence of my being.

Zafar Ali Khan, an Aligarh graduate (1895), entered the Hyderabad Civil Service as Assistant Home Secretary. A few years later, he edited *Zamindar*, which sold 20,000 copies twice a day in north India alone. This was due to its evocative writings on the annulment of Bengal's partition in 1911, the Turco-Italian war the same year,[68] the Kanpur mosque incident in April 1913,[69] and the rejection of the AMU scheme—the four key events shaping the political beliefs of a tiny but influential Muslim elite in northern India. Committed to the Islamic idea of *akhuwat* (brotherhood of Muslims), they placed their faith in the Khilafat as the raison d'être for welding Muslims scat-

---

[67] A. Siddiqi, *Begam Hasrat Mohani aur Unke Khutoot*. Translated by Nishat Zaidi.

[68] Italian troops landed in Tripoli (Libya) on 5 October 1911. In 1912, Bulgaria, Serbia, Greece, and Montenegro attacked Turkey, securing swift victories.

[69] See Mohamed Ali, *My Life*, p. 78n16.

tered all over the world into a compact whole under its aegis. They argued that the British were generally hostile to the Muslims and to their kingdoms, and it was, as a result, obligatory on the part of its citizens to defend them.

In 1912, Zafar Ali visited Constantinople to present to the Grand Vizier a part of the money raised by the sale of Turkish bonds. He went to Turkey again in early 1913 with the Indian Medical Mission to provide supplies to a camp in Anatolia for Muslim refugees. In India, he wrote against the government. 'A sacred portion of the Cawnpore Mosque,' he announced, 'was demolished in the midst of guns and bayonets. In this way the funeral of that religious liberty, whose effigy has been shown as living and moaning for more than a century, was performed with full military honours.' Towards the end of the year, his article entitled 'Come over Macedonia and Help Us' prompted the government to forfeit the security of the *Zamindar* together with the Zamindar Printing Press. In this and other writings his rhetorical style was overcharged with Persian and Arabic vocabulary. Generally speaking, he wrote like 'a cavalry in full charge'.[70]

Zafar Ali wrote poems mostly in jail. The political poem became, by and large, the chief attraction of *Zamindar*. It suffered from, wrote Aziz Ahmad, the historian of Islam, interminable shifting of personal ground and undeserved personal invective.[71] An intelligence officer talked of Zafar Ali visiting places in Punjab, and rousing forces of mischief, disorder, and anarchy. As regards *Hijrat* (the migration of Indian Muslims from the land of war to the land of peace, that is, Afghanistan), Zafar Ali assured his co-religionists that the Amir had not interdicted the *Hijrat*, that the prohibitory order was only temporary, and that people would be allowed to revisit Afghanistan after the cold subsided.

A resolution for Zafar Ali's unconditional release was moved in the Punjab Council on 4 August 1924, but John Maynard and Craik opposed it.[72] Consequently, he languished in Montgomery Jail for much of 1926, but produced a collection of poems—*Habsiyat*—that was published in Lahore. The collection is embellished with numerous

[70] Muhammad Sadiq, *History of Urdu Literature*, p. 404.

[71] Ahmad, *Islamic Modernism*, p. 101.

[72] Home Dept, Political, file no. 37-III, 1924 & KW; Home Dept, Political, file no. 37/V.

pieces of poetry, but they are remarkably simple and direct and reveal the day-to-day experience of a prisoner.

Outside jail, Zafar Ali raised points of order to embarrass the government in the Assembly. For instance, in 1938, he called for a clear enunciation of the government of India's position vis-à-vis the Secretary of State.[73] The same year, he debated the Federal Scheme and the League's stand that it would not be bound by a Congress–British agreement.[74] He also charged Bhulabhai Desai for announcing in London that Congress was prepared to accept federation within the framework of the Act of 1919.[75]

We conclude with Zafar Ali's description of the Peshawar 'martyrs' of 23 April 1930.

Malikul maut ko khatir mein na laney wala,
  Seena taney huye woh goliyan khaney wala,
Apne Iqbal ka naqara bajaney wala,
  Apne hi khoone shahadat mein nahaney wala,
Aisey Janbaaz Bahadur pe Khuda ki rehmat

  Fearless, he faced the angel of death,
Dauntless, he encountered the barrage of bullets,
  Joyous, he blew the horn of his valour,
Buoyant, he bathed in the blood of his martyrdom,
  God's blessings be upon this valiant hero.[76]

Although the tone of this kind of literature is sad, the poets during the Khilafat movement dwelt upon such themes as the fading glory of Islam, or the Muslim empires in a state of decline. The progressive poets were, however, cast in a different mould. They looked forward to their future without fear and with hope, and sought to derive comfort from the thought that all forms of exploitation must end in revolution.

---

[73] Home Dept, Political, (Reforms Office), file no. 86/17/38 G, 1938.
[74] Home Dept, Political, (Reforms Office), file no. 86/17/38 G, 1938.
[75] Home Dept, Political, (Reforms Office), file no. 86/11/38 G, 1938.
[76] For additional references to his poetry, see G. Minault, *The Khilafat Movement*, pp. 156–8.

7.   'Long Walk to Freedom'

It was in 1910 that I first visited an Indian jail. As I walked modestly behind the Jail Superintendent and Medical Officer along a row of cells, suddenly a painful of filth shot out of a cell and fell in a cascade over the Superintendent and his spotless silk suit! Amid the excitement and while buckets of water were being poured over this very senior officer, the struggling prisoner was dragged out of his cell and placed upon the whipping triangle which had hurriedly been brought. The aggressor was summarily flogged; the Superintendent retired to don new clothes, and I left the jail saying to myself, 'If that sort of thing is of frequent occurrence in jail work I'm not for it! But as I cycled homewards the thoughts kept recurring to my mind; 'What induced that prisoner to commit such an idiotic act?' and 'Was the resultant punishment calculated to do the offender any good, however necessary it might be to deter others?'
—F. A. Barker, *The Modern Prison System of India*, p. xv

Lenin addressed the communists of the East with the following words: 'You will have to base yourselves on the bourgeois nationalism which is awakening, and must awaken, among those peoples, and which has its historical justification. At the same time, you must find your way to the working and exploited masses of every country.' He spoke of translating the true communist doctrine into the language of every people; to carry out those practical steps immediately, and to join the proletarians of other countries in a common struggle.

In India, the Leninist doctrine struck a chord, though its interpretation varied. In the Congress itself views were dissimilar, but Jawaharlal Nehru spearheaded the radical, pro-socialist wing to usher in a major transformation of society that would weaken the capitalist–landlord stranglehold. In line with this thinking, the fundamental changes proposed at the Karachi session of the Congress in 1931 moved India forward socially and created a new dynamism in its ethos. With the Congress courting the industrial workers and peasants, its initiatives grew more radical. Land reforms were included in its package. This afforded an opportunity for organizing the rural masses. Elements from the intelligentsia too switched to the Left in droves. In Bengal, they were involved in controlling the labour unions so that they could declare a general strike—the preliminary to mass action for the overthrow of the Raj. In parts of Andhra, agricultural labour led major struggles in Krishna, Nellore, and Guntur districts, and were attracted to the cause of socialism and communism.[1]

In the 1930s, the world found itself in the depths of the Great Depression. Capitalism faced a severe crisis leaving behind a trail of social conflicts and political polarization, but Left unity failed to acquire that self-reliant autonomy to offer a realistic solution to the world-wide impasse. Although Bolshevism set the tone for turning the world into a socialist paradise, the cult of Joseph Stalin (1878–1953) gathered momentum and every so often an escalation of the intra-party tussle took place. Heavy rhetorical blows were exchanged, and leaders were blamed for betraying the working classes. As in other parts of India, it was in jail that most partymen in Kerala first heard of the attack on the USSR. They differed on their strategy until a party circular directed them to toe the People's War line on the war efforts.[2]

[1] Comrade M. Basavapunnaiah, *Reminscences* (Azamabad: Prajasakti Book House, 2010), pp. 35–6.
[2] T. J. Nossiter, *Communism in Kerala: A Study in Political Adaptation* (New Delhi: Oxford University Press, 1982), p. 85.

Fierce discussions took place in the cell, with the spotlight on the future relationship with the Congress.

The ideological divergences opened up a discursive space in which debates on Marxism and communism unfolded. The process was set in motion in Bengal after Nalini Gupta, M. N. Roy's emissary, established contact with Muzaffar Ahmad, Bhupendrakumar Datta, the young Jugantar revolutionary, and Munshi Alimuddin.[3] This was followed by the worldwide catastrophe of the War. Most supported the USSR and subordinated to it all other tasks. The masses were, in particular, filled with hatred for those who had seized their lands but at the same time felt liberated because the Soviet Union resisted Hitler's furious assaults. Creative writers used their imagination with great effect. Faiz Ahmed Faiz, for example, 'imbibed the ideas of the 1930s, more gradually but tenaciously, from books or smuggled pamphlets, travellers' tales, and the impalpable genie known as the Spirit of the Age. They rooted themselves in his own soil, he saw them and their shadows by familiar sunlight; they took possession of his imagination, a stronghold from which ideas are less easily dislodged, as well as of his mind'.[4]

The socialists believed they would prevail only by following a democratic course, whipping up mass enthusiasm first and then dominating state affairs from this position of strength. Nehru facilitated their birth, just as he contributed, years later, to their decline and ultimate disintegration. He himself did not join them, but advised a select few to remain organizationally inside Congress. Although he relegated his own dreams of a socialist state to a dim and shadowy vision, he sought to cement an alliance with the socialists and communists in a 'United Front against Imperialism'. As for the socialist response, the cream of the crop stood divided. Ram Manohar Lohia was bitterly opposed to Nehru's political hegemony and his Westernized ways. The Bombay socialists, especially those with a working-class background, were impatient with the Congress' policy to eschew agitation, while their counterparts in Bihar were caught up in caste and language disputes. Some of them were at times incoherent, emotional, and utterly capricious.

[3] S. Chattopadhyay, *Muzaffar Ahmad*, p. 105.
[4] Hameed, *Daybreak*, p. 1.

One man who reflected on this and many other aspects of the people's movement, or the lack of it, was M. N. Roy. A communist with wide-ranging global connections, he used his years in jail to construct his ideas that were the mainstay of political activism. 'Good men,' according to him, 'are seldom given a place in the galaxy of the great. It will continue to be so until goodness is recognised as the measure of genuine greatness.'[5] A vain hope! The communists scornfully dismiss Roy as an agent of British imperialism, who had to be fought against by any and every means. E. M. S. Namboodiripad and other Leftists made a similar evaluation.[6] Jyoti Basu alleged that he even accepted government funds to conduct his pro-War activities.[7] The following section does not get to the heart of the matter, so to speak, but captures a few moments in Roy's jail life.

Crime and Karma[8]

A kitten one day strayed into Roy's room. He gave it milk, and it stayed on. He soon became interested in animal psychology. At odd moments, he would observe the cat behaving in changed circumstances, and he would reflect on what might be the mental process behind its behaviour. He began writing a diary, the fragments of which offer a glimpse of his mind, his extensive range of interests from music to mathematics, and his broad sympathies.[9] K. M. Ashraf and Syed Mohammad Tonki, Headmaster of the Aligarh School (1958–60), the two Aligarh

[5]   M. N. Roy, *Men I Met* (Bombay: Lalvani Publishing House, 1968), p. 4.

[6]   'We learnt from the documents of the Third International that he had not only propounded the doctrine of decolonization but also committed various serious errors in handling the Chinese Revolution. Anti-fascism was just an apology for backing England and her allies in their war against Hitler' (Horst Kruger, ed., *Kunwar Mohammad Ashraf: An Indian Scholar and Revolutionary, 1903–1962*, Delhi: People's Publishing House, 1969, p. 14); *M. N. Roy's Memoirs* (The Indian Renaissance Institute, Allied Publishers Pvt. Ltd., 1964), p. 593; E. M. S. Namboodiripad, *How I Became a Communist* (Trivandrum: Chinta Publishers, 1976).

[7]   Oral History Transcript, p. 31, NMML.

[8]   Title of Roy's essay in *Fragments*, vol. 1.

[9]   Abraham. S. Erulkar, 'Introduction', in M. N. Roy, *Fragments*, vol. 1 (1965 Reprint), p. ii.

students, recalled what they read on the Russian Revolution (1917) and its consequences.[10]

India's covenant with the revolution is well-researched. We know of its best and brightest men and women embracing Marxism. Roy was active in Central Asia until his recall to Moscow after the Anglo-Russian Trade Agreement. He attended the Congress of 1922, served the Presidium of the Communist International's Executive Committee, moved to Berlin to collaborate with Maulvi Barkatullah (1854–1927) of Kabul's Provisional Government and other revolutionaries from Afghanistan and Russia, and was involved in the Howrah Conspiracy Case,[11] the Garden Reach Dacoity case, and the Beliaghata Dacoity case. P. Biggane, a CID officer, reported Comintern's satisfaction with Roy's work.[12]

Roy returned to India on 14 November 1930 against the advice of the veteran German communist, Heinrich Brandler, only to be arrested. Roy wrote several letters from jail, 'in the void, never knowing whether they will reach their destination'. The one that reached its destination had this message: 'This is a cruel world. It makes unnecessary troubles for harmless people like ourselves.' 'But,' he added, 'we must remake it.'[13] He took courage in both hands and indicted the government as an 'enormous tyranny'. To Justice Thom he quoted David Hume (1711–1776), the Scottish philosopher and historian, and Jeremy Bentham (d. 1832), founder of modern utilitarianism and leading theorist in Anglo–American philosophy of law. But the judge dismissed their views. Roy recollected:

> I had stood charged with a similar offence; and then, twenty years ago, without the benefit of the limelight of publicity and the backing of a whole galaxy of legal luminaries, I declared that the charge against me had no legal validity. I pointed out that the British Law Commissioners who examined Macaulay's draft of the Indian Penal Code were of the opinion that there was no evidence to the effect that the British Crown ever legally assumed the sovereignty of India. On that highest British

[10] Kruger, *Kunwar Mohammad Ashraf*, p. 343.

[11] The key figure was Bagha Jatin of the Jugantar Party. He and others were tried for treason, the charge being that they had incited various army regiments against the British.

[12] Home Dept, Political, file no. 11, 1923.

[13] 6 September 1931, M. N. Roy, *Fragments*, p. 3.

authority, I maintained that the sections of the Penal Code dealing with political offences were absurd. The British Crown could not be deprived of a sovereignty which it never possessed. I was the first to take up that position when put on trial for 'conspiring to commit treason'. No other Indian in a similar situation, since then or previously, took that position.[14]

Put simply, Roy agreed with Marx that great men did not make history. Scholasticism and the cult of hero worship, for which he decried Gandhi, had to be replaced by self-confidence and self-expression. 'Man always makes gods, and then worships them, thus debasing himself as well as his gods,' he observed. His views on persons, issues, and books were persuasive; he had a clear-cut stance on India's 'very shallow and woefully sterile' intellectual life; he wrote like a highly seasoned analyst on the evils of poverty and degradation; he had robust ideas on the shibboleth—Eastern Spiritualism versus Western Materialism, on Aldous Huxley's magnum opus, *Point Counterpoint*, Spengler's *Decline of the West*, and Pearl S. Buck's *Chinese Trilogy*, which he hailed as 'the best book on the subject written for a long time'. On religion and matters related to it, he prescribed:

> This country needs a Kemal Pasha, to begin with, to chop off the ridiculous tufts on the heads; to make the wearing of fierce moustaches punishable as culpable homicide; to drive the pampered, idle, gossiping, but outrageously maltreated women out in the streets to work down their fat or cure their anaemia, and to free themselves from the malignant curse of suppressed passion; to prohibit the irritating chanting of rigmarole in a language which few understand; and to do many other similar things.[15]

Politically, Roy offered solid grounds for declaring that the Congress had colluded with the British to perpetuate the rule of the dominant propertied and landed classes. Gandhi held that his spinning-wheel taught patience, industry, and simplicity, and was for India's starving millions the symbol of salvation, but Roy censured the 'holy ideal of loincloth and of voluntary poverty', pointing to 'the saintly deliverer'

[14] M. N. Roy, *INA and the August Revolution* (Calcutta: Renaissance Publishers, May 1946).

[15] 12 October 1933, M. N. Roy, *Fragments*, p. 65.

plying the divine spinning wheel in jail.[16] Arguing that Gandhi was offering an unrealistic solution to the post-War situation that was fraught with catastrophe, he scoffed at his 'conclave of cardinals', who were chosen not on account of any merit other than the ability to ply the prayer wheel. He wondered why 'the devoted souls with their prophet' did not 'go to the land of Dalai Lama'.[17]

Roy censured Gandhi's medieval ideals and 'obscurantist ideas',[18] and Nehrus dithering approach to issues that occasioned immediate solutions. 'A good man fallen among thieves,' was how he once referred to him. Nehru differed hugely with Roy, but respected his learning. He censured the government for treating 'a great opponent' shabbily for offences that had occurred many years ago,[19] and approached friends to aid the 'Roy Defence Committee'.

Roy's comments on 'intellectual stagnation' were superficial, and too greatly inspired by the Orientalists. India was not living, as he suggested, in the fifteenth century.[20] It was very much part of the industrialized era and the multiple currents of change that it engendered. Gandhi had raised public consciousness on these diverse currents to an extraordinary level, and there were clear signs of a new awakening that Roy could not see in jail. Besides, he was well aware of the burden of economic degradation and disparities, but not the magnitude of the challenge before the Congress leadership. He should have known that Royism would neither whet the appetite of the political classes nor be accepted as a remedy for India's ills.

'One must have a great sense of humour to avoid falling into a mood of bitterness,' remarked Roy. Indeed, notwithstanding the unpleasantness around him, he retained his sense of humour and shared it with friends and family.[21] Their letters to him were both a great source of enjoyment,

---

[16] 12 October 1933, M. N. Roy, *Fragments*, p. 13.

[17] 22 September, 1933, M. N. Roy, *Fragments*, p. 61

[18] M. N. Roy, *Men I Met*, p. 11.

[19] *Bombay Chronicle*, 9 November 1931, *SWJN*, vol. 5, p. 297.

[20] 21 January 1936, M. N. Roy, *Fragments*, p. 155.

[21] He was convicted of conspiracy against the King-Emperor and sentenced in January 1932 to twelve years' imprisonment. He was released on 20 November 1936, after serving all but eight months of his six-year sentence.

and of consolation in the dark moments through which he passed. In the first year, he read John Galsworthy (1867–1933), Thomas Hardy (1840–1928), Sinclair Lewis (1885–1951), and Pearl S. Buck (1892–1973), and took great delight in reading *Sesh Prasna* by Sarat Chandra Chatterjee (1876–1938), a work he thought stood well in comparison with those of Anatole France (1844–1924), French poet, journalist and novelist, Henrik Johan Ibsen (1828–1906), the Norwegian playwright, and Emile Zola (1840–1902), a French writer who exemplified the literary school of naturalism. He considered *Sesh Prasna* as 'a landmark in Indian Renaissance', and expected it to fetch the Nobel prize in literature. 'It has set agog the placid and sickening atmosphere of Bengali romanticism and mystic sentimentalism,' Roy said, placing *Sesh Prasna* above Tagore's *Gitanjali*. In a lighter vein, he advised a European friend: 'I warn you: if you learn Bengali and begin with translating a book not by Tagore, your prospect of visiting Santiniketan will vanish.'[22]

Placed in the B class where prisoners were not allowed the use of handkerchief, Roy's fortunes took a nosedive after he was moved from the District Jail in Kanpur to the Central Prison in Bareilly in mid-January 1932. He had an iron cot with a straw mattress, a table, a stool, and a shelf for his use, besides some plates. 'Just five weeks of the twelve years have passed,' he wrote in a despondent mood. 'Another eleven years and eleven months left. A glorious perspective, unless there were silver linings to the clouds.'[23] He was entitled to write only one letter a month, and could borrow only three books at a time, which to him was 'the worst possible calamity, and most unexpected. In 1932, when E. M. S. Namboodiripad was in jail, the works of Leon Trostsky were freely allowed but not those of Lenin or Stalin. He had read them between 1940 and 1942 when he was underground.[24] As for Roy's experience, blank paper, pens and even a pencil were withdrawn on the ostensible ground that jail was hardly a university and prison cells or barracks were not meant for scholarly pursuits. With months and years flitting away, Roy had the sense to take life easy and observe the jail rules like a good sportsman.[25] 'I am

[22] 17 October 1931, M. N. Roy, *Fragments*, p. 6.
[23] 16 February 1932, M. N. Roy, *Fragments*, p. 14.
[24] E. M. S. Namboodiripad, Oral History Transcript (794), NMML.
[25] 23 December. 1933, M. N. Roy, *Fragments*, p. 69.

fulfilling certain petit-bourgeois conditions which must be faced in this country. Take life easy, look around the world blossoming out in spring. There will be so much in every bus.'[26]

It was in jail that Roy wrote *The Historical Role of Islam*. Though only a sketch of a vast subject, it is full of ideas and throbs with life. He pictured Hindus and Muslims living together without being familiar with each other's culture and religion.[27] He wondered why this was so. Why, he asked, did the Hindu intelligentsia ignore Islam's 'immense revolutionary significance' and the varieties of Islam? Briefly and eloquently he marked out the position that the Sultans of Delhi (1206–1526) and the Mughals (1526–1857) had occupied. Islam and Hinduism found a mutual settlement whether the conquerors and the conquered so desired or not. He summed up:

> Islam was a necessary product of history—an instrument of human progress. It rose as the ideology of a new social relation which, in its turn, revolutionized the mind of man. But just as it had subverted and replaced older cultures, decayed in course of time, Islam, in its turn, was also overstepped by further social developments, and consequently had to hand over its spiritual leadership to other agencies born out of

[26] 16 February 1932, M. N. Roy, *Fragments*, p. 16. V. B. Karnik, 'Epilogue', *M. N. Roy's Memoirs*, p. 592.

[27] 'Indeed, there is no other example of two communities living together in the same country for so many hundred years, and yet having so little appreciation of each other's culture. No civilized people in the world are so ignorant of Islamic history and contemptuous of the Mohammedan religion as the Hindus. Spiritual imperialism is an outstanding feature of our nationalist ideology. But this nasty spirit is the most pronounced in relation to Mohammedanism. The current notion of the teachings of the Arabian Prophet is extremely ill-informed. The average educated Hindu has little knowledge of, and no appreciation for, the immense revolutionary significance of Islam, and the great cultural consequences of that revolution. The prevailing notions could be laughed at as ridiculous, were they not so pregnant with harmful consequences. These notions should be combated for the sake of the Indian people as well as in the interest of science and historical truth. A proper appreciation of the cultural significance of Islam is of supreme importance in this crucial period of the history of India' (M. N. Roy, *The Historical Role of Islam*, Calcutta: Renaissance Publishers, 1958, p. 3).

newer conditions. But it contributed to the forging of new ideological instruments which brought about the subsequent social revolution. The instruments were experimental science and rationalist philosophy. It stands to the credit of Islamic culture to have been instrumental in the promotion of the ideology of a new social revolution.[28]

In Dehra Dun Jail, Roy lived in one of a row of cells set like boxes along a wall. Soon, he fell into the prisoner's habit of counting days. After completing four years, he dreaded the prospect of another year of incarceration.[29] Like Nehru, who was every now and then chastened by the political turmoil around him, Roy used to withdraw into a shell. As with Felix Dzerzhinsky, there were so many nails in the living body of the prisoner that he no longer waited for anything. All he wanted was to be numb and not feel anything, not think, not be tormented between the terrible necessity and the helplessness. All that remained in the heart was the feeling of helplessness. To be guaranteed against disappointment, he fixed his gaze a year and a half hence,[30] and craved for 'some beauty of life—a comfortable hotel on pine-covered mountains, ravenous appetite at a well-laid table, and a lot of laughter'.[31] Lying in his musty cell, with its damp and dank mattress, he longed for a 'few months of civilized existence' in Europe and the luxury of 'splendid isolation'.[32]

When would he be free? The question tormented him. Nonetheless, he wanted friends to know that he had been writing and performing all along the task allotted to him, in full.[33] All the same, he wanted to get out as early as possible, to breathe fresh air and to view the world from the vantage point of his house. When would that happen? If only he knew! The last lap of Roy's ordeal threatened to be terrible. Death is no worse than five years of living death, he remarked. He was 'fagged out', but made the best of his life in the midst of all its cruelties and ugliness.[34] 'He wanted to breathe in a less suffocating atmosphere

[28] M. N. Roy, *The Historical Role of Islam*, p. 20.
[29] 21 July 1935, M. N. Roy, *Fragments*, p. 125.
[30] 20 December 1934, M. N. Roy, *Fragments*, p. 106.
[31] 22 March 1934, M. N. Roy, *Fragments*, p. 77.
[32] 19 June 1934, M. N. Roy, *Fragments*, p. 86.
[33] 19 June 1934, M. N. Roy, *Fragments*, p. 89.
[34] 29 November, 1935, M. N. Roy, *Fragments*, p. 146.

for his thoughts to become fresh and lively again.[35] 'No,' he uttered, 'I do not want to go to jail again, not if I can help.'[36] He wanted to launch a publishing house on the lines of the Malik Verlag to weaken the impact of the nationalist claptrap and reactionary romanticism, and circulate gendered literature to raise the standard of social revolt and cultural renaissance.[37] He was not the one to take hated enemies in brotherly embrace or treat old friends and tried treasures as untouchables.

Dehra Dun was all astir when Roy's release took place on 20 November 1936. After meeting the local men of influence, he attended the provincial conference in Bareilly, UP. A meeting with Nehru followed in December. At the Faizpur conference of the Congress in December 1936, the 'mystery man' visited communists, socialists, and others in an effort to convert them to his views. He seemed to be working hand in hand with Nehru and Bose,[38] and shared to the full the patriotic nationalism of the era of liberation.

Women as Political Actors

Left activism derived from Marxian ideology softened traditional differences in jails. Women sacrificed all kinds of cherished and religious privileges of caste, ceremonial piety, and privacy in prison. The cause of Swaraj swept all taboos and old customs before it. The most orthodox of Brahmin women mingled socially, even with *devadasis*, one of whom wept at the time of her release because her satyagrahi sisters had treated her as an equal.[39] There were others who were not locked into family life by socialization, tradition, and law, and either relegated these aspects to the background or renounced them altogether. Mridula Sarabhai (1911–1974) 'de-classed' herself; her co-workers shared the dining table with her.[40]

---

[35] 24 September, 1936, M. N. Roy, *Fragments*, p. 201.
[36] 20 November 1936, M. N. Roy, *Fragments*, p. 212.
[37] 20 July 1936, M. N. Roy, *Fragments*, p. 199.
[38] Home Dept, Political & K.W., file no. 4/40, 1936.
[39] Cousins, *Indian Womanhood Today*, p. 70.
[40] Aparna Basu, *Mridula Sarabhai: Rebel with a Cause* (New Delhi, Oxford University Press, 1996), p. 46.

Women, whose lives have changed our understanding of where they stood in prison life, recreated the day's events with the supplement of gossip and anecdotes. They found a purpose in their suffering, and overcame isolation and loneliness to soothe pain and fill their hearts with warmth. They would sing patriotic songs, their voices floating across the high walls. 'How wonderful is their enthusiasm!' Jawaharlal noted in his Prison Diary.[41] They would pray, fast, spin, read religious texts, and say to each other: 'Your sorrow is my sorrow, and your tears are my tears.' A white-haired grandmother, a sturdy and literate peasant woman and her middle-aged daughter heard their menfolk talk of Swaraj and of Gandhi's incarceration. They whispered to one another: 'If he is in jail then we must go there too.' The next day, they waited till their men had gone to the fields, and then went first to the nearest temple. They walked seven miles to the nearest town and there picketed a foreign cloth shop till they were arrested. They were contended only when they were behind prison bars, so afraid had they been that some of their relatives would find some way of frustrating their passion for patriotic sacrifice. This spirit flowed through the women like a flood.[42] When pushed to the limits, they would see a glimmer of humanity in one of the wardens, perhaps just for a second, but enough to reassure them and keep them going. Man's goodness, wrote Mandela in his autobiography, was a flame that can be hidden but not extinguished.[43]

Gandhi guaranteed to women the righteousness of whatever new actions had to be taken.[44] In addition, he decreed that only inter-caste marriages could be performed in his *ashram*, because they were possibly the solution since it would produce 'only one caste, known by the beautiful name Bhangi'. In general, he objected to intercommunity marriages, and prevented Vijayalakshmi Pandit from marrying Syed Hosain (1886–1949), a journalist close to Motilal Nehru. On the other hand, he let B. K. Nehru marry Magdolna Friedmann or Fori (b.1908), a Hungarian Jewish woman. Again, while Malaviya could not endure the thought of a Brahmin girl marrying a Muslim, he

[41] 12 February 1931, *SWJN*, vol. 5, p. 358.
[42] Cousins, *Indian Womanhood Today*, pp. 70–1.
[43] Mandela, *Long Walk to Freedom*, p. 749.
[44] Cousins, *Indian Womanhood Today*, p. 68.

blessed the marriage of Aruna to Asaf Ali.[45] There were other inter-community marriages too, though they did not always go down well with the parents. In 1945, Mohammad Yunus (1916–2001), nephew of Khan Abdul Ghaffar Khan, married a Christian woman belonging to Lahore's Rallia Ram family. He went to jail in 1941 and yet again in 1946.

Progressive writers made the most of each other's personal and literary companionship in jail, and, for this reason, narrowed gendered distinctions.[46] Conscious of the insidious way in which oppression entered their everyday lives, they retained the warmth of feeling. Romesh Chandra (b. 1919) married Perin Bharucha; Kalpana Dutt, a heroine of the Chittagong Armoury Raid of 1930, married Puran Chandra Joshi on 14 August 1943; Hajrah Begum, Secretary of the Punjab Women's Cell,[47] divorced her first husband and married Z. A. Ahmed; Vimla Faruqi (d. 1999) migrated from Rawalpindi to Delhi after Partition and joined the CPI a year later. She was wedded to Muqimuddin Faruqi (1920–1997). Faiz Ahmed Faiz married an Englishwoman. Rashid Jahan and Mahmuduzzafar broke the barriers of Awadh's feudal aristocracy. The latter lectured at Allahabad University and later at his alma mater, Lucknow University. His writings led to his arrest after the ban on the Communist Party in August 1940. Like Kalpana Dutt who organized relief work as an activist of the Mahila Atma Raksha Samiti, Rashid Jahan toiled hard to raise funds for the Bengal Famine, and donated her *mehr* to the party. After Independence, she was arrested and later freed owing to Nehru's intervention.[48] Her work is invaluable because of the contextual and dramatic details it provides about the gendered experiences, exploitation, and sexualization of the female body in a male-dominated

---

[45] G. N. S. Raghavan, *Aruna Asaf Ali*, p. 15.

[46] Suruchi Thapar-Bjorkert, *Women in the Indian National Movement: Unseen Faces and Unheard Voices, 1930–42* (New Delhi: Sage Publications, 2008), p. 142.

[47] She drew up plans to open chapters of the Progressive Writers' Association in major towns of UP like Kanpur, Benaras, and Lucknow, where the Communist Party wielded influence.

[48] This description is based on Rashid Jahan, *Shola-e Jwala* (Lucknow: India Publishers, n.d.); G. Minault, *Secluded Scholars*, pp. 273–5.

economy, and of the representation of subjects such as arranged marriage and familial oppression.[49]

Aruna and Asaf Ali were, so to speak, made for each other. For months the entire rhythm of their life was disrupted—like 'a plant whose roots have been pulled out of its soil'. Time in a prison stood immovable in its majesty,[50] and its grey monotony diminished the capacity for work.[51] Asaf Ali spent sleepless nights thinking of Aruna (she served more than four terms in prison—nearly four of the fifteen years of their married life). She went underground in September 1942. Imagining all sorts of things happening to her, Asaf Ali shared his anxieties with Gandhi.[52]

I fear it will have to wait till my return from the 'jatra'. There is a vacant cell next to the one I occupy. They hand a light in it every evening and take it down the next morning. Strange shadows play under the light as it awaits the arrival of the occupant who daily cheats the cell. It often reminds me of a poem of Robi Babu in which the solitary inhabitant of a hut daily garnishes and lights her dwelling, and with tears in her eyes waits through the night for the arrival of her lord. What a grand subject the poet would have in the cold, wind-swept, dimly lighted cell next door which is daily got ready for an ever-expected arrival. At night the lonely bars lengthen their shadows at cross angles and paint ghosts of lattice screens on the ground and the walls. The watch, as he paces his beat up and down, shouts 'all right' and awakens echoes all over the place. Who knows what lover of liberty is to be the inmate of this empty cell! But as I change my viewpoint and look at it from another angle, it appears to me a verisimilitude of life. In this great goal—the

[49] Nishat Haider, 'Theatre/Theory of Rashid Jahan, "Angareywali"', in *Gender, Space, and Resistance: Women and Theatre in India*, edited by Anita Singh and Tarun Tapas Mukherjee (New Delhi: DK Printworld, 2013), p. 197.

[50] B. R. Nanda, *In Gandhi's Footsteps* (New Delhi: Oxford University Press, 1990), p. 237.

[51] 9 December 1944, G.N.S. Raghavan (ed.), *M. Asaf Ali's Memoirs: The Emergence of Modern India* (Delhi: Ajanta, 1994), p. 317.

[52] 'Gandhian politics,' he noted in his diary, 'has invaded and conquered her imagination.' 'Those who love liberty,' he continued, 'must either live as prisoners, or like moles and foxes underground' (16 November 1942, G. N. S. Raghavan, *M. Asaf Ali's Memoirs: The Emergence of Modern India*, Delhi: Ajanta, 1994, p. 291).

Universe, there stands the empty cell of our Earth, ever ready to receive the new-born 'prisoner'. Shadows of Destiny dance in the prison house to receive the victim, and close in upon him when he arrives. With every breath Life, the Warder cries 'all right'. The prisoner fills the cell with his laughter, or sobs and sighs, according as his condition moves him.[53]

Kaifi (his nom de plume, 'Azmi', is derived from Azamgarh, his place of birth) and his Hyderabad-born wife, Shaukat, lived through turbulent times. Both mirrored the joy and expectancy of an era—boisterous, buoyant, and optimistic. The former was prominent in the Progressive Writers' Movement,[54] whereas Shaukat acted in Indian People's Theatre Association (IPTA) productions, and equalled the best that men could do, even to outstrip them in fields that had long been their preserve. She possessed the ability to weld instruction and entertainment. The association was formed in May–June 1943 at the national conference of the Communist Party of India in the wake of the Bengal Famine. It was to achieve more 'professional expertise' in the cultural work for 'freedom'—not only from the British but also from various societal norms within the wider panorama of world politics.[55]

Kaifi doggedly fought for victory and found many causes for which to fight, sang the joys and pains of the peasant and the millworker, exposed pretence, weighed everything anew, and voiced human sufferings and aspirations. He presented with fervour a wide variety of opinions and convictions other than his own, attacked oppression and convention, and bequeathed to his family a radical and eclectic inheritance. The Hindutva brigade's brutal religious hypocrisy was most disgusting and deadly in Kaifi's eyes. With his head held high and his voice commanding respect and attention, he was realistic about his work and himself.

[53] G. N. S. Raghavan, *M. Asaf Ali's Memoirs*, p. 193.

[54] One of the early works on the movement in Urdu was by Islam Ishrat, *Khalilur Rahman Azadi: Taraqqi-pasandi se Jadidiyat Tak* (Patna, 1988). *Josh Baani* 5–6 (Taraqqi Pasand Nazm) (Allahabad: Josh and Firaq Literary Society, 2011) is an invaluable collection.

[55] Sharmishta Saha, 'Witnessing Movement: The Women Artists of the Indian People's Theatre Association's Central Squad', in *Gender, Space, and Resistance: Women and Theatre in India*, p. 182.

Under Stalin, the increased preoccupation with sexual mores was part of a larger process of infiltration of official ideology into private life.[56] As the iconic Che Guevara (1928–1967) said: 'At the risk of seeming ridiculous, let me say that the true revolutionary is guided by a great feeling of love. It is impossible to think of a genuine revolutionary lacking this quality.'[57] Among the overseas activists, the American-born Evelyn Trent (1892–1970), Roy's first wife, faced expulsion in Paris in 1925, just before going to the United States. The India Office in Whitehall watched her closely, fearing that her visit would legitimize the Ghadar Party in California and encourage Sikhs from assisting the upheaval in that country.[58] Sarojini Naidu had said it all in December 1921: 'In the service of the nation, the voice of man and the voice of woman should not be divided. Neither might their action, neither might their aspirations, neither might they who walk humbly shall alone reach their sacrifices, neither might their lives, neither might their destinies and their liberty.'[59] This formula worked at times. Many have analysed these traits and sung their praises, and I need not repeat all this. Bhagat Purshottam Sevakram, a Gujarati saint from Bulsar, to whom Mahadev Desai was ardently devoted, affirmed:

All try to walk high, but none
Walks humbly. But he who walks
Humbly shall alone reach the Highest.

[56] Halfin, *Terror in My Soul*, p. 138.
[57] Waters, *Rosa Luxemburg Speaks*, p. 332.
[58] 2 September, 1935, Home Dept, Political & K.W., file no. 351, 1925.
[59] Home Dept, Political, file no. 461, 1921.

8. Sunlight and Shadow in Prison

Alexander Berkman, the American Anarchist, had nothing but disdain and disgust for his fellow-prisoners. They touched no chord in his heart. In India, on the other hand, many of the prisoners did not give up their sentimental idealism. This is, in short, my theme in this chapter. The other theme relates to prisoners leading a dog's life in prison and an impersonal system (not in every way, of course) that worked mercilessly and reduced human beings to animals kept behind bars.[1] I revisit their experiences to understand their commitment to freedom and duty to the nation.

From the grim happenings that we have elucidated, let us turn to the lighter moments when prisoners gossiped, joked, and amused themselves by parodying real life, or when excited voices, laughter and mock jeers resounded across the barracks. Besides the shy and modest kind were the boisterous prisoners bubbling with good humour and

---

[1] 24 September 1936, M. N. Roy, *Fragments*, p. 201.

unrestrained laughter. During the Non-cooperation Movement, S. M. Tonki (1901), an early graduate of Jamia Millia Islamia, recorded heated discussions on newspapers and various news items every day. In Agra Jail, a fellow inmate, Thakur Malkhan Singh of Aligarh, established an *akhada* for wrestling and physical exercise. *Mushairas* and *kavi sammelans* were held, and Basant celebrated.[2] In 1933, the year Adolf Hitler seized power in Germany, Haider Ali Khan, G. Srinivasa, editor of a Telugu weekly, and Madduri Annapurnayya became very close friends in Salem Central Jail and discussed politics on a daily basis.[3]

Gandhi wanted prisons to become happy places.[4] Motilal Nehru was supreme in the lighter sphere of anecdote and romance. He belonged to an unusual gregarious group and developed to a high degree the art of cooperation. He talked and laughed, and recited Hafiz Shirazi (1315–1390). Ganesh Shankar Vidyarthi witnessed him and twenty others playing *gulli danda*. Hussain Zaheer, a scientist, and C. B. Gupta, the future Chief Minister of UP, played rummy. Accustomed to a mudbath, Purshottamdas Tandon (1882–1962) retained his frugal habits. He started his speech with a 'but' and never entirely agreed with anyone. One of his jail mates talked of him as the 'most queer [sic] personality'.[5] His diet consisted mainly of fruit which he could obtain in juice.

A fair number of poets and writers were imprisoned in the Lucknow Jail in 1920–1 such as Raghupati Sahay 'Firaq' (1896–1982), Niyaz Fatehpuri (1884–1966), and Arif Husain Haswi. Their Urdu magazine, *Nigar*, achieved literary distinction and enjoyed popularity for decades. The very first issue carried the poems of Allama Kalb Ahmad Mani Jaisi (1888–1963) and Fani Budauni (1879–1961). Firaq wrote a few literary articles in Hindi and sent them to Munshi Prem Chand, who published them in Hindi magazines. He received Rs 60 for two

---

[2] S. M. Tonki, Oral History Transcript (421), NMML.

[3] Mirza, *A Legendary Communist*, p. 209.

[4] M. K. Gandhi, *Mahatma Gandhi's Jail Experiences: Told by Himself* (Madras: Tagore & Co., 1922), p. 73.

[5] Choudhry Khaliquzzaman, *Pathway to Pakistan* (Pakistan: Longmans, 1961), p. 64.

or three of those articles, but spent the money buying cigarettes in a furtive way, or used them for pressing needs.

Vallabhbhai Patel and Syed Mahmud (1889–1971), Jawaharlal Nehru's contemporary at Cambridge, competed for honours in *takli* spinning—and, in fact, that the former was seen one night twiddling his fingers even in his sleep as if he were working a takli![6] Patel, of course, played bridge after lunch, but Pant got on his nerves for being slow in placing his cards.[7] Badminton was the latter's favourite game, but his tall frame and weight restricted his on-court movements.[8] In Peshawar Jail, Mohammad Yunus, Ghaffar Khan's associate, 'built castles in the air, only to tear them down and build new ones.'[9] Pattabhi Sitaramayya, former Congress president, and Azad often talked across the screen. The latter's avidity for scientific books and pursuit of history, Eastern and Western, indicated his intellectual engagements. Packets of cigarettes were part of his baggage. He longed for jasmine tea whenever he ran short of it.

Mohamed Ali took pleasure in gorging on the *rasagolla*s that Motilal Ghose, editor of *Anand Bazar Patrika*, sent him; Vijaya Lakshmi Pandit invited the inmates of the other barracks to lunch on Dussehra and to sing and dance;[10] Patel, Syed Mahmud, and Ranjit Sitaram Pandit (d. 1944) celebrated Nehru's birthday; Qazi Jalil Abbasi (1912–1996) played chess with a prison guard, read *The Good Earth* by Pearl S. Buck, the American novelist, and *Mother* by Maxim Gorky (1868–1936), the Russian writer;[11] M. N. Roy was distressed by a crop of flowers—the red, purple and lavender ones—dying. But he expected more to grow—all in his tiny cell on the narrow strip of ground along the foot of its outer wall.[12] Faiz Ahmed Faiz attempted

---

[6] 12 September 1930, *SWJN*, vol. 4, p. 386.

[7] M. Chalapathi Rau, *Govind Ballabh Pant: His Life and Times* (New Delhi: Allied Publishers, 1981), p. 270.

[8] Chalapathi Rau, *Govind Ballabh Pant*, p. 269.

[9] Mohammad Yunus, *Letters from Prison* (New Delhi: Vikas Publishing House, 1969), p. 19.

[10] Vijaya Lakshmi Pandit, who began her third term of imprisonment on 12 August 1942, met with a few of the old familiar faces.

[11] Qazi Jalil Abbasi, *Kya Din The* (New Delhi, 1985), pp. 94–105.

[12] 22 September 1935, M. N. Roy, *Fragments*, p. 135.

to grow flowers from packets of seed requisitioned from distant Scotland, while a fellow-prisoner of more mundane tastes devoted his garden to raising chicken.[13]

Rajaji missed his wife, relatives, friends, and the sweet music of the village nadaswaram that came from happy homes in the hamlets outside the prison wall. The music of those pipes brought with it 'an irresistible rush of happy recollections', and reminded him of 'a *vahana* of happy youth, of joy and hope'.[14] He let himself wander in that happy dream-world. He did not have access to newspapers, but read Shakespeare, Voltaire, the Mahabharata, and biographies of Christ, Socrates, and Prophet Mohammad.[15] The well-bred, self-restrained, and god-fearing Shafiqur Rahman Kidwai, a teacher in Jamia Millia Islamia, compensated this loss.[16] He was an ardent nationalist. The disagreement between him and his father reached such a point that the son could come home only by stealth; he got into the house by the backdoor with the help of his sisters and everything was done to prevent the father from knowing that the son had come.[17] All in all, Rajaji's three months in jail were among 'the happiest periods of life'.[18]

In Hazaribagh Jail, Swami Sahajanand, a peasant leader and an ascetic of the Dashnami Order, lectured on the Gita, whereas Rajen Babu read, for the first time, the principal Upanishads. Maulana Mahmud Hasan (1851–1920), principal of the Deoband seminary, had declared in Delhi in November 1920 that Hindu–Muslim cooperation was vital so long as they worked hard together against the British. Rajen Babu made friends in jail, and brought out a hand-written journal called *Qaidi* and another one entitled *Karagar*, with Kalika Kumar Sinha's sketches and cartoons. He learnt weaving, and in six months wove about 100 yards of *nawar*, and 15 yards of cloth.[19] Asaf Ali went through abridged versions of the *Bhagavat Puran* and

---

[13] Kiernan, *Poems by Faiz*, p. 33.
[14] 19 January 1922, Rajagopalachari, *Jail Diary*, p. 37.
[15] 10 February 1922, Rajagopalachari, *Jail Diary*, p. 64.
[16] 11 March 1922, Rajagopalachari, *Jail Diary*, p. 88.
[17] Oral History Transcript (407).
[18] 17 March 1922, Rajagopalachari, *Jail Diary*, p. 91.
[19] R. Prasad, *Autobiography*, pp. 323, 324.

Mahabharata,[20] while K. M. Ashraf having taken the seven sacred turns round the fire at his own marriage, claimed he had the credentials to defend each community's freedom and culture.[21]

Ram Krishna learnt German and other European languages in jail, wrote poetry in Bengali, and drew 'numerous' cartoon sketches. What's more, 'he ... developed into an atheist, a free thinker, a new philosopher, an individualist of the uncompromising order, a thoroughly rational being, an ultramodern Messiah and what not'. These words came from Gobinda Charan Kar, a Kakori prisoner of Naini Prison. Kar knew that Manmath and Mukundi Lal lived in Agra, and that Sachinda, Jogesh Babu, and Bakshi Babu had set up home in Lucknow and Allahabad, respectively. V. S. Dublish, who was lodged in Port Blair, preferred the Andamans so that he could move around freely.[22]

Political prisoners presented a common front that extended to laughing with one another, deciding together, often disagreeing and giving in, each indulgent to the other, on what to do and what not to do. Husain Ahmad Madani, Jairam Daulat Ram, and Swami Krishna Nand protested against *jharhti* in the Karachi Jail. Again, when issues of *azan* (call to prayer) came up in the same jail, Hindus and Muslims went on hunger strike.[23] Sarojini Naidu had a friend who possessed powers of clairvoyance so that she believed she could clearly see things happening at another place as well as in the future. Listening to this, Gandhi said: 'If God was to offer me the power of extrasensory perception, I do not think I would accept it. If there is happiness in store for me tomorrow, why lessen the joy of it by knowing about it beforehand, and if there is unhappiness coming, why spoil today's sleep in anticipation of what is coming tomorrow.'[24]

Stories about the gourmet habits of Shaukat Ali and other maulvis went round. Another story from the princely state of Rampur, to which the Ali brothers belonged, was this: Nawab Hamid Ali

---

[20] 26 September 1944, G. N. S. Raghavan, *M. Asaf Ali's Memoirs*, p. 258.

[21] Kruger, *Kunwar Mohammad Ashraf*, p. 354.

[22] Home Dept, (Jails), file no. 104, 1935.

[23] Mohammad Mian, *Prisoners of Malta*, p. 130.

[24] Sushila Nayyar, *Mahatma Gandhi's Last Imprisonment: The Inside Story* (Delhi: Har-Anand Publications, 1996), p. 61.

Khan's (1875–1930) table was laden with the best and choicest cuisine. As they entered, a few maulvis thundered that eating at the table violated the *Sunnat*, the Prophet's preferred way. Accordingly, the nawab ordered the servants to set the tablecloth on the floor. But Mohamed Ali, who did not welcome their hypocrisy, suggested that they be offered bread and dates for dinner. When the maulvis sat down to the meal, they felt let down, because they had already smelt the aroma of exotic meats. Mohamed Ali said, 'Bismillah, start eating please. This meal is one hundred per cent *Sunnat*. The Prophet's spirit will be pleased at your austerity; and this, after all, is what you desired most!'[25]

Sometime in 1941, Jayaprakash Narayan's wife Prabhavati came to meet him. As planned, he wanted to send a message to his colleagues *via* a coded letter to strengthen the Socialist Party and to step up political activities. That day a CID officer came along, and sat close by, and listened in on their conversation. Catching on, he complained that his shoe had a tear, and he wanted a new pair. Prabhavati replied that that she would if she could have his measurement. He took out a piece of paper and placed his foot on it. 'Pencil an outline of my foot,' he said. Suddenly, the officer snatched the sheet and put it in his pocket, telling him that he would ask his officer to get a shoe of his size and give it to him on behalf of the jail. In truth, that paper bore a missive in secret ink, which the government later published in the newspapers.

Gandhi talked of food constituting the 'eternal apple of discord' in South African jails. He noticed some people kindling the embers of racial antagonism which were ever smouldering, or using their propagandist and myth-making skills to spew venom against the Muslims.[26] He also found the revolutionaries divided;[27] a split

---

[25] Yunus, *Letters from Prison*, p. 149.

[26] V. D. Savarkar, *The Story of My Transportation for Life*, (Bombay: Sadbhakti Publications, 1950), pp. 547–9. He was transferred from the Andamans to Ratnagari in 1921 and 1923.

[27] This point was made by Sachindranath Sanyal, once the Chief Lieutenant of Rash Behari Bose (1886–1945), one of the organizers of the Ghadar Party and later the Indian National Army (INA) (Pande, *A Centenary History*, p. 598).

between them came about with the Chittagong Uprising on 18 April 1930. Surya Sen (1894–1934), 'the rebel against Imperialism', was captured in 1933, tried, and hanged a year later. So was Tarakeshwar Dutt. Following the intervention of Gandhi and C. F. Andrews (1871–1940), Kalpana Dutt's sentence was commuted.

Indulal Yagnik entered the Sabarmati Jail on 6 April 1923. He and Gandhi had many discussions, and over time their divergences increased, so much so that he freed himself from the atmosphere of blind faith and went to Bombay.[28] There is no dearth of other examples, such as a 'nerve-shattering' scene between Gandhi and Rajaji in Poona Jail when 'the little man' shouted in uncontrollable rage with eyes flashing fury: 'Don't dare to shatter the fundamentals of my faith.'[29] For better or worse, a free fight among the satyagrahis came about in the Ferozepur Jail in February 1941. When Gandhi learnt of this, he sent Rajkumari Amrit Kaur (1899–1964) to mediate. At Nasik, a dispute of a special kind took place—regarding whether or not it was proper to smuggle newspapers into the jail. The Kumarappa brothers (J. C. Kumarappa and Bharatan Kumarappa) chose to abide by the jail rules, but others asserted their right to read the papers. The elder Kumarappa (1892–1960), who was first jailed in 1931, threatened to inform the superintendent if the smuggling continued.[30]

Doubts and deviations were held to be natural to the intelligentsia. Hence the noise, complaints, quarrels, and free fights—to say nothing of the abuses hurled back and forth.[31] Many of the progressive writers harboured feelings of resentment towards each other. One example would be the break-up of the friendship between Sajjad Zaheer and Ahmed Ali, the author of *Twilight in Delhi* (1940).[32] This apart, progressive writers mark out, with varying degrees of emphasis, the larger context in which tyranny within and outside the prison walls was understood and articulated. But they did not come out of jail empty-handed. Socialism gave many of them a sense of security and

[28] Yagnik, *Autobiography*, vol. 2, p. 10.

[29] To Padmaja and Leilamani Naidu, 5 May 1932, *Sarojini Naidu*, p. 285.

[30] Morarji Desai, *The Story of My Life* (Madras: Macmillan India, 1974), vol. 1, p. 101.

[31] Vijaya Lakshmi Pandit, *Prison Days*, p. 20.

[32] Coppola, 'Zaheer v Ali', pp. 212–14.

superiority over their fellow-Indians. Convinced that the British were not dissimilar from the Spanish or the French when it came to cruelty and destruction, they protested. Chandrawati, an undertrial prisoner in Agra Jail, made short work of all rules and regulations.[33] Bishwanath Dubey wore a beard as disguise to hide his identity and move about freely. He and other communists and revolutionaries freely communicated with friends outside, both through smuggled correspondence and by verbal messages conveyed by visitors.

In this story of courage and defiance, the grey monotony of the cell wore some political prisoners out.[34] Savarkar apologized. Syed Mahmud went a step further. On 6 October 1944, he informed the government that he did not favour the Quit India Resolution, and agreed to keep aloof from politics if freed.[35] Gandhi made him apologize for his injudicious conduct. Jawaharlal Nehru rebuked him. He said to him: 'Life is not a very gentle or considerate teacher. If one allows oneself to drift about on the surface of the waters, the waves and the tides are apt to knock one against the rocks, but a good swimmer can even tide the storm.'[36] Alas, Syed Mahmud turned out to be a poor swimmer.

Divide and Rule

The classification of population into castes and religions conformed to colonial assumptions about society in general. Managing prisons also required dividing them along caste and community lines. Thus, the Report of the Committee on Prison Discipline recommended that no convicted prisoner be authorized to cook; accordingly, a Brahmin and Muslim were recruited for each and every prison.[37] In Bombay Presidency, an increase in the proportion of Christian and Hindu prisoners and a diminution in the relative proportion of Muslim

[33] Hindustan Times, 29 June 1932.
[34] G. N. S. Raghavan, M. Asaf Ali's Memoirs, p. 317.
[35] V. N. Datta and B. E. Cleghorn (eds), A Nationalist Muslim and Indian Politics: Selected Correspondence of the Late Dr. Syed Mahmud (Delhi: Macmillan, 1974), pp. 230–44.
[36] To 'Betty darling', 16 June 1933, SWJN, vol. 5, p. 481.
[37] Report of the Committee on Prison Discipline, p. 34.

prisoners took place in 1876, as compared with 1875.[38] And, as in the Census enumeration, a table in 1913 detailed the convict's religion.[39] Likewise, column 5 of the report on the NWFP jails is entitled 'Religion of convicts admitted'.[40] The 1928 *Administration Report* lists prisoners as Muslims, Hindus, Sikhs, and Christians.[41] Although Gandhi saw a faint echo of the dissimilarity between one being a Hindu and another Muslim, between one belonging to the upper and another to the lower classes, he dwelt on transcending caste, class, and religious barriers, on equality or equal rights, and on the overcoming of prejudices.[42] Once, after Ramazan, he came out to gaze at the *Id* moon and wished Hasrat Mohani *Id Mubarak*.[43] The human spirit knew no boundaries of nationality or race. The essential friendliness, neighbourly, and almost comradely spirit stayed with the prisoners.

Prisoners came from virtually all regions speaking and writing one language—the language of freedom, sharing the same basic virtues. The care and affection which Yusuf Meherally bestowed on his fellow prisoners knew no bounds. During the Quit India commotion, Kisan Mehta from Bombay was lodged in Yervada Jail in B class, along with about 1500 prisoners. To protest against the treatment meted out to them they started a hunger strike. Prior to that, Mehta had written to prominent leaders detained in 'A' class. For eight days there was no response, but on the ninth day Kisan Mehta could see Yusuf Meherally, who had already manoeuvred to arrange for a medical certificate for him. Mehta was, naturally, touched by Yusuf's affection and profound

[38] *Annual Report of the Bombay Jails, for the Calendar Year 1876* (Bombay: Government Central Press, 1877), p. 2.

[39] *Administrative Report of the Bombay Jail Department, for the year 1915* (Bombay: Government Central Press, 1916), pp. 30–1.

[40] *Administration Report of the Jails of the North West Frontier Province, 1928* (Calcutta: Central Publications Branch, 1929), p. 4.

[41] *Administration Report of the Jails of the North West Frontier Province, 1928*, p. 4.

[42] *Administration Report of the Jails of the North West Frontier Province, 1928*, p. 144.

[43] Yagnik, *Autobiography*, vol. 2, p. 113.

concern. Meherally sent soap, toothpaste, tooth powder and other necessities for his fellow inmates.[44]

'Interactional Spaces'

Oscar Wilde, in September 1896 wrote: 'There are, however, kinder elements in this evil prison air than before; sympathies have been shown to me, and I no longer feel entirely isolated from humane influences, which was before a source of terror and trouble to me.'[45] Scholars talk of the 'interactional spaces' embodied in a certain kind of prison environment balanced by a 'culture of lenience', the following of rules, the ordering of the physical space, a set of institutional beliefs around what a prison should be like, and a set of intense interpersonal dynamics between and among the controller and the controlled.[46] Thus the medical officer in Bloemfontein became Gandhi's friend. There were other kind and lenient officers, but they were exceptions. Even a 'humane disciplinarian' was at a discount in official circles.

Smuggling of books and letters was a common practice. Khairabadi's book, written on tattered pieces of cloth and on dried leaves, was smuggled out in bits and pieces, and then sent to his brother in Calcutta, where the ships from the Andamans docked.[47] Letters were smuggled out of Vellore Central Jail by the Madras Students' organizations. Inayatullah Khan Mashriqi (1888–1963), a maverick Khaksar, tried sending out unauthorized letters to his followers. Letters of Keshav Chandra Gupta, a high-security prisoner in Agra Central Jail, and addressed to a revolutionary of Ajmer, contained invaluable information.

In actual fact, the Fatehgarh Jail staff unearthed an organized system of smuggling.[48] In Gorakhpur, Iftikhar Husaini Faridi smuggled

[44] Madhu Dandavate, *Yusuf Meherally: Quest for New Horizons* (Bombay: Popular Prakashan, 1986), p. 109.

[45] Mason, *Oscar Wilde*, p. 890.

[46] Mahuya Bandyopadhyay, *Everyday Life in a Prison: Confinement, Surveillance, Resistance* (New Delhi: Orient BlackSwan, 2010), p. 287.

[47] Ashraf, *Panel Settlement*, p. xvii.

[48] Home Dept, Political, file no. 3/9, 1942.

out instructions to enlist satyagrahis, whereas a warder carried revolutionary literature from Rajdeo Singh to Bareilly Jail. To prevent such things from happening, the authorities numbered and initialled notebooks. 'Unauthorized' letters to outsiders were sent, as in Alipore Central Jail by Ganesh Ghose, Purnanda Das Gupta, and Govinda Banerjee of the Jugantar Party. In Trichinopoly, prisoners on arrival warned the subordinate staff that they would retaliate after Congress returned to power. Elsewhere, they held meetings, arranged interviews surreptitiously, resorted to impersonation, and put together bits of information for onward transmission.

Of the interactional space, I conclude with Firaq, who had resigned from the Provincial and the Indian Civil Service in response to Gandhi's call for non-cooperation. He and seventy to eighty others were arrested and despatched to Agra Jail during the agitation against the boycott of the visit of the Prince of Wales. They were huddled together in the same barracks. Some poetry lovers started weekly mushairas. Here is the concluding verse of Firaq's ghazal composed for the first poetic symposium:

Mark, Firaq, the poetic meet of captives in the jail,
Who couldn't be dismembered despite being dispersed.[49]

The mushairas continued for seven or eight weeks. Firaq said: 'This doesn't mean that these victims of the British tyranny were free from all cares inside the jail. Almost every one of us suffered the pangs of inward grief and anxiety, though none of us spoke about them. Every face wore a forced smile.'[50]

Acquittal

Acquittal did not protect the prisoner either against the trumping up of a fresh accusation or the arbitrary law of deportation that dispensed with the inconvenient formality of a charge and the still

---

[49] K. C. Kanda (ed.), *Firaq Gorakhpuri: Selected Poetry* (New Delhi: Sterling Publishers, 1990), p. 28.

[50] Kanda, *Firaq Gorakhpuri*, p. 28.

more inconvenient necessity of producing evidence.[51] In 'The Ballad of Reading Gaol', a long poem on the harsh rhythm of jail life, Oscar Wilde feared being 'a welcome visitant' in a world that did not want him, 'a *revenant* (ghost), and one whose face is grey with long imprisonment and crooked with pain.'[52] In India, on the other hand, scores of individual prisoners remained faithful to their ideals and to an enlightened and humanistic conception of nationhood. As for families, they rejoiced in the return of a husband, son, or brother. Children jumped and scuffled in excitement. Local factions banded together to celebrate one of them bearing the mantle of long misfortune.[53] Thus, leading townsmen welcomed homeward-bound young men convicted in the Mainpuri Conspiracy Case (Ram Prasad Bismil was connected with it).[54] Similarly, Ganesh Shankar Vidyarthi arrived to a rousing reception at Narwal (40 kilometres from Kanpur) in May 1922. He was covered with *batasha*s (sugar bubbles) by an elderly woman.[55]

The revolutionary Maharaj (T. N. Chakraborty) led processions, heard slogans of cheers, and addressed the rural poor around the post office or the bazaar.[56] Also in Bengal, when the first batch of women prisoners was released, the people took them out in procession. The District Congress Committee (DCC) saluted them.[57] In Lahore, the release of a batch of women brought a mammoth crowd outside

---

[51] Aurobindo Ghose, in *Karmayogin*, 31 July 1909, Home Dept, Political (Deposit), September 1909, file no. 28/8.

[52] Mason, *Oscar Wilde*, p. 891.

[53] 'At home, my family members eagerly waited to embrace and bless me after this long absence. What a delightful homecoming I had! After I had met each and every one, the young and the old, we all sat together until late at night. I remember how amused they were when I regaled them by narrating funny stories and anecdotes about events that occurred during my longish sojourn within those prison walls' (Yunus, *Letters from Prison*, p. 157).

[54] 'The Khilafat Movement in the United Provinces', in *Regionalizing Pan-Islamism*, p. 60.

[55] Moti Lal Bhargava, *Ganesh Shankar Vidyarthi* (Publications Division, Ministry of Information and Broadcasting, Government of India, 1988), p. 76.

[56] T. N. Chakraborty, *Thirty Years in Prison*, p. 186.

[57] Manmohini Zutshi Sahgal, *An Indian Freedom Fighter Recalls Her Life*, edited by Geraldine Forbes (New York: East Gate Books, 1994), p. 85.

the jail.[58] Last, but not the least, a few prisoners broke down when Hajrah Begum (b. 1910) entered the Deoli Detention Camp to meet Z. A. Ahmed. Once this was over and Ahmed was released, an elaborate meal in Lahore was laid out to make him feel at home. Feasting continued for four or five days.

The ways of the world hardly changed over time. In May 1945, Wavell's visit to London triggered the release of the Congress President and the CWC members, an event widely rejoiced. Among scores of people, Firaq was freed. But he was grief-stricken by the death of his brother a few days before and wrote an elegy in his memory. A warm welcome awaited Azad at Howrah Railway Station. That moment he thought of his departed wife, and remembered the lines of William Wordsworth (1770–1850): 'But she's in her grave and oh; The difference to me.'[59]

[58] M. Z. Sahgal, *An Indian Freedom Fighter Recalls Her Life*, p. 84.
[59] Azad, *India Wins Freedom*, p. 100.

9. 'The Vessel Will Sink When the Load of Sin Is Great'

In jail, Mr. Gandhi was brought down by the warder to the superintendent's room in which the superintendent was sitting in a chair while Mr. Gandhi was kept standing throughout his interview with Mr. Rajagopalachari. Questioned by Rajaji, Mr. Gandhi is reported to have said that he was given goat's milk and bread, the milk being given all at a time. He had cut down his three meals to two. Mr Gandhi was not allowed to see Mr. (Shankerlal) Banker (1889–1985) who was in the same prison. Mr. Gandhi was kept in one of the cells intended for solitary confinement and looked in during nights....

Leader (Allahabad), 5 April 1922

Mr. Gandhi is given precisely the same diet to which he was accustomed when he was free, namely, goat's milk, bread, oranges, sugar, tea and raisins. He brought his own raisins to prison with him which he used until they were finished and a fresh supply was provided for him by the jail authorities. It is untrue to say that he is locked in at night. He has separate quarters of his own, one cell to sleep in and the other to work in during the day.

Home Dept, Political, file no. 489/IV, 1922

Gandhi and Nelson Mandela walked that long road to freedom to discover that after climbing a great hill, one only finds many more hills to climb. They had no time to rest; only a few moments to steal a view of the glorious vista surrounding men and women, and to look back on the distance they had come. With freedom came responsibilities, and they dared not linger, for their long walk had not yet ended. Freedom was not pushed from behind by a blind force; it was actively drawn by a vision. 'I am just stretching my limbs on the mattress,' Gandhi wrote to Tagore in early January 1932, 'and as I try to steal a wink of sleep I think of you. I want you to give your best to the sacrificial fire that is being lighted.'[1]

This was true of Mandela as well. Both found compensation for their sufferings in the devotion of their followers who recognized their work and worth and moulded their own lives heeding their conscience. They created their image in such a way that ordinary mortals did not comprehend their actions and settled for eulogizing their prophet-like or Christ-like qualities. For example, many of Gandhi's friends were deeply affected by his gentleness of spirit,[2] and treated him with a mixture of respect, affection, and detachment. This gave Gandhi his optimism in the gloomiest and darkest of circumstances.

Leo Tolstoy (1828–1910) believed that the principle of passive resistance, based as it is on concord and love, could not be made coercively binding. Taking their cue from him, Gandhi and Mandela

---

[1] 3 January 1932, CWMG, vol. XLVIII, p. 489.

[2] Gandhi said on 2 June 1919, 'I have no [Rev. JJ] Doke here. I have no Kallenbach, [Henry] Polak is in England.' At the marriage of Henry and Millie Polak, Gandhi was the best man. There are more than 200 letters from Gandhi to Kallenbach on record. 'Love and more love' is the running theme of their association. They used to address each other affectionately by nicknames in their correspondence. While Kallenbach was the 'Lower House', Gandhi signed his letters to his Prussian friend as 'Upper House'. Gandhi's relationship with Kallenbach was a male bonding of a special kind, a platonic relationship with a difference. There is no reason to read more into his letters to Kallenbach, his partner in spirit. He wrote to him, 'I am not with you in body but I am always with you in spirit' (5 April 1909). His 'extraordinary love' for his companion is expressed as 'our mutual attachment' in another letter. Gandhi tells Kallenbach to hold his breath 'because the expression of love is an indication of our having lived before in bodies other than the present ones.'

resisted evil but substituted persuasion for brute force. They argued that religious doctrines could only be propagated among men and women by peace, love, and concord. The Bible says, 'Blessed is the man who remains steadfast under trial, for where he has stood the test he will receive the crown of life, which God has promised to those who love him.' The Quran, likewise, points out that Allah protects (*maghfirat*) those facing the divinely ordained trial with truth and patience.

Though separated in time, there were striking similarities between Gandhi and Mandela in their defiance of unjust laws, and in the strict adherence to non-violence in thought, word, and deed, no matter how great the provocation. Indentured Indians, many of whom had left their native land in fierce indignation and despair, were regarded as a lesser species of humanity—servile and incompetent. They were jailed, beaten, fined, and deported. An indignant Gandhi rescued them from a life of misery, indignity, and harassment to one that would grant them political and civic rights. He aimed to build an inclusive society, in which Indians and South Africans would have a stake and whose strength would be a guarantee against disunity, backwardness, and exploitation. 'Our quarrel is not with men but with measures,' he said.[3]

As in the subcontinent, the South African regime was sufficiently powerful to crush the freedom fighters. This Mandela realized. Under the circumstances, non-violence became a practical necessity rather than an option to him.[4] What made his vigorous and daring responses unique is that he contested the apparently unassailable might of white rule, harnessing 'people's power', and giving them what they wanted. Not always did events run on his side, but his hour was ultimately struck in his twenty-sixth year of custody. He brought in the first breath of fresh air and freedom. Arnold Toynbee opined: 'What we mean by greatness, of any degree, in a human being is, I should say, the power, in some measure and in some field, to move other human beings.' Both Gandhi and Mandela achieved this amazing feat during their lifetime.

---

[3] *The Hindu*, 3 January 1932, *CWMG*, vol. XLVIII, p. 488. B. R. Nanda (ed.), *Mahatma Gandhi: 125 Years* (New Delhi: Indian Council for Cultural Relations, 1995).

[4] Mandela, *Long Walk to Freedom*, p. 147.

There were, however, hurdles to be crossed. For one, the government sentenced Gandhi several times during his twenty-one years in South Africa. He lived in a bare 70 sq. ft cell, and subsisted on 'the diet of the most degraded aboriginal native felons...'[5] The unfortunate Indians got nothing while the white convicts were given a bedstead to sleep on, a toothbrush to clean their teeth, a towel to wipe their faces, and also a handkerchief. Whenever Gandhi paced up and down the floor, the warder shouted, 'Gandhi, stop walking about like that, my floor is being spoilt.' He stood by to keep watch. If by chance he did not know Gandhi, he would shout, 'Sam, come out now.'[6] When he heard of friends in Pretoria being sentenced to six months' caging with hard labour, he pleaded with the Magistrate to impose this penalty upon him too, as he had led the opposition against the Ordinance. He was shocked that his followers were being more harshly treated than he himself, and it was with bowed head and deep humiliation that he left the Courts, sentenced only to two months' simple imprisonment.[7] In February 1909, Gandhi was rearrested for a three-month term. Not only did he remain calm and quiet, but he acquiesced in all the bodily suffering his warder imposed on him with the result that the warden himself eased up in the end.[8] When charged on three counts on 11 November 1913 before Dundee's Resident Magistrate, Gandhi elected to go to gaol.

In Volkstrust, Gandhi quarried stone and swept the compound. In Johannesburg, he was made to walk in the clothes of an ordinary prisoner, paraded through the streets, and tossed into an overcrowded jail: 'The more the Government oppresses us, and the more we bear it, the earlier would our release come,' he responded.[9] Two of Gandhi's

---

[5] M. K. Gandhi, *Speeches and Writings of M. K. Gandhi, with an Introduction by C. F. Andrews, a Tribute by Mr G. A. Nathesan, a Biographical Sketch by Mr H. S. L. Palak* (Madras: Natesan & Co.; second edition, 1918) p. iii.

[6] Every Indian man was referred to as Sam, or Sammy, in those days and much after, even as every African male was John, every African woman, Annie, and every Indian woman, Mary.

[7] *Speeches and Writings of M. K. Gandhi*, p. 77.

[8] M. K. Gandhi, *Mahatma Gandhi's Jail Experiences*, p. 77.

[9] John Haynes Holmes, P. G. Bridge, and F. E. James, *Mahatma Gandhi: The World Significance* (Calcutta: C.C. Basak, n.d.), p. 129.

fellow prisoners in Johannesburg jeered and laughed. Then, the two exchanged obscene jokes, uncovering each other's genitals. On another occasion, a strong, heavily-built person lifted Gandhi up in his arms and threw him out of the lavatory. He caught hold of the door frame and saved himself from a fall.[10]

Tagore spoke of Gandhi's prison terms as 'arrest cures'. In Bloemfontein, Gandhi hailed isolation as a blessing, and looked forward to a year of uninterrupted study. That is when he read Thoreau, Tolstoy, Ralph Waldo Emerson (1803–1882), the American essayist and poet, and Thomas Carlyle (1795–1881). On the other hand, the Bible, the *Manusmriti*, the *Ramayanasar*, the Mahabharata and the Bhagawad Gita illuminated his life and elevated his spirits to new heights. He scanned the Mahabharata in Gujarati—which was of 5000 pages.

Gokhale's India

The ryots of Godavari district wrote movingly:

> If, at prayer call, every Mussalman's eyes turn to Mecca, and every Hindu's eyes to Banaras, at the clarion call of duty to the motherland, the eyes of both the Hindu and the Mussalman turn to the Yeravda jail, the shrine where India's greatest son is undergoing that baptism of suffering that is fast heaving up the spirit of our national independence, and, we pray that you will be pleased to convey to him our homage of love, devotion, and loyalty.[11]

India's political turmoil continued until the end of the war when prices soared and unemployment deepened. Instead of embarking on a policy of political and economic liberalization, the government took recourse to strong-arm tactics. A number of high-minded men and women, whose temperaments and orientations would probably have kept them remote from politics in quieter times, were drawn into active public life. In 1915, Annie Besant conceived the idea of Home Rule. Sarojini Naidu joined her; as a student, she had met her on the ship sailing to

---

[10] Joseph Lelyveld, *Great Soul: Mahatma Gandhi and His Struggle with India* (New York: Alfred A. Knopf, 2011), pp. 55–6.

[11] 30 December 1923, in *Mohamed Ali in Indian Politics*, vol. 1, p. 373.

Great Britain. M. A. Jinnah, the immaculately dressed barrister, was their close friend. He belonged to Bombay's cosmopolitan culture, and to a family far removed from the Islamist rhetoric.

Gandhi, who had returned to India in 1915 with an excellent reputation and had had the pleasure of meeting Jinnah in Bombay, was quite prepared to work with Chelmsford, the Viceroy, (1916–21). But the brutal action of General Dyer (1864–1927), a temporary Brigadier-General, dug an almost impassable ditch. Keeping in mind General Smuts' justification for a crackdown, Gandhi argued that any government worth its salt would not resort to torture or make people crawl on their bellies. By drawing this analogy with Dyer's crawling order in Amritsar, he elevated the ordinary aspects of prison administration to national insults, and thus transposed jail conditions into metaphors for the condition of all of India under British rule.[12] In 1931, when Gandhi was released to set the stage for the Second Round Table Conference, he used the same metaphor at the meeting of the Commonwealth of India League: 'We are prisoners. You Englishmen and Englishmen are our jailors ...'[13]

It would not be wrong to say that from the days of the Rowlatt Satyagraha, Gandhi sketched in an inspiring outline of his life with the assumption that he would have to pass through the ordeal of being locked up in order to redress the wrongs.[14] The ordeal was not over even after he abandoned the Non-cooperation Movement on 12 February 1922. With the flare-up of violence in Chauri Chaura, a village in the Gorakhpur district (UP), he lived with the burden

[12] Sherman, *State Violence and Punishment in India*, p. 46.

[13] 30 October 1931, *CWMG*, vol. XLVIII, p. 250.

[14] Gandhi, *Speeches and Writings of Gandhi*, pp. 464–5. The *Satyagrahi*, which Gandhi brought out in Bombay, on 7 April 1919, spelt out: 'We are now in a position to be arrested at any moment. It is, therefore, necessary to bear in mind that if anyone is arrested, he should, without causing any difficulty, allow himself to be arrested.... No defence should be offered [in court] and no pleaders engaged in the matter. If a fine is imposed with the alternative of imprisonment, the imprisonment should be stopped. If only fine is imposed, it ought not to be paid; but his property, if any, should be allowed to be sold.'

of disunion preying upon him.[15] In such a situation, he linked the exaltation of suffering with the asceticism of Sufism, that is, acceptance of pain as a necessary stage in the human being's spiritual advancement.[16] Hence, a day before his trial, he asked Andrews not to seek permission to visit him in jail. That would be a privilege, and he would have none. He was happy as a bird: 'The religious value of good discipline is enhanced by renouncing privileges.'[17] Ranjit Pandit, inspired by Gandhi's example, refused favours from the 'petty gauleiters'.[18] On 10 May 1920, he had married Swarup, who changed not only her last name, but also her own personal name, becoming Vijaya Lakshmi. Jawaharlal Nehru called his sister 'Nan'.

Gandhi regarded the time spent behind prison bars as a crowning achievement. For that reason, he was not eager to know what was happening outside.[19] When Shankarlal Banker, one of his most dependable allies, moved to another section in the same jail,[20] he reiterated: 'My stay here is a good school for me, and my separation from my fellow workers should prove whether our movement is an independently evolving organism or merely the work of one individual and, consequently, something very transient.' He had no fears; as a result, he neither buckled under pressure nor was hurt by bodily hardships.[21] He explained that 'when the conviction goes deeper than the intellect, you will brave all danger and risks and live the true life, and you will at once find that it is its own reward'.[22] He would say

[15] To Mohamed Ali, 7 February 1924, Mahadev H. Desai, *Day-to-Day with Gandhi*, vol. 4, p. 52.

[16] Hamid Enayat, *Modern Islamic Political Thought* (London: I. B. Tauris, 2005), p. 183.

[17] 17 March 1922, Fulop-Miller, *Lenin and Gandhi*, p. 309.

[18] 18 November 1942, Vijaya Lakshmi Pandit, *Prison Days*, p. 94.

[19] To Ajmal Khan, 14 April, Fulop-Miller, *Lenin and Gandhi*, p. 317.

[20] He and Gandhi were brought to Yeravda on 18 March, a Saturday, and moved to an unknown destination the following Monday. They were escorted to a special train at Sabarmati and taken to Yeravda via Khnirki. As soon as they entered the prison, they had to leave the spinning wheel and the basket of fruit.

[21] Holmes, Bridge, and James, *Mahatma Gandhi*, p. 147.

[22] To Harry Deutsch, 12 Jan 1933, http://flicker.com/photo/littlejohn collection/3366102776.

his morning prayers and sing some hymns he knew by heart. Prayers, he said, played a large part in a 'self-purificatory sacrifice'. Spinning brought him nearer to the poorest of the poor, and in them to God.

Gandhi felt that he was privileged to receive the same sentence as Tilak—a sentence he considered as light as any judge could impose on him. This not only vindicated Krishna's comforting words in the Gita: 'Even here, in this life, the universe is conquered by those whose mind is established in equanimity', but also confirmed the Biblical verse: 'Rejoice in hope, be patient in tribulation, be constant in prayer'. Patriots and reformers all over the world have had the capacity to put up with pain when they take it up in the true spirit.[23] Gandhi, for one, hankered after the pure spirit of fearlessness or *tapasya*. He expected civil resisters to do likewise—to learn as much as possible about jails[24]—and be there often for the present cause only, and for wrongs inflicted in future. They had to fight it out for their rights, face the worst, deny themselves the privilege of being let off, and in the process inspire the public to win swaraj.[25] They had to brave the attendant risks such as uttermost penury, loss of all possessions, and *lathi* blows, and not be either contaminated or dissipated by worldly gains. Among the instructions he gave to the satyagrahis were: (*a*) to avoid classification of prisoners—in no case should any attempt be made to ask either for a higher or a lower class and not to take advantage of the special facilities offered to 'A' class prisoners; (*b*) to strictly observe jail rules so long as they were consistent with human dignity.[26]

Thousands saw Gandhi organize his tasks in their proper order, change slogans in a judicious fashion, and make timely transitions in his strategies, without losing sight of the long-term goal of freedom as a whole. The thrill of Gandhi's short trial and his statements from the dock struck a chord; it seemed that 'Jesus of Nazareth himself was again being tried and convicted in this fashion'.[27] The entire court rose when Gandhi entered—a frail, serene, indomitable figure in a coarse and scanty loincloth. This was like a family gathering and not a

[23] Home Dept, Political, file no. 3/17, 1933.
[24] Holmes, Bridge, and James, *Mahatma Gandhi*, p. 113.
[25] Home Dept, Political, file no. 190/1923.
[26] November 1940, *CWMG*, vol. LXXIII, p. 158.
[27] N. S. Hardiker, in *1921 Movement: Reminiscences*, p. 107.

law court.[28] He went smilingly to prison, bringing the government to grief.[29] A poem published in an American magazine asked a question that stirred and troubled the consciences of men and women of goodwill.[30]

Who is it sits within his prison cell
The while his spirit goes astride the world?

The decision to launch Civil Disobedience was Gandhi's notable act of defiance. People pored over the daily newspapers and joined his crusade with faith and fervour. They realized then that non-violence was not a form of negation but a definite scheme of resistance. Civil disobedience came to be termed *satyagraha*, the tenets of which were: to be prepared to endure imprisonment, suffering, and penalties for the cause; to never ask for any monetary help; and to implicitly obey the leaders of the campaign.[31] Hearing distant cries of 'Bande Mataram', defiant slogans, and voices raised in anger, Shudha Mazumdar asked her little sweeper girl what was happening down the road. All she said was, 'Only Gandhi.'[32]

Nevertheless, against the predominant opinion of the political classes, Gandhi met Irwin, the Viceroy (1926–31), 'a strange conjugation and prelude to many other such meetings: the aristocratic ruler of a declining empire wooing the nationalist rebel'.[33] The negotiations plastered over the cracks for the time being and provided Gandhi a breathing space to rally his forces. But when they broke down, he concluded that he would secure swaraj by force of an irresistible destiny or mission. The government wrecked his plan by putting him in jail. Shudha Mazumdar in her memoirs writes: '"He has been arrested and taken to Yervada Jail," Chorda announced mournfully one morning. Then we came to know of the message

[28] Sengupta, *Sarojini Naidu*, pp. 169–70.

[29] *Bengalee*, 19 March, *Report*, week ending 25 March 1922.

[30] Roy Walker, *Sword of Gold* (Bombay: Orient Longmans, 1969), p. 99.

[31] S. Mazumdar, *Memoirs of an Indian Woman*, p. 206.

[32] S. Mazumdar, *Memoirs of an Indian Woman*, p. 206.

[33] A. J. P. Taylor, *English History, 1914–45* (Oxford: Clarendon Press, 1965), p. 275.

he had left—that neither the people nor his colleagues should be daunted. He was not the conductor of the fight; that was God who dwelt in the hearts of all. Only faith was necessary; then God would lead them....'[34]

Isolated in a cell while officialdom teased with promises from week to week, month to month, Indulal Yagnik gives us an idea of Gandhi's routine in jail:

> On the very first day, Gandhiji told me about his daily programme asking me to join in as I desired. He used to pray in the morning at 4 o'clock and in the evening at seven. Up to 7 in the morning he used to read the *Upanishads* and other religious literature. Then, he used to take his meals with fruit and hot goat's milk. Up to 11 o'clock and now and then in the afternoon he used to spin on the spinning wheel. In the afternoon, taking his bath, he drank milk, read and took rest. In the evening at four, he took his last meal and read up to about 7 and till 8 o'clock talked with his colleagues while walking in the garden. Following that, he used to massage his body with oil and go to sleep soon after 8 o'clock.[35]

On his release, Gandhi made it apparent that he would have no qualms about fasting to the finish if he was arrested or denied the opportunity to serve 'Harijans'.[36]

Wilful Neglect?

Gandhi wanted to be classed as a run-of-the-mill prisoner, but most Indian legislators thought that he was entitled to an 'A' class status.[37] He was not one to complain, but his kinsfolk and friends complained that the jail authorities ill-treated him. This the government denied,

[34] S. Mazumdar, *Memoirs of an Indian Woman*, p. 206.
[35] Gandhi to Jawaharlal Nehru, 2 January 1932, in *Together They Fought: Gandhi–Jawaharlal Correspondence, 1921–1948*, edited by Uma Iyenger and Lalitha Zackariah (New Delhi: Oxford University Press, 2011), p. 167.
[36] Gandhi to Jawaharlal Nehru, 2 January 1932, in *Together They Fought*.
[37] Home Dept, Political, file no. 24/19, 1933.

and rightly so.[38] In 1930, Gandhi benefited from a 'culture of lenience' in terms of ordering the physical space, modification of rules and of institutional beliefs.[39] He received Rs 100 for 'maintenance';[40] his furnished rooms were fitted with electric light and had a wide verandah and a small garden in front; he slept in the open; ate fresh fruit of his choice, dates, and drank goat's milk. The guards treated him with deference; he behaved, as always, courteously towards them. A serene and radiant Gandhi listened to Mahadev Desai's *bhajan*, followed by his favourite hymn about who the true Vaishnava is.[41] Kasturba Gandhi, too, had certain special privileges.[42]

At the same time there were severe restrictions that only a man like Gandhi could bear with silence. Visitors were, for example, denied access. In July 1930, Dr Ansari was not allowed in, fearing that he would undo the good work of Tej Bahadur Sapru (1875–1949), delegate to the Round Table Conferences (1930–2), and Mukund Ramrao Jayakar

---

[38]   Home Dept, Political, file no, 489/IV, 1939. The article was published in *Young India* of 18 April 1922. The government replied to the charge in detail: 'Mr. Gandhi is given precisely the same diet to which he was accustomed when he was free, namely, goat's milk, bread, oranges, lemons, sugar, tea, and raisins. He brought his own raisins to prison with him which he used until they finished and a fresh supply was provided for him.... It is untrue to say that he is locked in at night. He has separate quarters of his own, one cell to sleep in, and the other to work in during the day. The sleeping cell he is allowed to keep open at night. Half the yard is reserved for him to exercise and the space is ample for the purpose, as Mr. Gandhi has stated ... on several occasions, Mr. Gandhi has not asked for any newspaper and his request to be allowed to retain some of his private books was granted as soon as it was made. A pillow in addition to the usual bedding was supplied when it was asked for. A commode for use at night was placed in the cell on medical grounds ...'

[39]   Bandyopadhyay, *Everyday Life in a Prison*, p. 287.

[40]   This amount was debited under the head '29-Political Central Refugees and State Prisoners—other Refugees and State Prisoners' (G. F. S. Collins to Secy., Home Dept, Political, 10 June 1930, Home Dept Political, file no. 32 [1], 1930).

[41]   To Padmaja and Leilamani Naidu, 8 May 1932, *Sarojini Naidu*, p. 286.

[42]   Harry J. Greenwall, *Storm over India* (London: Hurst & Blackett Ltd, n.d.), p. 198.

(1873–1959), a lawyer and legislative assembly member (1926–30).[43] In February 1932, the government rejected the request of B. S. Moonje (1872–1948), the Hindu Mahasabha President, to discuss his plan of starting elementary military schools in Gujarat.[44] Even President Roosevelt's personal envoy was not allowed to meet Gandhi.

The Inspector-General of Prisons withdrew the facilities Gandhi enjoyed in Yeravda,[45] the 'shrine where India's greatest son is undergoing that baptism of suffering that is fast heaving up the spirit of our national independence.'[46] Nor was this all. With Gandhi's presence creating unrest around Poona's military population, he mulled over the proposition of moving him to an alternative site.[47] They even thought of transporting him to the Andamans or Aden.[48]

> I am however to say that the Governor-in-Council considers that the moral effect of Mr. Gandhi's internment would be far greater and that it would have a more valuable effect in showing the determination and power of Government to crush the Civil Disobedience Movement if Mr. Gandhi were removed to the Andamans, or possibly Aden might be considered, in order to place him entirely beyond reach of political exploitation.[49]

Yet, despite the pleading of Andrews who pressed very strongly that the Mahatma should not be put back in prison,[50] Bengal's Governor refused to let him visit his province and the NWFP.[51] The administration laid

[43] Before the first Round Table Conference in London, Sapru and Jayakar acted as mediators. They put in their best to build bridges between the Viceroy and the Congress leadership. Gandhi, having raised the level of confrontation to new heights during the Dandi March, agreed to attend the conference.

[44] Home Dept, Political, file no. 5/32, 1932.

[45] Home Dept, Political, file no. 56, 1934.

[46] From the ryots of Godavari District, 30 December 1923, in *Mohamed Ali in Indian Politics*, vol. 3, p. 375.

[47] Home Dept, Political, file no. 31/73, 1932 and file no. 56, 1934.

[48] Home Dept, Political, file no. 31/73, 1932.

[49] Home Dept, Political, file no. 31/73, 1932.

[50] 26 October 1933, Home Dept, Political, , file no. 159, 1933.

[51] Gandhi to Governor, 6 June 1934; Governor to Gandhi, n.d., Home Dept, Political, , file no. 50/5/34, K.W. A pro-Congress regime would, the

itself open, not once but on more than a few occasions, to a serious charge of being insensitive to Gandhi's pivotal position and popularity with the masses. It preferred ordinances to the dialogue mode.[52]

Nilla Cram Cook, a 'beautiful American girl', bathed in the Ganga at Banaras before her conversion on her twenty-second birthday. From the time she began studying the philosophies of Indian religions in Greece, she longed for release from the bondage of earthly existence and found her salvation in Gandhi's wisdom. She regarded him as another Christ. Dressed in flowing Grecian robes, shoeless, hatless, and stockingless, Miss Cook, who had married a young Greek aristocrat in Athens; from whom she was separated, she adopted Gandhi's diet of cereal and goat's milk.[53] She met him every afternoon, stayed until after supper at sunset when the jailor came 'to disband the imperial court and take the uncrowned emperor back to his cell'.[54] She and the others sat on the ground around Gandhi before a white khadi tablecloth. When she toured Chitaldrug, a remote town in the Mysore wilds where a white woman had not been seen before, she read Gandhi's comment on village sanitation, made unleavened cakes, washed clothes without soap, and controlled her temper when crowds collected around the windows and peered in.[55]

Unlike Gramsci who lived in almost permanent isolation and with no facilities for studying, Gandhi wrote letters once a week or more. The ones in Gujarati and Hindi were sent to the oriental translator, unless translated by the district magistrate.[56] The Censors, having scrutinized the incoming and outgoing 'foreign' mail, passed the innocuous letters on for delivery, and sent the rest to the Home department. In 1942–3, they divided letters from overseas into three

---

government thought, complicate the all-India situation and leave an impact on Punjab (Telegram dated 21 November 1934, Viceroy to Secretary of State for India, Home Dept, Political, file no. 11/2, 1934).

[52] Home Dept, Political, file no. 14/12, 1931.

[53] Greenwall, *Storm over India*, pp. 197–8.

[54] Nilla Cram Cook, *My Road to India* (New York: L. Furman, inc., 1939), p. 343.

[55] Cook, *My Road to India*, p. 353.

[56] The Superintendent of the Prison censored the letters. Vernacular correspondence which could not be translated in the prison was sent to the oriental translator to government for translation unless the District Magistrate, Poona, could have it translated in his office.

main categories: fan mail—this was by far the largest and comprised the usual sort of stuff written to famous men, requests for autographs, advertisements for patent medicines, and so on; letters of a generally anti-British nature supporting Gandhi's latest stand; and letters criticizing Gandhi's 'Quit India' move.[57] There was practically nothing in them to interest the intelligence department; it was seldom that foreign mail disclosed information of value.[58] As for books, Harry J. Greenwall, the author of *Storm over India*, saw the following books:

> *Married Love* by Marie Stopes
> *Reversed Councils and Other Organized Plunders* by Krishnamurthi Iyer
> *Right Food: The Right Remedy* by C. C. Froude
> *The Fast Way to Health* by Maximilian Oskar Bircher-Benner
> *The Art of Creation* by Edward Carpenter
> *Civilization: Its Cause and Cure* by Edward Carpenter (two copies)
> *The Science of Power* by Benjamin Kidd
> *The Subjection of Women* by J. S. Mill[59]

The books read were exceptional in range. Zohra Ansari and Rehana Tyabji taught him Urdu. The result was remarkable: Gandhi's Urdu was improving towards the end of June 1932. He became acquainted with the nuances and intricacies of Islam, in addition to what he already knew about Hinduism, Christianity, and Buddhism. With a view to opening quite a few ways to a dialogue between religions, he advised Mirabehn to read Syed Ameer Ali (1849–1928), a jurist and author of *The Spirit of Islam*, and *A Short History of the Saracens* by Marmaduke Pickthall (1875–1936), the English translator of the Quran, and Mohammad Ali (1874–1951), a leading figure of the Ahmadiya movement and translator of the Quran with a commentary in both English and Urdu. Why this solemn advice? 'To correct,' Gandhi wrote, 'some of the notions you have formed.'[60] He was groping and searching, and not once did he claim to have uncovered the ultimate truth.

---

[57] Home Dept, Political (I), file no. 156, 1942.
[58] Home Dept, Political (I), file no. 156, 1942.
[59] Greenwall, *Storm over India*, p. 195.
[60] 7 July 1932, *Bapu's Letters to Mira* (Navajivan Trust: Ahmedabad, 1949), p. 166.

Gandhi read to locate the meeting points in an assortment of religious traditions. He read the Bhagawad Gita, his 'Kamdhenu',[61] and advised one of his co-prisoners to go through one chapter every day. 'You will not realise the value today,' he said to him, 'but as time passes, you will be able to understand the meaning and significance of this advice and you would then value the study as much as I am doing.'[62] He explained that what seemed an assault against religion in certain quarters was in reality an attack upon a one-sided image of religion, launched, mistakenly, from the point of view of an alternative scientific ideal. He reasoned that the Upanishads produced great 'peacefulness', as did the sentence: 'Whatever thou dost, thou shouldst do the same for the good of the soul.' 'What hardships could trouble me externally,' he asked, 'if I were such to make God live in my heart?' In Yeravda Jail, he translated parts of the Upanishads, and the works of the Bhakti saint Kabir (1440–1518):

> He who is valiant of heart fleeth not from the face of peril,
> And he who fleeth from peril is craven and base:
> Behold, the battle is joined,
> Fierce, fierce is the onslaught;
> Anger, passion and pride,
> Ambition, lust and desire the battle is joined
> Are the foes who ride wildly upon us
> At our side fight our friends,
> Self-rule, truth, piety, peace,
> The warrior's sword is the Holy Name
> And we brandish it wide:
> In that war
> Cravens are 'never seeen',
> But the valorous fight in the van.[63]

Meanwhile, Dharasana became the scene of the breaking of the Salt Laws. The Salt Depot at Wadala came under siege. George Slocombe, a British journalist, witnessed what happened at the Wadala Depot. After meeting Gandhi in jail, he wrote that he incarnated the soul of India.[64]

---

[61] In Hindu mythology, Kamdhenu is a wish-fulfilling cow.
[62] Shankarlal G. Banker, Oral History Transcript (153), pp. 69, 70.
[63] Walker, *Sword of Gold*, pp. 129–30.
[64] Walker, *Sword of Gold*, p. 130

The imprisoned Gandhi in Yeravda turned to the uplift of 'Harijans'. To those who complained, he replied that having entered the gates of prison, he was precluded from guiding Civil Disobedience and was hence concentrating on the work that he was still able to do. In November he set out on a long 'Harijan' tour, during which he travelled 12,500 miles and collected eight lakh rupees.

The Aga Khan Detention Camp

Leaving on one side, for the moment, Gandhi's thoughts on Quit India, let us turn to the anger and despair during the War years. Thousands marched to police stations and prisons demanding that they be arrested. By May 1941, the number of persons imprisoned reached 14,000.[65] Vijaya Lakshmi, then in Naini Jail, saw more and more of them come into the men's section every day. She heard police lorries drawing up outside. Sometime she heard the sound of boys being thrashed on the other side of the yard. She also heard of students being arrested in large batches, being thrashed, and released later.[66] A fresh burst of nationalist energy was triggered by the conviction or detention of 42,475 persons for anti-War offences from 1 April to 16 April 1942.[67] Long before Gandhi gave the 'Quit India' call, 264 security prisoners languished behind Bengal's prison bars. Three of the AICC members lived like ordinary prisoners without mosquito curtains or warm clothing in winter.[68] Those were the years for which there are first-hand accounts of the merciless degradation of prisoners at the Lahore Fort Torture Camp.[69] Azad has recorded his tough and strenuous life.[70]

---

[65] Moon, *Gandhi and Modern India*, p. 212.

[66] 28 September 1942, Vijaya Lakshmi Pandit, *Prison Days*, pp. 69–70.

[67] File no. 18/19, 1942, AICC papers.

[68] 26 December 1945, in *Towards Freedom*, edited by B. Prasad, p. 503.

[69] Sardul Singh Caveeshar, *The Lahore Fort Torture Camp* (Lahore: Hero Publications, 1946).

[70] Azad explained that the experience of prison life at that time was in many ways different from what he had experienced in the past. Earlier the prison rules permitted meetings with friends and relatives and personal correspondence was not stopped. Newspapers were supplied and more could be secured on payment. In special circumstances there were more facilities. So

Gandhi's associates carried on like brave soldiers. When he went on fast after an early morning breakfast on 9 February 1943, a sorrowful nation prayed. Three Indians on the Viceroy's Executive Council resigned.[71] Around a tube of toothpaste members of the Nehru household wrapped several newspaper clippings reporting the progress of Gandhi's fast and put the tube back into its container—that was how the news travelled to Vijaya Lakshmi Pandit, who was in prison.[72] At first, the British resorted to severe repression, for they were 'too embedded in their conservative rut to recognize that for every one person they imprisoned, two would rise to take their place.'[73] After a while, they avoided the arrest of the rank and file,[74] and freed persons 'of no importance'. This was done to keep the releases from and admittance to jail about equal.

Meanwhile, the long and interminable Gandhi–Viceroy correspondence produced no tangible result. Linlithgow's inglorious viceroyalty ended on 20 October 1943. Personal tragedies, including the death of Mahadev Desai, for whom Gandhi had enormous respect and affection, saddened him. He had lived with Gandhi from 1917 to 1942. Gandhi said of him: 'Remaining the disciple, Mahadev became my Guru. I visit his Samadhi to remember and emulate his worthy example. Pray God, let us walk in his footsteps.' Gandhi lost Kasturba on 22 February 1944, before his release. They had been married for

---

far as correspondence and meetings were concerned he had always enjoyed more facilities. As a result, even when bound hand and foot in shackles, ears were not blocked and eyes were not blindfolded. In spite of incarceration one felt as if one were living the same life that one lived outside. But this time an entirely new situation confronted him. Not only did all the outside faces disappear altogether but the voices also suddenly died. About the companions in a catacomb it has been said that they were all of a sudden deprived of all company. They were also subjected to the same blow; the world they lived in was no more.

[71] H. P. Mody, N. R. Sircar, and M. S. Aney.

[72] Nayantara Sahgal, *Prison and Chocolate Cake* (London: Victor Gollancz, 1954), p. 121.

[73] Seton, *Panditji*, p. 102.

[74] A. Gorev and V. Zimyanin, *Jawaharlal Nehru* (Moscow: Progress Publishers, 1982), p. 84.

sixty-two years and were a couple 'outside the ordinary'. A grief-stricken Gandhi observed 91 hours' silence, and asked the government to grant a small plot of land in the Aga Khan Palace compound for the families and associates to visit the place where their bodies were cremated.[75] In May 1944, a severe attack of malaria caused the authorities to free their most formidable adversary. 'The wheel of Fate,' Tagore had said on his deathbed, 'will someday compel the English to give up their Indian Empire.' It did.

Whenever the children and grandchildren of German historian Leopold von Ranke (1795–1886) gathered around him, he would say, 'I have another and older family, my pupils and their pupils.' Likewise, in the Aga Khan Detention Camp, as in the ashrams where Gandhi spent so many years of his life, he had his share of pupils, admirers, and disciples. Individually and collectively, they could have made life in the Camp austere and grim. But they did not. Mirabehn created a clay temple of all faiths, Sushila Nayyar (1914–2000), Gandhi's personal physician, wrote verses from the Ramayana in large letters, and Gandhi taught Kasturba Gandhi the tune of one of the hymns—'the 74-year-old couple enjoying their honeymoon' (Sarojini Naidu). Others played badminton. In this setting, Gandhi had the leisure to look at a spider's web at the fountain and wonder how the spider crossed from the periphery to the central column of the fountain and wove its web.[76]

Gandhi's conversations inspired close friends and associates. One such tête-à-tête took place with Sushila Nayyar on life and death. 'Bapu' did not want to anticipate release. So she said: 'As you say, we shall think of these matters when we are released. Who knows whether we may not have to stay here by the side of Mahadevbhai?' 'That is right,' Bapu said, 'if all of us sleep by Mahadev's side, I shall be very happy.' Sushila Nayyar said, 'No, Bapu not you. All of us, by all means, except you.' Bapu said: 'It is not right for you to express such sentiments. By doing so you weaken my "Do or Die" resolve.' Sushila Nayyar remarked, 'You as our General have to direct us to go forward and face dangers. You know there is no one else who can lead the people in the battle of non-violence.' Bapu was annoyed. He said, 'You want to be super-general and tell the general what to do. That is what

---

[75] Home Dept, Political, file no. 19/2, 1944.
[76] Nayyar, *Mahatma Gandhi's Last Imprisonment*, p. 117.

I told Mahadev, too. He, too, talked like you. The general knows where he should send his men and where he should go himself. Have you read *Mukta Dhara*? How the prince in it stopped his brother from going forward to offer self-immolation. He tells him, 'No, this is my job.' Then Bapu narrated the story of William of Orange,[77] and concluded, 'If I come to feel that it is my time to go and all of you try of dissuade me, it will dissipate my energy. Fortunately, I can still think clearly, but a day can come when I may begin to wonder, "This is what Mahadev said. Sushila, Ba,[78] Pyarelal, all of them say so; perhaps they are right." Our scriptures, too, say that if a man who feeds a hundred lives and fifty dependent on him die, it is all right. Because if the one who feeds the hundred dies, all the hundred will starve. But I do not agree with that philosophy. The man who feeds others may feel that by continuing to live under certain conditions, he will not be able to do the job of feeding others. He will become a burden to himself and to others. Then it is useless to stop him from facing death. All those whom he feeds may stand on their own feet when he is no more. Don't misunderstand me. I do not wish to die. Don't you see that I am studying Urdu and carrying on other studies with the enthusiasm of a lad of 15? I play with you. I enjoy everything that is worth enjoying, but if a time comes when I feel helpless, then what can I do?'[79] This is no fairy tale; it reflects Gandhi's state of mind and his inner quest for spiritual escape. He expressed his intense love for Mahadev Desai, longing for their life together, and yearnings to be free.

Gandhi had other stories to tell. Once, somebody noticed that his smile was not of the troubled soul. It broke around the mouth and passed quickly, like a veil thrown for a fraction of a second across the settled melancholy of the face.[80] He paused, looked at the skies, and then sized up the audience. He narrated how people took the risk of hiding poems, letters, and photographs for decades, and provided lively and evocative sketches of friends and his mentor, the venerable became more and more aware of following in the footsteps of Gopal Krishna

[77] He and his wife were crowned joint monarchs of England, Scotland, and Ireland in 1689. Their accession is known as the 'Glorious Revolution'. William III of Orange ensured the Protestant faith's primacy in Britain.

[78] Kasturba Gandhi was affectionately called 'Ba'.

[79] Nayyar, *Mahatma Gandhi's Last Imprisonment*, pp. 95–6.

[80] Holmes, Bridge, and James, *Mahatma Gandhi*, p. 68.

Gokhale (1866–1915), the leading light in Poona's Deccan Education Society and founder of the Servants of India Society in 1905. Gandhi maintained that Gokhale had many friends, but no one to whom he could pour his heart out. But he had faith in Gandhi, and discussed practically every important subject with him.[81] After recounting this, Gandhi smiled quietly or burst into laughter. It is hard to imagine how he could recall those years in such detail. Perhaps, the unforgettable nature of certain incidents was stored in his memory, and he remembered them in terrible or tragic moments in life or when his associates wanted him to talk about his ideals and heartfelt dreams.

One evening, on 12 September 1943, Gandhi resumed his story about his time in London. In the room he hired he would have porridge and a pint of milk and a little bread for breakfast. At midday he would settle for a six-penny lunch in a restaurant, and in the evening two apples and bread. He studied all day. A tutor prepared him for the London Matriculation examination, but he needed help with Latin. He went down the first time in an examination for which he had toiled hard for three months. At last, one day the landlady handed him a telegram that brought news of his success.

According to the Indian calendar, 26 September 1943 was Bapu's birthday. He did not want any floral decorations, but Sarojini Naidu ignored his protestations. The Jail Superintendent brought in flowers, and garlands were made out of them. After Bapu went to sleep, they were hung up on the staircase leading down to the compound. On the landing between the steps and on the verandah leading from his room, the place was brightened up with rangoli (decorations in coloured powders). All this went on till well after midnight.[82] Ba distributed food to the poor, though Bapu protested on the grounds that government money should not be spent in this fashion. Sarojini Naidu brushed aside his objections and told Bapu, 'Tomorrow you will have lunch like a civilized human being. You will have a special soup, then cauliflower, bread, and raw vegetables. Everything will be served in courses in the right style.' Bapu smiled.

Ba wore a new sari with a red border of yarn spun by none other than her husband. Manubehn and Sushila Nayyar also dressed in

---

[81] Nayyar, *Mahatma Gandhi's Last Imprisonment*, p. 104.
[82] Nayyar, *Mahatma Gandhi's Last Imprisonment*, p. 112.

red-bordered saris. There was no lavish feast. With Gandhi reminding them of their brethren dying of starvation in the Bengal Famine of 1943, they ate coarse grain like bajra.[83] The sepoys had decorated Bapu's room and the verandah with flowers and leaves. All the inmates sat down for prayers, singing a hymn, 'O God our Help in Ages Past'.[84]

Meeting of Minds

A prisoner had no choice, and his or her body was not in his or her own keeping.[85] As the Ganga of his knowledge flowed, Gandhi explained that 'the valiant taste of death but once' had a deeper meaning conveying the perfect truth according to the Hindu conception of salvation. It meant freedom from the wheel of birth and death. If the word 'valiant' may be taken to mean those who are strong in their search after God, 'they die but once, for they need not be reborn and put on the mortal coil'.[86] Submissive endurance of pain and suffering was the hallmark of all worthy souls.

John Stuart Mill (1806–1873), the British philosopher, enumerated 'truths' that were cruelly liquidated in the dungeon and at the stake. Gandhi, on the other hand, opened up new horizons to help his admirers and pupils in a variety of ways. Jamnalal Bajaj (1889–1942), social reformer and Gandhi's follower, could spin on the *charkha*. He did that for ten and a half hours on Gandhi's birthday. He wrote and

---

[83] It is estimated that between 1.5 million and 4 million people died in the famine. The theme haunted Urdu poetry. For example, 'A Question' by Akhtar-ul-Iman begins with the lines, 'Throw this dust body into the deep/ Dark bosom of the earth', and concludes with

> Will these soft plants, supple branches
> Go on growing
> So that we can pick them up one day
> And put them to sleep in autumn's lap?
> —*Query of the Road: Selected Poems of Akhtar-ul-Iman with Extensive Commentary* (edited by Baidar Bakht, Delhi: Rupa & Co., 1996, p. 140).

[84] Nayyar, *Mahatma Gandhi's Last Imprisonment*, pp. 298–9.

[85] Letter to Mirabehn, 22 April 1932, *Bapu's Letters to Mira* (Ahmedabad: Navajivan Trust, 1949), p. 181.

[86] Letter to Mirabehn, 22 June 1932, *Bapu's Letters to Mira*, p. 189.

received letters; played cards or chess; read hardbacks in Hindi, Marathi, and English; and took pleasure in the company of Kishorilal Mashruwala (1890–1952), Gandhi's disciple; and Khurshed Framji Nariman and K. M. Munshi (1887–1971), both Congress politicians. Like Rajaji, he confessed to an extraordinary tranquility and even joy such as he had rarely felt before.[87] Jamnalal started the Flag Satyagraha in 1923.

M. N. Roy was mistaken in his belief that the 'social backwardness of Gandhism is cultural backwardness; its intellectual mainstay, superstition.'[88] We might once again refer to the words of Rosa Luxemburg who stated in an essay she wrote in 1903, twenty years after the death of Marx, a 'system of ideas which is merely sketched in broad outline proves far more stimulating than a finished and symmetrical structure which leaves nothing to be added and offers no scope for the independent efforts of an active mind'.[89]

How did Moraji Desai's committing of the Gita to memory, reciting it every day, and meditating on it make him culturally backward or superstitious?[90] So what if Indulal Yagnik moved freely in the colourful imaginary world of yoga and the Upanishads and of the idealism of sacrificing saints and sadhus and Ramakrishna Paramahamsa?[91] Every day, he wrestled with the mutually opposite dreams of worldliness and spiritualism, read Christ's biography along with If Winter Comes, a novel, Rousseau's Emile, Maeterlinck's plays, and the works of Goethe. Every day he read bits of the Gita and the Puranas, and wrote children's stories on Rushabhadev on the basis of the Bhagavat Purana.[92] In Yervada, Gandhi reminded him of Gautam Buddha moving during Chaturmas with devotees in the morning and evening 2,500 years ago. He felt as if he had added the new mantra of suffering to his message of charity.

Indulal Yagnik heard the tunes of Devadutta from far away and felt for a moment the bright light of a Paighambar (Messenger) in his

---

[87] This paragraph is based on B. R. Nanda, In Gandhi's Footsteps, p. 186.
[88] M. N. Roy, Fragments, vol. 2, p. 211.
[89] Waters, Rosa Luxemburg Speaks, p. 107.
[90] Moraji Desai, The Story of My Life, vol. 1, p. 112.
[91] Yagnik, The Autobiography, p. 10.
[92] Yagnik, The Autobiography, pp. 111–12.

white clothes. By establishing contact with God, he derived definite inspiration and its impact percolated in every moment of his life,'and I had a clear perception from the *darshan* of the great soul in the idol of Mahatmaji who adorned the evening at the ashram, the limit of pure suffering, the insistence on immovable truth and the glimpse of *satya* and great soul. And with that very idea bending my heart I close this chapter of his imprisonment bowing in reverence at his feet.'[93]

In response to the promptings of his heart, Gandhi chose Acharya Vinoba Bhave as the first satyagrahi. He was arrested and lodged in Nagpur Jail where he taught Sanskrit and wrote *Swaraj Shastras* on the lines of Harold Laski's *A Grammar of Politics*. Dr Bharatan Kumarappa, a fellow prisoner, translated it into English with the help of Dada Dharmadhikari and Gopalrao Kale. During his detention at Vellore, Bhave learnt Tamil, Telugu, Kannada, and Malayalam. Kumarappa taught him these languages and Vinoba, in turn, introduced Tulsidas' *Ramayana*. When he chose not to be silent, he would speak on the Gita. Bhave followed this pattern of life througout his fifteen-month detention in Seoni Jail in the Central Provinces.[94]

In actual fact, the foundation of jail life was a powerful form of consensus that put a high premium on unanimous decisions. But such a consensus was not easy to sustain when two or more clearly articulated parties pursued conflicting aims. In such a situation, Gandhi did his very best to reconcile differences, more so when it mattered to him personally. Thus in 1938 he went out of his way to mollify the feelings of Mahadev Desai, who had offered his resignation. Gandhi adopted his own style to dissuade him from doing so:

What a gift in the morning? Even before the final mistake is rectified other mistakes follow one after the other. I would suffer thousands of mistakes rather than bear the separation. It is better to die at the hands of a devotee.... So there is no reason for you to go ... except cowardice there is nothing in your letter. If you leave me, do you think Pyarelal would live here? If Pyarelal goes would Sushila stay with us ...?[95]

[93] Yagnik, *The Autobiography*, p. 209.
[94] The information is based on Shriman Narayan, *Vinoba: His Life and Work* (Bombay, 1970), pp. 145–7.
[95] Gandhi to Mahadev Desai, 31 March 1938, *CWMG*, vol. LXVI, p. 455.

As we come to the end of this section, let us remember Gandhi's precious and wonderful ability to direct the interest of women in pursuing a range of causes. Both in religion and politics, the source of every action is some individual person. He inspired women to straddle the domestic and the public spheres. Gandhi worked on the assumption of a cosmos of interrelated, equal persons who deserve to be autonomous and with his claims that a good society cannot be characterized by domination and hierarchy.[96] Thus, the mother of the Ali brothers, the wife of Maulana Hasrat Mohani, Begum M. A. Ansari, the Istanbul-born Atiya Fyzee (1877–1967), whose father was attached to an Indian merchant attached to the Ottoman court, and many other ladies came out of purdah and jumped into the fray. The begums of Mohamed Ali's family drew large audiences in Bijnor, Saharanpur, Fatehgarh, Benares, Jaunpur, Ghazipur, and Azamgarh. Avantikabai Gokhale and Kamaladevi Chattopadhyay were among the first women satyagrahis a decade later. During Civil Disobedience, they, along with men, acted 'as souls not as sexes'.[97] They shared the burden, the pain, and the sacrifices with 'soul-force' as their weapon and safeguard. Men and women marched in public, served terms of severe imprisonment, suffered lathi charge, and went through court proceedings.

Sarojini Naidu headed the Rashtriya Stree Sabha, an independent women's organization with Goshiben Naoroji Captain, granddaughter of Dadabhai Naoroji, and Avantikabai Gokhale. She was struck by Gandhi's single-mindedness, consistency, his good faith, and largeheartedness. As the symbol of India's ideological unity,[98] he provided millions like her with a purpose in life. A 'poet in action', he delivered from bondage proud citizens whom he had taught to stand erect.

Mickey Mouse

'Ah! You must be Mrs Naidu? Who else dare be so irreverent? Come and share my meal!' Gandhi said to her. He had gone to London

[96] Ronald J. Terchek, *Gandhi: Struggling for Autonomy* (New Delhi: Vistaar Publications, 1998), p. 67.
[97] Cousins, *Indian Womanhood Today*, p. 68.
[98] Pyarelal, *Mahatma Gandhi: The Last Phase*, vol. 1 (Ahmedabad: Navjivan Publishing House, 1956), p. 185.

to organize an ambulance corps during World War I. That's when they met on 8 August 1914. And so began a friendship that lasted and developed through the years. She revealed the man, and, though the picture was not always pleasing, it was at any rate human. In fact, Gandhi's simple and austere life inspired in her the combined feeling of reverence and awe, though the world did not know, so she said jokingly, what it cost to keep him in poverty. She herself wore coarse khadi. She could joke with Gandhi on *brahmacharya*, chastity. Once, when an article appeared in *Young India* suggesting several ways of avoiding the temptation of being with women, the writer advised, among other things, the wearing of dark glasses. As Rajaji always wore very dark glasses, Sarojini Naidu made naughty remarks about him in which both Gandhi and Rajaji himself joined. Rajaji's views were as staunch as Gandhi's, but both put up with her teasing.[99]

Gandhi called her *Bharat Kokila*. They were closely and constantly linked together. Endowed as Gandhi was with the liveliest sensibility to feminine influence, his life of self-discipline, self-development, and, as he aptly called it, self-abandon, enabled him to weld together in his own person the masculine and feminine qualities into a single whole, free from tension.[100] Gandhi deliberately surrounded himself with women to prove that his mastery over 'lust' was not achieved by avoiding them.[101] He enjoyed being nicknamed 'Mickey Mouse' by Sarojini Naidu, whom he never had seen on the screen. But did Naidu follow Gandhi's rules of diet? She cried out: 'Good heavens, all that grass and goat's milk? Never, never, never!'[102]

'I am back in my old cottage in the corner of the Walled Garden of Seclusion ... the Garden alas,' wrote Sarojini Naidu during Civil Disobedience.[103] She had for company Kamaladevi Chattopadhyay,

[99] Vijaya Lakshmi Pandit, *The Scope of Happiness: A Personal Memoir* (New York: Crown Publishers, 1979), p. 67.

[100] Horace Gundry Alexander, *Consider India: An Essay in Values* (Bombay: Asia Publishing House, 1961), p. 58.

[101] Louis Fischer, *The Life of Mahatma Gandhi* (New York: Harper and Row Publishers, 1983 edn), p. 440.

[102] Padmini Sathianadhan Sengupta, *Sarojini Naidu* (Bombay: Asia Publishing House, 1966), p. 344.

[103] To Padmaja and Leilamani Naidu, 2 May 1932, in *Sarojini Naidu*, p. 269.

who was lodged 'in a dark gloomy room, full of murky air and putrid smells; bats hanging from the ceiling occasionally startled her by sudden flights from corner to corner.'[104] Without grumbling or sulking, she informed Gandhi of the plight of women in the barracks. Solitude and inaction ate deeply into the spirit of Mridula Sarabhai as she eagerly waited for the mail from home, which was often delayed because Gujarati letters took longer in censoring. She maintained her poise and equanimity.

Besides sharing experiences, opinions, and inner feelings, Sarojini Naidu wrote the poetry of love and pleasure, laughter and tears whenever Gandhi embarked on a fast. She was by his side on 20 September 1932, the day of the fast against the Communal Award.[105] 'The Little Man,' she reported to Jawaharlal Nehru from Calcutta in mid-November 1937, 'is sitting unconcernedly eating spinach while the world ebbs and flows about him breaking into waves of Bengali, Gujarati, English and Hindi.... He is really ill ... not only in his brittle bones and thinning blood but in the core of his soul ... the most lonely and tragic figure of his time.'[106] If many saw Gandhi as a saint, others thought of him as 'a fanciful dreamer of inconvenient and impossible dreams', that is, Hindu–Muslim unity. Sarojini Naidu was concerned about the 'communal readjustments' and wondered, from her sickbed in The Golden Threshold[107] if the 'Gandhi Magic' and the 'Jawaharlal Nerves' were ever going to work.[108]

In 1942, Sarojini Naidu sensed thunder in the air, and anticipated mass arrests. She prepared herself for this in her Bombay house. The bell rang at 4 a.m. The police came in. Her hunch proved right. She and others were led into prison on 8 August to lead a monotonous existence.

---

[104] K. Chattopadhyay, *Inner Recesses*, p. 157.

[105] The British Prime Minister, Ramsay Macdonald, announced the Communal Award on 16 August 1932, granting separate electorates in British India for Muslims, Sikhs, Anglo-Indians, Indian Christians, and Europeans. It also allocated separate electorates for the Depressed Classes.

[106] Sarojini Naidu to Jawaharlal Nehru, 13 November 1937, in *A Bunch of Old Letters*, p. 255.

[107] The Golden Threshold was the residence of Naidu. It was named after her collection of poetry.

[108] Sarojini Naidu to Jawaharlal Nehru, 29 March 1938, in *A Bunch of Old Letters*, p. 282.

Now and then, of course, there were brighter moments: one of them occurred when Rajaji visited Gandhi in jail. The last time he had seen him, Gandhi had been reading *The Hound of Heaven*, and Sarojini Naidu had been sitting by him trying to explain what it all meant.

'Well', said Rajaji, 'have you finished that dog poem?'

On 10 February 1943, Gandhi commenced another of his fasts. A number of unsavoury things have been said about it. One of them is that the state of his health chart varied according to the political situation, and that when the Viceroy looked like yielding, Gandhi grew rapidly worse, and when it was quite evident that the Viceroy was adamant, Gandhi took a marked turn for the better. Sarojini Naidu, on the other hand, said that towards the end of the seventh day, Gandhi had, to all appearances, died. He had been sinking rapidly since the morning, and as the dusk deepened the worst seemed to happen; his breathing ceased, his pulse faltered and stopped. It was as though a light had gone out of the world, she said. But she could not explain how he came back. All she could suggest was that it was a supreme effort of will. She told her daughter of the problem and paradox of 'the marvellous little Mickey Mouse who has nibbled his way back to life from the lightly spread and knotted nets of death'. She also discussed his 'horrid scrubby little chin growth that made him look like a gnome and he had himself shaved and trimmed to "look nice" because he thought I was being rude about his appearance'.[109]

In this chapter, I have neither been concerned with Gandhi's sincerity [or otherwise] nor with the fallacies and the contradictions of his message. I realize that his message cannot claim the indisputable authority of revealed truth, but I suggest that it should be judged on its own merit. It is not without significance that even in the twenty-first century some parts of the Western world are swayed by the doctrines of Gandhi. He has been a reliable guide in life to the likes of Nelson Mandela and other pacifists across the world. He has inspired anti-apartheid, environment-friendly groups, and the Palestinians, who are concerned not with metaphysical speculations but with the courage and tenacity with which he led the liberation struggle.

---

[109]   To Leilamani Naidu, 3 March 1943, in *Sarojini Naidu*, p. 309.

Gandhi is relevant today not because he is the bearer of India's spiritual message to the West, but because he has contributed substantially to the common heritage of humanity—the philosophy of living together separately. His vision of a life free from the vulgar—materialistic extravagances of capitalist society is still valid. That makes *Hind Swaraj* a manifesto for our times. His thoughts on satyagraha and non-violence, the *pièce de résistance* of Gandhism, are not mere abstractions but are precepts whose real meaning can be easily read by putting them into practice. Lastly, the world today can benefit from and recognize the value in interfaith dialogue and global cooperation. This, I believe, is the central pivot of Gandhi's philosophy.

There is no denying that some of Gandhi's formulations were riddled with contradictions, and that the assertion of sectarian, communitarian, and caste identities foiled his major plans and interventions. His elusive shibboleths did not appeal to the Dalits, the tribals, and the religious minorities, who gradually distanced themselves from him. They saw his talk of love, truth, goodness as abstract categories that defied definition. While a detailed critique of Gandhi is not a part of my present purpose, one cannot help pointing to his monumental 'failure'—the partition of the subcontinent. This event, with all its attendant violence and bloodshed, throws a flood of light on Gandhi's idyllic picture of Hindu–Muslim relations during the pre-colonial days. In his own days, he underestimated the potential of violence in society. He protested against them like a saint but did little to contain it like a statesman. In short, his ideas did not help to stem the tide of hate, violence, and civil strife. Yet, neither India nor the world at large can shun his message.

In conclusion, I underline three points. First of all, Gandhi deployed the symbolism of political prisoner in his crusade, and jail as a metaphor to depict India's enslavement. He contended that India was a vast prison, and the Viceroy its irresponsible superintendent with numerous jailors and warders under him. India's four hundred million were not the only prisoners, but there were others similarly situated under other superintendents.[110] To Gandhi, the *jailkhana* equalled persecution, torture, and loss of life. 'The discomforts of prison life,' he wrote, 'will be throughout our lives the most cherished of our memories, like

---

[110] B. Prasad, *Towards Freedom*, p. 150.

the scars of warriors', and mentioned the qaidis in Delhi, and the prizes of honour and virtue, rewards, and distinctions that were given to them. Their role and contribution, he said, confirmed India's fitness for swaraj.

Gandhi raised the spirit of heroism to new heights.[111] Besides khadi, the cow, and the Khilafat, he used non-coercive methods to link the rural and the urban, the rich and the poor, the educated and the uneducated. While in the Sabarmati Jail, he took up the cause of the six prisoners of Mulshipeta who had been subjected to lashing. A compromise was reached. After this, Gandhi several times observed, for the happiness and the health of comrades, the penance that had been postponed because of Mulshipeta.[112]

Ironically, the great votary of non-violence inspired prisoners in Sylhet Jail to turn truculent.[113] Thus when Jairamdas Daulatram refused to submit to a search in 1922, he let loose a barrage of words. As a result, he was confined to a solitary cell for a week. Certain that the penalty was not new—'they have been paid in all times and in many lands'—Gandhi, who championed his cause, was convinced that God gave him and others the strength to challenge the authorities, and that they would not capitulate, though they may have to die. Inspired by such examples, 'refractory and mutinous' state prisoners refused to be searched.[114]

To conclude, the main purpose of the jail system was to create the fear of God in the minds of nationalists, but the chief result was its gradual weakness and ultimate collapse. Gandhi's interventions and withdrawals had, in each case, been decisive. He compelled the government to improve the lot of the prisoners. And Jawaharlal often talked about jail reforms. As in other political matters, the Mahatma had shown him the way.

[111] The Rowlatt Committee recommended that the government should have powers to make arbitrary arrests and inflict summary punishments for the suppression of revolutionary activities in certain parts of the country. Accordingly, a bill was introduced in the Imperial Legislative Council in February 1919. On 24 February, Gandhi conveyed his decision to launch satyagraha, followed by the appeal to join him. On 6 April, a hartal was widely observed.

[112] Yagnik, *Autobiography*, vol. 2, pp. 129–33, 134.

[113] Home Dept, Political, file no. 98, 1932.

[114] *Young India*, 9 February 1922, Home Dept, Political, file no. 654, 1922.

10. 'Thy Flag Will Be Laid in the Dust'*

The Nehrus in Prison

Life in prison is not meant to be exciting—it is about as uneventful as the existence of the average turnip—and if some exciting event does take place once in a while, the veil of mystery must not be removed and no whisper of it must percolate to the outside world. Inside the jail—and outside—the massive gates and the high walls of the jail separate two worlds. Almost one might say that it is like one living world and the hereafter—but few, if any, want to rush to the hereafter, and none love the jail so much as to wish to remain here. Two worlds! You could also compare the two to the animal and the vegetable kingdoms. The object of jail appears to be first to remove such traces of humanity as a man might possess and then to subdue even the animal element in him so that ultimately he might become the perfect vegetable! Soil-bound, cut off from the world and its activity, nothing to look forward to, blind obedience the only 'virtue' that is instilled, and spirit considered the

---

* Amar Nath Dutt, member from the Burdwan division, quoted in the Legislative Assembly debate on 14 September 1929.

great sin—is it any wonder that the prisoner approximates to the plant? Of course this does not apply to the likes of me who come for short periods, but the others who spend years and years here, wherein do they differ, I wonder, from the plant? And if after long years they are let off how do they feel in the strange new world of bustle and activity?

—Jawaharlal Nehru to Vijaya Lakshmi Pandit,
25 June 1930, *SWJN*, vol. 4, p. 361

The prerogatives of information and position permit certain families to contend that the dawn of freedom would have eluded the country had they not parted with their comforts. Apart from appropriating the multilayered contest between the peoples and the colonial state,[1] they have deftly scripted their images through a variety of means such as statues, memorials, and first-day covers. Indira Gandhi, who spent 243 days in prison, boasted that she did not know of any other family that was so involved in the freedom struggle and its hardships;[2] Nayantara Sahgal talks of the meeting of national and family history so that the 'entire family—grandparents, parents, uncles and aunts, and also a servant—ended its old life and started a new one in thrall to a country whose destiny it now took to be its own'. She narrates, furthermore, how the emotional connection transformed their lifestyle and goals.[3] Elsewhere, she mentions B. K. Nehru (1909–2001) visiting Jawaharlal Nehru in jail in 1935, with his newly wed wife, Fori (b. 1908), born in Budapest to a Jewish mother. When she had earlier come on a visit to India and stayed with her future in-laws, she was demure, dressed in a sari and learning to speak Hindi, but when she saw the tub in the bathroom, she cried out in delight 'Hallelujah'.[4] While they talked, the warder came in and laid a hand on the prisoner's arm to take him back to his cell. Fori could not bear this and began to cry. Jawaharlal Nehru looked back and said to her, 'No tears. In this family we keep a stiff upper lip.'[5]

[1] U. K. Singh, *Political Prisoners in India*, p. 2.
[2] Pranay Gupte, *Mother India: A Political Biography of Indira Gandhi* (New York: Charles Scribner's Sons, 1992), pp. 129–31.
[3] Nayantara Sahgal, *Jawaharlal Nehru: Civilizing a Savage World* (New Delhi: Penguin Books India, 2010), pp. 2–3.
[4] C. Mehta, *Freedom's Child*, p. 10.
[5] C. Mehta, *Freedom's Child*, p. 17.

Did Jawaharlal's scepticism on religion and faith deepen behind the thick walls of the numerous jails he frequented? If so, what did he think of the growing religious influence in the public domain or its effect on inter-community relations? What insights did he gain from his historical explorations that resulted in the publication of several books? What did he make of the friendships in jails? Lastly, did those months and years strengthen or weaken family ties?

This chapter seeks to trace the composite identity of the Nehrus through their experiences in and outside of colonial jails. B. K. Nehru, one of them, refers to the lesser-known members of the illustrious family in the following words: 'They too suffered the consequences of opposition to foreign rule. They too went to jail, had their property confiscated, got beaten up and sometimes shot by the police, as did thousands of other Indians who fought for independence.'[6] My narrative is, however, centred on Jawaharlal and Motilal, though I pay some attention to the political fortunes of other family members, whose lives combined the benefits of privilege with the satisfaction of being on the side of freedom and freedom from caste and religious conventions with the confidence and assurance of being a part of a long and proud tradition. What is more, their sufferings in jail brought an otherwise elite family close to the people, who could not think of Allahabad without the Nehrus. And they could not think of Allahabad without Anand Bhawan.

Anand Bhawan was like the ancestral house of a clan in the Highlands of Scotland. It was much more than a structure of brick and mortar, more than a private possession. Within its walls great events took place and momentous decisions were taken. Kisan sabha meetings were held on the tennis court where not long ago tennis parties had taken place. From the verandahs one could look out on a vast expanse of garden—full of gladioli, daffodils, sweet peas, chrysanthemums, delphiniums, and roses. Hundreds of birds flitted about, adding their sweet songs and flashing colour to its beauty. Indira looked upon trees as life-giving and a refuge; she loved climbing and hiding in them. Motilal, her grandfather, wanted friends and family to share the good life with him. Jovial, easy-going, and generous, it was hard to imagine the host lonely, or bored, or despondent. The effect of one of his occasional anecdotes would be to make his listener warm to humankind and its failings.

---

[6] M. Z. Sahgal, *An Indian Freedom Fighter Recalls Her Life.*

The Nehru family has a photograph of Motilal, a Saraswat
Brahman, in his formal cutaway coat of English broadcloth and grey
striped trousers, with a stiff shirt, high collar, and a satin tie. His rather
full face had a handle-bar moustache—which he soon shaved off.
The picture was taken in 1899. Artists portrayed him as a vigorous
man with the clear-cut and domineering mask of a Roman senator,
his bearing irresistibly youthful till the very end. He lived on Elgin
Road until 1900. Thereafter, he moved to a forty-two-room house on
Church Road in the Civil Lines and decorated the new house with
expensive European artefacts. Swarup Rani Thussi, a shy Kashmiri
girl, often heard the tinkle of ice cubes as her husband sat next to a
low wooden lamp holding the gin and tonic in his hand. During the
40 years preceding March 1921, he had seldom missed a drink for
11 months in the year. He abstained for a month simply to avoid
getting enslaved to the habit.[7] 'I know you will feel polluted if you eat
at my table,' he said to one of his uncles, 'but it won't hurt you to drink
a whisky-and-soda with me.'[8]

Motilal led a social life with a fine clutch of interesting personalities
living nearby and a constant stream of others attached to the High
Court, the University, and, above all, the great confluence of the sacred
rivers in Allahabad. They dropped by to sit around the tiered fountain
in the centre of the courtyard, or take a dip in the indoor swimming
pool in a great, cavernous, damp-smelling room. At one end of the
pool there was a large carved stone crow's head from whose mouth
fresh water poured to fill it. Sapru could not swim; hence, he would
not move from the first step in fifteen inches of water. Manmohini
Zutshi's mother recounted an incident when one of the women lost
her gold ring in the pool. Jawaharlal was asked to dive in and get it out.
How he teased his sisters-in-law! They had to beg and plead with him
before retrieving the ring.[9]

Motilal's guest list had everyone who was anyone in Allahabad—
politicians, journalists, poets, and British administrators. A prominent

[7] To Gandhi, 10 July 1924, *SWMN*, vol. 4, edited by Ravinder Kumar
and Hari Dev Sharma (Delhi: Vikas, 1986), p. 47.

[8] Krishna Nehru Hutheesing, *We Nehrus* (New York: Holt, Rinehart and
Winston), p. 21.

[9] M. Z. Sahgal, *An Indian Freedom Fighter Recalls Her Life*, p. 6.

guest was Harcourt Butler (1869–1938), UP's Lieutenant-Governor. A lover of music, dance, and good food, he enjoyed life as it came his way. The Raja of Mahmudabad was his generous host. When it was Motilal's turn to play host, his guest list had Manzar Ali Sokhta, T. A. K. Sherwani, and Puran Chandra Joshi (b. 1907), the future communist leader. His affection for Hakim Ajmal Khan was like that of an own brother.[10] He loved him for his searching, lucid, and incisive mind. They, in turn, were captivated by Motilal's aristocratic manner, his humour tempered with good taste in poetry, and his sophistication, which, under no circumstances, degenerated into 'showing off'. They judged him to be too worldly, domineering, acerbic, and wilful—flaws of character which, in their minds, were redeemed by his gracious and courteous bearing.

There was nothing bohemian about Motilal Nehru's lifestyle. Stories of linen being washed in Paris were apocryphal, but not the tale of his acquiring a set of Bohemian glass, the kind just purchased by King Edward VII. 'Who in Allahabad is going to appreciate these?' wondered Swarup Rani, who was accustomed to her husband's princely habits, 'and why should we be like King Edward?' Gandhi considered her a personification of dignified bravery and sacrifice. As knives and forks appeared on the dining table, social conversation veered around Shakespeare and the nineteenth-century Romantic poets. Guests took their turn on the *takhtposh*, and chewing *pan* (betel leaf) from the *pandaan* (pan box), they listened to ghazals or *thumri* and *dadra*. On a wintry night, they would move into the large living room with the tabla and sarangi. Come Muharram and they would put away their musical instruments in memory of the great martyrdom of Imam Husain, the grandson of the Prophet of Islam. These gestures survived well until the 1930s, when Shia–Sunni animus, along with Hindu–Muslim conflicts, disturbed Awadh's ambience.

Anand Bhawan was noisy and full of laughter, and if an outsider had witnessed the family talk and joke and laugh, he would not have thought they had many cares or worries to trouble them, much less that they were mentally anguished. There was little sleep those days. The Nehrus held discussions, narrated old and new stories, joked and

[10] M. Z. Sahgal, *An Indian Freedom Fighter Recalls Her Life*, p. 26.

laughed. The younger ones were simply delighted with this excitement and riotous living. Egotistical and self-important, they relied
on Motilal Nehru for his urbanity, high poetical feeling, and elegant
tastes. In days of affluence or in days of hardship, they remembered
both his awe-inspiring temper and infectious laughter. And whenever
Sarojini Naidu was in town they turned to her scintillating wit, irre-
pressible vivacity, and *joie de vivre*. Music flowed from her lips, as it did
from her pen. Charming, kind-hearted, and friendly, she had a generous disposition. In 1940, Gandhi visited Anand Bhawan. Nayantara
Sahgal served garlic to him. She carried it at arm's length destesting
its strong smell. Sarojini Naidu saw her and said, 'There is no need to
be so snooty, young lady. If you want to have a complexion like the old
man's when you're his age, you'd do well to eat some of it yourself!'[11]

Faith and Modernity

Starting with Pandit Raj Kaul, a Sanskrit and Persian scholar, the daily
lives of the Nehrus were a seamless blend of tradition and modernity.
Once upon a time, they were concentrated in Lahore, followed by
Lucknow and Allahabad, where the Ganga meets Yamuna and the
fabled subterranean stream Saraswati. At all these places they reflected
the enquiring and assimilative ethos of the Indo-Gangetic heartland.
Time crept on inexorably. Like many others, they adapted themselves
to new ways. Whether it was the fact of ancestry or location, they
developed an eclectic outlook on life and on interpersonal relationships. Neither man nor nation, Fyodor Dostoevsky (1821–1881) had
written, can exist without a sublime idea. 'Your whole education, your
upbringing, and the makeup of your mind cannot permit you to think
in terms of caste, creed, or colour,' Sapru reminded Jawaharlal a year
before Independence.[12] With very few exceptions, the Nehrus spoke
the secular language, whatever their private religious beliefs. Motilal
Nehru carried the richness and appealing quality of his outlook.
Convinced of the use of reason, he rejected irrational behaviour and
institutions. Watching his butler serve Motilal Nehru a dish of eggs,

[11] N. Sahgal, *Prison and Chocolate Cake*, p. 27.
[12] Henriette M. Sender, *The Kashmiri Pandits: A Study of Cultural Choice in North India* (Delhi: Oxford University Press, 1988), p. 264.

an orthodox Hindu visitor remarked in horror, 'Panditji, you are not going to eat those eggs!' 'I most certainly am,' he replied, 'and in another few moments I am going to eat their mother too.' He inspired the Nehrus to do the same, many of whom represented the triumphant, rationalist, humanist 'Enlightenment' of the eighteenth century. Sapru, Jagat Narain Mulla, and Bishen Narain Dar introduced newness and vitality into activism by putting together the two great compromises with the Muslims: the Jahangirabad Pact of 1915 and the Lucknow Pact of 1916.[13] Like bourgeois liberals and revolutionary proletarian socialists, Jawaharlal Nehru believed that human society and the individual could be perfected by the application of reason, and were destined to be so perfected. On the other hand, 'the various religions have especially helped in petrifying old beliefs and faiths and customs', he wrote in 'The Last Letter' on 9 August 1933, 'which may have had some use in the age and country of their birth, but which are singularly unsuitable in our present age.'[14]

Religious rituals were, admittedly, deep-rooted and pervasive. Swarup Rani kept intact the family practices. At the same time, she avoided interfering in her husband's lifestyle. Married at fourteen, she went along with his decision not to perform a purification ceremony on his return from England in 1899, and agreed to the invocations at Jawaharlal's wedding being sung by a group of young girls rather than the Pandits. Later in life, she stood by Indira Nehru when some people condemned her proposed marriage to Feroze Gandhi, a Parsi. 'My grandmother said that since neither Feroze nor I were much concerned with religion, she did not see that it mattered what either of us were. If we were religious, then it might matter, but not being so, it did not.'[15] Such instances reveal the direction of Motilal Nehru's unorthodox ways as well. He was like that not because he was anglicized or that he wanted to follow Western ways to fall in line with the British, but because of his composite cultural legacy. He turned pictures of Hindu nationalists upside down, opposed the All-India Hindu Sabha on the

[13] Sender, *Kashmiri Pandits*, p. 261; Francis Robinson, *Separatism among Muslims: The Politics of the United Provinces, 1860–1923* (Cambridge: Cambridge University Press, 1975).

[14] Jawaharlal Nehru, *Glimpses of World History*, p. 951.

[15] Seton, *Panditji*, p. 103.

grounds that it would minimize all chances of Hindu–Muslim unity, sap the foundation of the Congress itself, and come in the way of cultivating a pluralist point of view. For this, he was damned as a beefeater and a destroyer of cows. Yet, he took it all calmly. This was one of the many qualities that raised him many notches in public estimation.

Like his father, Jawaharlal Nehru did not submit to irrational authority, be it religion or any dogma. At the same time, he accepted, more out of convenience rather than conviction, a few social and religious customs. Thus, he took part in his father's *shraddha* ceremony as a mark of respect for his mother's religious susceptibilities. Both his sisters married outside of the Brahman community, and he defended Krishna's marriage to Gunottam 'Raja' Hutheesing, a non-Brahman. He wrote:

> I would welcome as wide a breach of custom as possible. The Kashmiri community—there are exceptions, of course, in it—disgusts me. It is the very epitome of petit-bourgeois vices, which I detest. I am not particularly interested in a person being a Brahman or a non-Brahman or anything else. As a matter of fact, I fail to see the relevance of all this; one marries an individual, not a community.[16]

Gandhi assumed that the satyagrahi's only weapon is God; Jawaharlal Nehru, an agnostic, did not agree. Similarly, Gandhi thought of fasting as the final panacea prescribed by *dharma*; Nehru hardly ever used fasting as a political option. He once said that India's spirit was in the depth of his conscience while the mind of the West was in his head by virtue of his education in Harrow, Cambridge, and all over London.[17] Driven or dominated by the urge to see reason in thought and action, he explained his explicit disavowal of interest in religions.

> I am becoming more and more hostile to the religious idea. Exceptions apart, it seems to me the negation of real spirituality and only a begetter of confusion and sentimentality. I should like to keep myself away, as far as possible, from all religious rites and ceremonials, all the hallmarks of religion—indeed to be wholly non-religious. Regard for mother, and

---

[16] Gupte, *Mother India*, p. 193.

[17] 'A Dialogue with Jawaharlal Nehru' by Mohamed H. Heikal, file no. 1097, Misc., AICC Papers.

a desire not to hurt her feelings at this time of life, occasionally make me agree to participation in some ceremony. But even so it is an unwilling and ungracious participation and I am not sure if it is not better to do without it.[18]

Yet, Nehru conceded that old-established traditions could not be scrapped or dispensed with. Traditions, he wrote in *The Discovery of India*, had to be accepted to a large extent and adapted to meet new conditions and ways of thought. He thus tried 'to conjure Bharat Mata as the body politic, composed of the bodies of millions of Indians, as an image that can convince and carry both himself as the speaker and the crowds that he addresses into a future of independent nationhood.'[19] During his sixth prison term, a friend sent him a picture of a famous old statue of Buddha at Anuradhapura in Sri Lanka. He kept it on the table in his jail cell; it soothed him, gave him strength, and helped him overcome depression. While Buddhism or any other dogma did not interest him as such, he found the Buddha to be an attractive person. 'It is moving to think of this agnostic,' writes one of Jawaharlal's many biographers, 'gaining strength to endure his loneliness through contemplation of the Buddha's serenity.'[20] He regarded Asoka as the paradigmatic ruler; for him, the Buddhist period was a veritable 'golden age', marked by a unique internationalism, tolerance, compassion, and a vigorous openness to 'foreign' influences and ideas. It is to Asoka and the 'golden period' that he constantly harks back, be it in the adoption of the Asoka *chakra* in the national flag or the policy of Panch Shila. 'That wheel is a symbol of India's ancient culture, it is a symbol of many things that India had stood for through the ages,' he told the Constituent Assembly.[21]

Lado Rani, mother of Manmohini, came from a traditional Kashmiri family. When faced with the modern way of life in Motilal's household, she started taking English and art lessons. Like the Kayasthas, and the Amils of Sind, the Nehrus were supremely eclectic and left their

[18] To Gandhi, 25, July 1933, *SWJN*, vol. 5, p. 491.

[19] Ananya Vajpeyi, *Righteous Republic: The Political Foundations of Modern India* (Cambridge, MA: Harvard University Press, 2012), p. 179.

[20] Beatrice Pitney Lamb, *The Nehrus of India: Three Generations of Leadership* (New York: Macmillan Company, 1967), p. 113.

[21] Lamb, *Nehrus of India*, p. 190.

imprint on north India's culture. This is true of the family of Ladli Prasad Zutshi, nephew of Motilal, and of Lado Rani. At his suggestion, some family members moved to Lahore. Here, one of their four daughters, Manmohini, became a social rebel and political activist.[22]

The Trial Ahead

The Nehrus had a choice in politics—to make their peace with government and add to their riches. At first, Motilal was inclined to do just that, but the Calcutta Congress in September 1920 changed it all. Shudha Mazumdar, a young lady from Bengal, who heard people discuss the Non-cooperation Resolution, noted:

> The Ali Brothers supported it. 'Pandit Motilal Nehru,' whispered my companion reverentially, and I could hardly tear my eyes away from that proud patrician face when I remembered that wonderful portion of his Presidential address from the previous year: 'What is our ultimate goal? We want freedom of thought, freedom of action, freedom to fashion our own destiny and build up an India suited to the genius of her people.... We must aim at an India where all are free and have the fullest opportunities of development, where women have ceased to be in bondage and the rigours of the caste system have disappeared ...'[23]

Soon enough, the gay and carefree chitchat of yesteryear, and the Spode china and Venetian glass, the stock of choice wines, and the prized horses and dogs disappeared. Manmohini Zutshi recalled: 'All bank accounts, securities and so forth, were transferred to my father's name so that Mrs Motilal and the immediate family would not suffer any hardship. Life changed drastically. Carriages and horses were dispensed with...'[24] Once, one could walk into Anand Bhawan and see Harcourt Butler and other British luminaries raising their whisky glasses and smoking the choicest cigars. But now the guests were khadi-clad. The hosts themselves donned khadi clothes.

Imagine the evening of 7 December 1921 when an audacious but nervous Indian policeman made his way to arrest the two Nehrus. For

---

[22] M. Z. Sahgal, *An Indian Freedom Fighter Recalls Her Life*, pp. xiv–xv.
[23] S. Mazumdar, *Memoirs of an Indian Woman*, p. 154.
[24] M. Z. Sahgal, *An Indian Freedom Fighter Recalls Her Life*, p. 29.

the family women, their arrest marked the beginning of a new life, a life of uncertainty, of sacrifice, of heartache and sorrow. In *House of the Dead* by Dostoevsky the exile in Siberia was the period in which the narrator's knowledge of good and evil, and the variegated causes of the decay of human personality, came to him. The lack of faith, skill, and integrity in the jail officials made him value the Marxian theory that the State was really the coercive apparatus that enforced its will.[25] But the presence of vast crowds at the railway stations or at public meetings gave him comfort. Krishna attributed her brother's popularity to his giving up his wealth and leading a simple life.[26] A friend congratulated him on his 'lucky escape from Nabha land', and hoped that he would not put his head into the noose too often.[27] Political activism meant arrest, detention, and prosecution. Wrote Vijaya Lakshmi Pandit: 'Another birthday spent in prison. So many good years of his life wasted—I feel rebellious when I think of all he has had to go through.'[28]

Nehru linked prison with the colonial project of enforcing conformity on the convicts, some of whom were warders or overseers because of fear, or in anticipation of reward and special remissions.[29] He was stung by reports of the destruction of young lives, and by the humiliation of families and friends through brute force.[30] Furthermore, he became aware of entrenched race prejudices at all levels of jail management and the differentiation of Indians into A, B, and C class prisoners. This led him to request his father not to send him delicacies such as the Mau melons when imprisonment, flogging, firing, and martial law were the lot of those outside.[31] He disapproved of the special facilities (with regard to diet) extended to the accused in the Meerut Conspiracy Case, with the exception of Messrs Benjamin Bradley (1898–1957), a British communist, and Philip Spratt (1902–1971), also a British communist jailed with a short break from 1929–34.[32]

[25] J. Nehru, *An Autobiography*, p. 225.

[26] Hutheesing, *We Nehrus*, p. 10.

[27] B. R. Nanda, *The Nehrus* (Delhi: Oxford University Press, 1962), pp. 222–3.

[28] 10 November 1942, in *Prison Days*, pp. 91–2.

[29] 25 April 1930, *SWJN*, vol. 4, p. 330.

[30] 25 April 1930, *SWJN*, vol. 1, p. 584.

[31] 28 May 1930, *SWJN*, vol. 4, p. 353.

[32] Statement on Meerut Prisoners, 22 May 1929, *SWJN*, vol. 3, p. 343. See also Hajrah Begum, Oral History Transcript (613), pp. 36–7, NMML.

A French saying goes that 'on the eve of the revolution, revolution seems the most improbable thing', an idea Raghupati Sahay 'Firaq' (Firaq Gorakhpuri, 1896–1982), expressed in a couplet: 'Mark the march of revolution, Firaq/How slow it seems, and yet how fast!' Indeed, the Quit India Movement brought Jawaharlal Nehru back into prison—'rooted in the same spot, with the same few individuals to see, the same limited environment, the same routine from time to time'. There is a tale, perhaps apocryphal, yet poignant, to the effect that upon being released from prison after long confinement for speeches he had made, Jawaharlal went directly to a large meeting, stood up and said quite unaffectedly, 'As I was saying …'

On 25 March 1945, Jawaharlal Nehru completed 960 days in Ahmadnagar Fort—a long chunk of one's life. 'The longest lane has a turning somewhere and so we turn to—another prison,' he wrote to Krishna. 'The release will come,' he stated elsewhere in his moralistic style, 'early or late, when the time is ripe for it. To live in expectation of it, either for those inside prison or outside, is folly.'[33] This signified his acceptance of the tyrannies of prison life as duty and obligation. Were those stretches in jail worthwhile? They were from the point of view of the masses who looked upon Nehru as a *desh-bhakt* from an early age, and who sacrificed his youth and its charms to guide the kisans and the underprivileged. Jawaharlal himself wanted to mould the future 'as it emerges from the slime and mud of the present, as a potter with his clay', and added: 'An empty conceit probably, but nevertheless good for the soul.'[34]

Jail life changed the basic parameters of Nehru's life, and there were hardly any new images or ideas to develop a new fully acceptable identity. Like everyone else who lived an existence full of abnormality in that haunted world, he viewed outside happenings as through a glass, with phantom and almost unreal figures moving hither and thither,[35] and the ghosts of the dead yesteryear rising up,

---

[33] Jawaharlal Nehru to Krishna, 19 April 1945, in *Nehru's Letters to His Sister*, p. 181.

[34] Jawaharlal Nehru to Krishna, 10 November 1942, in *Nehru's Letters to His Sister*, p. 95.

[35] 25 September 1935, *SWJN*, vol. 7, p. 26.

bringing back poignant memories.[36] He felt unsettled because of the double lives—the ordered and circumscribed existence and the free life of the spirit, with its dreams and visions, faith and desires,[37] and this thought occupied him from the time he walked up and down, five measured paces this way, and five measured paces back. Occasionally, a burst of activity took place around him, though he mostly led a life of languid ease rather than one of rush and bustle. 'Those who have had the advantage of prison experience know at least the value of patience,' he said to Betty,[38] 'and if they have profited by their experience, they have learnt adaptability, and that is a great thing.'[39] 'Life is an odd game at best and it grows odder. It serves little purpose to complain against its vagaries or to allow them to fill our minds.' The only right way to treat it 'is with a certain friendly and yet superior contempt. We can never allow ourselves to become victims of its pranks.'[40] With these soft words Krishna's wise brother counselled her to cheer up.

The spirited Jawaharlal kept good health during his first imprisonment, but he did not feel at all well in 1932, his sixth prison term, and in 1944. He had to fight the growing lethargy with yoga. One of the exercises was to stand on his head for a few minutes every day, a practice he continued until the last years of his life. Gandhi advised a close disciple with the words, 'Light the fire of yoga and consume yourself in it.'[41]Ansar Harvani (1916), who had two terms in jail with Jawaharlal, described his exercises. This is what he wrote:

> In the morning, he used to do his Yoga exercises. After that he used to have his bath. Then all of us used to have our breakfast, together. Then he used to read newspapers. Then he used to sit down and read his books and do his writing work. Then lunch. After lunch, he never had rest. After that also, he used to read and write. Then at about 5 o'clock, he used to have again a bath. Then he used to play badminton... In jail,

[36] J. Nehru, *An Autobiography*, p. 598.
[37] J. Nehru, Prison Days, *SWJN*, vol. 8, p. 877.
[38] Krishna Nehru was also affectionately called 'Betty'.
[39] To Krishna, 1 March 1934, *Nehru's Letters to His Sister*, p. 42.
[40] To Krishna, 27 December 1942, *Nehru's Letters to His Sister*, p. 101.
[41] Gandhi to Premabehn Kantak, 28 October 1940, *CWMG*, vol. LXXIII, p. 136.

he was rather a bad sportsman. Whenever he lost a point, he used to throw away his racket and shout too. After that, since electricity was not there—we used to be supplied only kerosene lamp in which it was not possible to do night reading—he used to sit down and talk to us and discuss various political, social economic problems.[42]

Being sick was like being in hell. To be really ill in jail is about the worst punishment. Illness struck Ranjit Pandit in Bareilly, 'one of the worst prisons'. While he pulled through, his wife, Vijaya Lakshmi Pandit, had to make do with the rations of the poorest quality—mixed with grit and dirt, tiny stones and even an odd spider or two thrown in for good measure.[43] Patel suffered from spastic colon; doctors diagnosed G.B. Pant (1887–1961) with giddiness of the head, pain in the spine, and double hernia; Azad lost weight. M.N. Roy was seriously ill in June and July. What troubled him was the intense heat. 'Owing to the state of my health,' he wrote on 8 August 1932, 'my daily life of late has been still more monotonous than before. So, there is very little to write in detail … I stopped the pleasant pastime of spinning three months ago, owing to illness.'[44]

Jawaharlal would not let his spirits be dampened. He dug with vigour, played with the soft earth, and watched the seedlings peep out from its surface and look with yearning towards the sun. The 'most brilliant and very lovable' Ranjit told him the names of new birds.[45] They watched the migratory flights from Mansarovar in Tibet, or the new generation of birds coming out of their nests. In Ahmadnagar Fort Prison,[46] Jawaharlal collected fine stones of all manner of

[42] Ansar Harvani, Oral History Transcript (596), NMML; and his *Before Freedom and After*.

[43] 21 April 1943, Vijaya Lakshmi Pandit, *Prison Days*, p. 115.

[44] 8 August 1932, M. N. Roy, *Fragments*, p. 31.

[45] 17 August 1942, Vijaya Lakshmi Pandit, *Prison Days*, p. 16.

[46] It is difficult to say who first had the idea of using the fort as a prison, but during the First World War the British had hidden in here detainees whose whereabouts, for a variety of reasons, had to be kept secret. The prisoners lived in blind casemates whose narrow windows just below the ceiling were now completely bricked up. The casemates gave on to an inner courtyard, fifty metres from wall to wall, with bare cracked ground and a single stunted tree with withered leaves hidden in one corner.

colours, built a museum, and planted thirty or forty kinds of seed in the otherwise bare quadrangle. If Gandhi had known, he would have shared what he had said to Mirabehn: 'Your affinity for bird, beast, trees and stone is your greatest support. They are never-failing friends and companions.'[47]

Again, in Ahmadnagar, Jawaharlal and Asaf Ali raised a garden in the quadrangle of the barracks, and spent long evenings discussing *The Discovery of India*.[48] Claiming that his appraisal would act more as soporific than stimulant,[49] Azad prophesied that Jawaharlal, having proved his mettle at the Lahore Congress in December 1929, would guide India out of the confined past into the light of a rational and wide-awake, dynamic, and fast-progressing India.[50] Yet their conflict of viewpoints, desires, and loyalties stayed. They tried finding harmony and equilibrium, and in this endeavour they succeeded. The quest was the same, in prison or outside, and Jawaharlal penned his past feelings and experiences to gain peace and psychic satisfaction.[51]

Jawaharlal's mind kept ticking. How shall we put up with ourselves in this great struggle, and what part shall we accept? Like Rosa Luxemburg, he realized that it would not do to moralize about the great elemental forces that manifested themselves in, say, a hurricane, a flood, or an eclipse of the sun. These had to be accepted as data for investigation, as subjects of study. Given his own sense of ideas and movements in history, he followed them without losing sight of the main trend, and concluded that someday India and the world may be transformed.[52] That is when he saw the stars better and the rays of the morning sun reached him sooner than they did the valleys.[53] The suspension of Non-cooperation upset him, but his faith in Gandhi was hardly ever shaken. He carried on in his usual way more than two decades later when the government put him in Gorakhpur

[47] Gandhi to Mirabehn, 21 September 1940, *CWMG*, vol. LXXIII, p. 40.

[48] 30 November 1944, G. N. S. Raghavan, *M. Asaf Ali's Memoirs*, p. 309.

[49] 14 November 1944, G. N. S. Raghavan, *M. Asaf Ali's Memoirs*, p. 307.

[50] 28 January 1944, G. N. S. Raghavan, *M. Asaf Ali's Memoirs*, p. 313.

[51] Jawaharlal Nehru, *An Autobiography*, p. 208.

[52] Waters, *Rosa Luxemburg Speaks*, p. 337.

[53] Prison Diary, 1 September 1922, *SWJN*, vol. 1, p. 334.

Jail, held the trial inside the prison, and imposed on Jawaharlal the heaviest sentence.

> Life grows harder for all of us and the soft days of the past already belong to an age that is gone. When will they return? No one knows. Or will they return? We must adapt ourselves to life as it is and not hunger for what is not. Physical risk and suffering are often all petty compared to the troubles and tempests of the mind. And whether life is soft or hard, one can always get something out of it—but to enjoy life ultimately one must decide not to count the cost.[54]

The 1942 campaign required aggression, defiance, daring, and challenge. Jawaharlal erred on this side rather than on the side of caution. He concluded that the best of works became useless and even harmful the moment satyagrahis avoided jail.[55] In those stirring times, he sent for roses to mark New Year's Eve, and went about humming 'Auld Lang Syne'. A fellow prisoner commented: 'What an Englishman he is at heart! And what a tragic irony that he should draw on himself the wrath of the British imperialists every now and again, and find himself immobilized at this crucial moment of history.'[56] In a lighter vein, Jawaharlal missed seeing women for exactly 785 days—not even from a distance. He began to wonder—what are women like? How do they look—how do they talk and sit and walk? He found answers only after the prisoners were allowed interviews after nearly two and a quarter years.

Compromise and Dissent

Politics was a chaotic and contaminated pursuit, but Gandhi moved Jawaharlal 'like a thunderbolt shaking us all, and like a flash of lightning which illumined our minds and warmed our hearts'. He brought freely into the open his amazing powers to stimulate and stir the dream of swaraj.[57] Some of this even crept into the gaol. 'Swaraj is coming!'

[54] To Krishna, 2 December 1940, *Nehru's Letters to His Sister*, p. 67.
[55] 'Agrarian Programme for the UP', in *A Nationalist Muslim and Indian Politics*, p. 106.
[56] 1 January 1943, in *M. Asaf Ali's Memoirs*, p. 312.
[57] 28 July 1930, *SWJN*, vol. 4, p. 370.

cried the ordinary convicts; they waited impatiently for it. The warders, who came in contact with the bazaar gossip, expected swaraj to
come in the near future.

Jawaharlal's devotion to Gandhi did not lead him to suppress
disagreeable facts. He admitted blemishes on his part, contested
some of his ideas, and demonstrated impatience with the suspension of Non-cooperation. Inwardly, he felt that the masses had been
betrayed. So did Rajaji, a sober voice in Congress politics. He saw
nothing but darkness all around.[58] The younger men saw Gandhi's
capitulation as an act of betrayal. Munshi Premchand (1888–1936)
felt disenchanted with political regression. The writer who had
given up his career in the provincial education service and thrown
in his lot with Gandhi and the national stir bemoaned the absence
of the spirit of the new India and the pulse of its new life. He
wrote in February 1923: 'You ask me which party I support. I do
not support either party. Because neither is at the moment doing
any effective work. The party I am a member of is that party of
the future which will devote itself to the political education of the
lower classes.'[59]

Jawaharlal was aware of the many substantial grounds, fully
present to Gandhi's sharp mind, for taking certain unpopular
decisions. He shared Gandhi's passionate quest for swaraj and
Hindu–Muslim unity, and grasped, to borrow a quote from
Vladimir Ilyich Lenin (1870–1924), that 'nothing is final; we must
learn from circumstances', and concluded that life and politics were
much too complex to be thought of in straight terms. He perceived

[58] 18 February 1922, Rajagopalachari, *Jail Diary*, p. 71.

In Yervada jail, when all the political prisoners were placed in the European yard
for a day, we told him how angry people were for his suspension of the Bardoli
campaign of total non-cooperation and civil disobedience, on the plea that there
was violence in Chauri Chaura. He quietly explained to us that, if he had not
done what he did, the whole movement would have gone on wrong lines and gone
beyond control. He confidently declared that what had been achieved in a single
year of the movement would not have been possible by normal methods of agitation for thirty years. Without doubt, the seeds of future campaigns were really
sown by the movement in 1921–2. (Morarji Desai, *The Story of My Life*, p. 111.)

[59] Premchand, *Rangbhumi*, p. viii.

the grandeur of the Gandhian revolution the very first time he went to prison. Gandhi, in turn, accepted him on the basis of the enigmatic rapport though apparently they had very little in common. The 'enigmatic relations' themselves were the logical consequence of their essentially similar feelings and ideals.[60] On 27 December 1936, Gandhi announced: 'If Jawaharlal is not in jail. It is not because he is afraid of it. He is as capable of walking into prison doors as of mounting the gallows with a smile on his lips'.[61] During Civil Disobedience, he prized Jawaharlal's loyalty,[62] and in the critical negotiations with Stafford Cripps, he wanted Jawaharlal's wishes to be ascertained at every stage.[63] He did this now and on other occasions and risked incurring the displeasure of the Congress right-wingers.

Prison and Family

Allahabad means 'City of God'. Pilgrims come from everywhere to Prayag, especially during the great Kumbh Mela, held every twelve years. And every year smaller numbers attend the Magh Mela. They plod patiently along in the heat and dust, and are serenely happy and content at the prospect of being cleansed of every vestige of sin by the holy waters. Sustained by an unwavering faith and belief, they endure the resultant miseries with repining.

Once upon a time, Allahabad hosted many families in search of 'fresh fields and pastures new'. The Kashmiri Pandits were probably the most successful of them, reaping the rewards from the seat of government, the nucleus of the university system, and, above all, the locale of the High Court. By the turn of the twentieth century, they were a close-knit community, united by their memory of the 'motherland which gave birth to the great Rishis and Munis whose blood is coursing through our veins and is sustaining us in the struggle for life'. This was so from the time Ganga Dhar, Motilal's grandfather, who had joined the

---

[60] M. N. Roy, *Men I Met*, pp. 11, 12.
[61] P. N. Chopra, *Towards Freedom*, p. 4.
[62] To Jawaharlal Nehru, 24 October 1940, CWMG, vol. LXXIII, p. 127.
[63] Horace Alexander, *Gandhi through Western Eyes* (Delhi: Asia Publishing House, 1969), p. 202.

Table 10.1   (a) Jawaharlal Nehru in Jail

	Sentence	Date of Imprisonment	Days	Place
1.	Six months	6 December 1921–3 March 1922	87	Lucknow District Jail
2.	Eighteen months	11 May 1922–31 January 1923	265	Lucknow District Jail
3.	Two years (suspended)	22 September 1923–4 October 1923	12	Nabha Jail (Nabha State)
4.	Six months	14 April 1930–11 October 1930	180	Naini Central Prison, Allahabad
5.	Two years and four months	19 October 1930–26 January 1931		
6.	Two years	26 December 1931–30 August 1933	612	
7.	Two years	12 February 1934–4 September 1935	569	
8.	Four years	31 October 1940–3 December 1941	398	Gorakhpur Prison, UP
9.	Indefinite detention	9 August 1942–15 June 1945	1040	Ahmadnagar Fort, Bombay Province
		Total	3262	(Nine years less twenty-three days)

Table 10.1   (b) The Week out of Jail

October 11

3.30 p.m. Released from Naini Central Jail.
Attended office and went round Allahabad immediately after.

October 12

8 a.m. Hoisted National Flag at Swaraj Bhawan. Issued short message to the country.
12 noon. Met Congress workers of Allahabad.
4 p.m. Taken out in procession by citizens.
7 p.m. Addressed monster public meeting.

October 13

10.15 a.m. Left for Mussoorie. Wrote long circular letters to PCCs in the train. Met workers at principal stations and delivered short speeches to the assembled crowds.

(Cont'd.)

Table 10.1 (b)   (*Cont'd.*)

October 14, 15, and 16

Spent in Mussoorie with the family; met prominent workers and deputations from various parts of the country. Issued messages to the men and women of the NWF and instructions about boycott of foreign cloth, statement on colours of the National Flag.

October 17

Left Mussoorie, addressed largely attended public meeting at Dehra Dun. Served with notice under Section 144 after his speech. Met workers of Dehra Dun. Left by the evening train.

October 18

Received municipal address at Lucknow. Met workers. Notice under Section 144 issued but not served. Left by car for Allahabad, meeting workers at Rae Bareli and Pratapgarh.

October 19

Addressed office and issued appeal to the public and mill owners for boycott of foreign cloth. Notice under Section 144 served. Presided at District Volunteers Conference. Received Pandit Motilal Nehru and family at Prayag Station at 5.30 p.m., attended meeting at Purshottamdas Park at 7 p.m., arrested under Section 124-A on his way from the meeting to Anand Bhawan.

Jawaharlal made the following statement to a press representative immediately after his release on October 11: 'I am very much alive and kicking. I hope to do my little bit to hasten the dissolution of the British Empire and take part in its final obsequies.'[64]

East India Company in Delhi. Adversities such as the 1857 revolt could have weakened family ties, but Ganga Dhar did not let that happen. He moved from Delhi and settled in Agra. After him, Nand Lal assumed family responsibilities. He was the one who brought up Motilal. And between the two, there 'grew up a knot of affection, a happy blend of the filial and the fraternal, of which the Hindu joint family, with all its faults, furnishes probably the best example.'[65]

Bansi Dhar, son of Ganga Dhar, went abroad and returned to India in 1895. Motilal travelled four years later. Like his predecessors, he set great

---

[64]   File no. 17, 1930, part 1, AICC Papers.

[65]   B. R. Nanda, *Gokhale, Gandhi and the Nehrus: Studies in Indian Nationalism* (London: Allen & Unwin, 1974), p. 86.

store by education, projecting himself as the bearer of learning, taking pride in their love of literature, art, and music, and drawing comfort from their healthy attitude to life, their exquisite code of manners, and their delightful sense of fun. The Nehrus ate well, 'being better at appreciating whenever possible the good things of this life than at accumulating merit for another.'[66] One of them indicated this awareness of being special. 'We were Kashmiris whereas everyone else was "they".' The Nehrus grew up guided by this unwritten code of behaviour.

At the age of 26, Motilal headed an extended family, which he saw as an integrated entity and wanted each one of them to be 'universally loved and respected'. He was generous towards them and attended to their needs. He regarded Ladli Prasad Zutshi as one of his own children, arranged his marriage, and incorporated his nephew's family into the larger extended family. Any form of success brought a smile on his face. 'What single family in India can boast of such a galaxy of intellect among its scions as the Nehru family?' he wrote triumphantly. 'Why, we should conquer the world with these and other descendants who I am sure will go on adding fresh lustre to the family name as years go by?'[67] When Manmohini was arrested in 1930, he was happy that three generations of his family were then in jail.

Motilal expected Indu (Indira) to grow up to be a Nehru worthy of the name. She was young and intelligent. In 1942, she and her husband Feroze Gandhi (1912–1960), 'a stocky, fair young man', organized a demonstration in Allahabad. For this they were put in Naini Prison. Indira shared prison life with her aunt Vijaya Lakshmi Pandit from 11 September 1942 to 13 May 1943. 'We were all one family

[66] 'A domestic event, however, just then absorbed my attention. This was the birth of a little sister. I had long nourished a secret grievance at not having brothers or sisters when everybody seemed to have them, and the prospect of having a baby brother or sister all to myself was exhilarating. Father was then in Europe. I remember waiting anxiously for the event. One of the doctors came and told me of it and added, presumably as a joke, that I must be glad that it was not a boy, who would have taken a share in my patrimony. I felt bitter and angry at the thought that anyone should imagine that I could harbour such a vile notion' (Jawaharlal Nehru, *Before Freedom: Letters to His Sister*, edited by Nayantara Sahgal, New Delhi: HarperCollins, 2000, p. 10).

[67] Motilal to Bansi Dhar, 9 October 1912, *SWMN*, vol. 1, p. 175.

living together in the manner of those days,' Vijaya Lakshmi Pandit boasted. An illustration of the strong *biradari* solidarity is the feast at Anand Bhawan (Abode of Happiness), on the occasion of her brother's marriage to Kamala Kaul (1899–1936) on 8 February 1916. A judge of the Allahabad High Court had built this house; Motilal had purchased it in 1900.

> In accordance with custom, after the return of the *barat*, the entire Kashmiri *biradari* (and nobody else) had to be invited to dinner. It did not matter whether the host knew or did not know the invitees and it did not matter whether the guest was rich or poor, educated or uneducated, good or bad; he had obligatorily to be invited. Separate invitations were not sent out to individuals; the guest list, which only contained the names of the heads of families, was sent around to each of them, it being understood that the invitation was meant for all the members of the family including children. The list was written in Urdu and the manner of acceptance was to write the Arabic letter *swad* against the name of the invitee. What this letter meant I do not know but it illustrates the extent of Islamic influence on the Kashmiri community. One of the guests who used to be invited to these community feasts was a well-known drunk, Bishambar Nath Aga, who came presenting a pitiable sight, for his clothes were tattered and dirty, his face unshaven and he himself unwashed. He belonged to a very respectable family but had become so uncontrollable an alcoholic that there was no point in giving him any money or trying to help him in any other way. Nevertheless, such was the solidarity of the community that he was never excluded from any community function. All that happened was that he used himself to sit down at the far end of the *saf* (row).[68]

The group identity of the Kashmiri Pandits, though fractured over time, survived in large measure.[69] When the young were lodged in prison, their elders wrote letters to them which were full of good cheer, affection, and optimism. Jawaharlal, in particular, comforted the

[68] Mushirul Hasan, *The Nehrus: Personal Histories* (London: Mercury Books, 2006), p. 18.

[69] Hutheesing, *Nehru's Letters to His Sister*, p. 11.

women.[70] Family and its traditions mattered to him a great deal. Thus he selected the name of Rajivratna, his grandson, from lists that were sent to him for approval at the Naini Central Prison.[71] He mentioned to Indira Priyadarshini (as Jawaharlal called his daughter):

> To some extent you cannot get rid of the family tradition, for it will pursue you and, whether you want to or not, it will give you a certain public position which you have done nothing to deserve. This is unfortunate but you will have to put up with it. After all, it is not a bad thing to have a good family tradition. It helps looking up, it reminds us that we have to keep a torch burning and that we cannot cheapen ourselves or vulgarize ourselves.... If your grandfather's example strengthens and inspires you in any way, that is your good fortune. If your feelings towards your father or mother also help you in that way, well and good.[72]

The Nehrus had been a trifle arrogant. But, as B. K. Nehru mentioned: 'We have much to be arrogant about!' Indeed, the Kashmiri Pandits claimed to have shaped both Allahabad's social and cultural landscape and its cross-communal tradition.[73] At the same time, there were other individuals and groups who represented the aspirations of Allahabadis. They represented a variety of interests and acted in public life accordingly. Similarly, views on nationalism changed from time to time, although local publicists took advantage of any national issue to advance their cause. The combination thus achieved brought about certain general or specific changes in the political temper.

Harivansh Rai Bachchan, the eminent Hindi poet, recalled Malaviya walking from Bharati Bhawan to the Home Rule League office, with thousands following behind. He also recounted the grief caused by Tilak's death, as also the feeling of pride that he too, a boy of thirteen, put his shoulder to the bier alongside the others. When

---

[70] Hutheesing, *Nehru's Letters to His Sister*, p. 13.
[71] In Sanskrit, Rajiv means lotus, as does Kamala, the name of Jawaharlal's wife. Ratna means 'jewel', one of the meanings of Jawahar.
[72] Hasan, *The Nehrus*, p. 19.
[73] 'Short History of My Family' by Motilal Nehru, and 'Welcome Address to Maharaja of Kashmir', *SWMN*, vol. 1, pp. 240–1; Sender, *Kashmiri Pandits*, p. 263.

he came back from the committal ceremony, he felt as if he was back from a pilgrimage. Bachchan had seen Gandhi and the Ali brothers take their seats on the dais, 'a meagre Sudama between mighty Arjuna and Bhima!' Everyone was astonished that such an emaciated frame of bones could challenge the British Empire. He left the impress of 'fearless self-confidence, hope and a thirst for action' on their faces. More and more people wore homespun and 'Gandhi topis'; some students gave up their studies, some lawyers their practice, and some government servants their jobs. News spread of local families joining them. They echoed whatever Gandhi said; then news of miracles began to spread—Gandhi was seen speaking simultaneously in several places or cotton had been found growing on neem trees, and the public believed in such rumours.[74]

The excitement at Anand Bhawan inspired Hari (d. 1961), a Dalit boy. He appeared before the English magistrate who asked him his age. Hari did not know what to say. But this much he knew: 'I had started shaving daily when Panditji [Jawaharlal] returned from college in England.' His freedom was taken away for a year. When it was restored, the Nehrus awaited his return. At last a *tonga* clattered into the portico and an unrecognizable roly-poly form bounced out of it. The spare, sprite-like little man had disappeared and in his place emerged a prosperous-looking substitute. During his enforced idleness, Hari had gained two stones which he was destined not to lose. Prison had proved a happy holiday for him. His rotundity became a joke and all the other servants in the Nehru household declared that they too, wanted to spend a few months in jail if such was the result of martyrdom![75]

There was, in fact, no mistaking the euphoria at Anand Bhawan, 'the steadfast symbol it had been before, defiantly flaunting the tricolour and defying defeat.'[76] Motilal had already set the course for political

[74] Harivansh Rai Bachchan, *In the Afternoon of Time* (New Delhi: Penguin Books, 1998), pp. 91–2.

[75] Sahgal, *Prison and Chocolate Cake*, p. 88; Seton, *Panditji*, p. 113.

[76] On 27 March 1930, Motilal gifted Anand Bhawan (thereafter named Swaraj Bhawan or Abode of Freedom) to the nation. Intimately connected with the freedom struggle, within its walls great events occurred. They flaunted their patriotism by flying the Congress flag: a saffron band for Hinduism and a green band for Islam, divided by a spinning wheel representing cottage industry on a white middle band representing unity.

activism: he chaired the first Provincial Conference of the United Provinces on 29 March 1907, attended the Congress at Allahabad in 1910, and seconded a resolution proposed to William Wedderburn (1838–1918), Scottish civil servant and President. In September 1918, he mooted the idea of starting a newspaper and talked of securing a truly nationalist tone and policy. He translated this idea into practice after the Jallianwala Bagh incident. Sensitized to imperial arrogance, he was horrified by the government casting aside the chance of friendship with the Moderates with whom it had quite a bit in common, and applauded Gandhi for pleading with the men in power to be worthy of themselves. The Leader was premised on the principle that 'the duty of those who honestly profess contrary views is for each party to instruct the public in its own propaganda and leave the rest to the inexorable law of nature—the survival of the fittest'.[77]

Motilal led the Swarajists in the Central Legislative Assembly. In 1924, he earned many accolades for suggesting a Round Table Conference to draw up India's new constitution. In August 1928, he drafted the Nehru Report that embodied Congress' quest for swaraj. This was a far cry from the previous decade when the senior Nehru had tried restraining his son from adopting an extreme course and, a year later, had exhorted him not to precipitate a crisis in the family and in professional work. But Motilal changed his political course. Soon, he and his son shared a 'horribly uncomfortable' cell—about 11 square feet. In their combined pursuit of nationalist goals, they radiated an aura of optimism, energy, and adventure that remained undiminished in the dreary monotony and harshness of jails. Motilal remained his cool, calm, and collected self.

Life in prison turned out to be an important and touching period of mutual discovery for father and son. They understood each other's point of view in a manner that the demands of a busy public life had made difficult earlier.[78] While Motilal suffered the pangs of separation after completing the formalities of his son's admission to Harrow, he expected his son to play a large part in human affairs. He arranged everything accordingly. Once, after returning from a long trip in Europe, he told Jawaharlal that he had sown the seed of his future

[77] Motilal to Bhagwan Das, 1 November 1918, SWMN, vol. 1, p. 182.
[78] Ravinder Kumar, 'Introduction', SWMN, vol. 1, p. 39.

greatness, and that he did not have a shadow of a doubt that he had a great career ahead of him. His instincts were based on the confidence that for an aristocratic family like his all things were possible. Like a true patriarch, he wrote on 20 October 1905:

> You must bear in mind that in you we are leaving the dearest treasure we have in this world and perhaps in other worlds to come.... It is not a question of providing for you as I can do that perhaps in one single year's income. It is a question of making a real man of you which you are bound to be. It would have been extremely selfish—I should say sinful—to keep you with us and leave you a fortune in gold with little or no education. I think I can without vanity say that I am the founder of the fortunes of the family. I look upon you, my dear son, as the man who will build upon the foundations I have laid and have the satisfaction of seeing a noble structure of renown rearing up its head to the skies.[79]

The son reciprocated in various ways. What was Motilal's greatest quality? Gandhi replied: 'Love of his son.' 'Was it not love of India?' the Mahatma was asked. 'No,' he replied, 'Motilal's love for India was derived from his love for Jawaharlal.'[80] He nursed his father in jail, washed his clothes, and swept and dusted the gaol barracks. Motilal was impressed. 'Hari (my personal servant) could well take a leaf out of Jawaharlal's book in the matter of serving me. From early morning tea to the time I retire for the night, I find everything I need in its proper place ... anticipates everything and leaves nothing for me to do. I wish there were many fathers to boast of such sons.'[81]

Motilal was released on 11 September 1930, and motored to Radha Swami Santholia's house, on the banks of the Hooghly, very close to the temple of Kali at Dakshineshwar. Charles Tegart, a police officer who had initially refused to let Jawaharlal visit Calcutta, relented after a while.[82] Motilal died on 6 July 1931 and was cremated on a pyre of

[79] Mushirul Hasan, *The Nehrus: Personal Histories* (London: Mercury Books, 2006).

[80] B. R. Nanda, *The Nehrus*, p. 343.

[81] B. R. Nanda, *The Nehrus*, p. 39.

[82] Even if Jawaharlal had given an undertaking, he would not have been allowed to carry it out by the local leaders who would drag him back into politics (Home Dept, Political, file no. 32 [III], 1931).

sandalwood. Gandhi gave an inspiring funeral oration. His soothing and healing presence saw the Nehrus through their ordeal. Women did not normally attend funerals, but Motilal's widow, silent, dry-eyed, and courageous, turned up at the cremation.

Quite early in life, the young Jawaharlal cherished a steadfast affection for his parents, and judged his father, in particular, as a tower of strength. Wondering if he had repaid his love and care, he felt ashamed at his record. On his *barsi* he mentioned, 'Almost all my latest memories of him are jail memories, and being again in prison my mind goes back to him again.'[83] His loss made it difficult for him to settle down as easily as he had done in the past. The historian Ravinder Kumar, summed it up well:

> The bond of affection between Motilal and Jawaharlal was characterised by a blend of admiration, esteem and regard on the part of Jawaharlal; and a deeply tempered love, parental and solicitous, on the part of Motilal. Yet in the texture of his personality, no less than in the cast of his features, the young Jawaharlal drew much upon his mother as he drew upon his father. Particularly did Jawaharlal inherit his sensitive eyes, the eyes of a Hamlet, introspective and soulful, searching and questioning, from the gentle Swarup Rani, who in a quiet and unobtrusive manner, filled the Nehru household with the warm presence of a devoted wife and a loving mother.[84]

The Nehru Women

'Causes save one,' a woman told Gretta Cousins. This was particularly true of many women, whose line of least resistance was self-sacrifice. They did not naturally move towards fighting for their own freedom, but achieved empowerment through throwing themselves into a 'cause'. The cause, however, had to be related to the attainment of some aspect of progress or emancipation.[85] Once in prison, they turned it 'into a temple and the way thereto into a path of pilgrimage.'[86] Motilal

---

[83] 25 February 1931, *SWJN*, vol. 5, p. 361.
[84] Kumar, 'Introduction', *SWMN*, vol. 1, p. 5.
[85] Cousins, *Indian Womanhood Today*, p. 58.
[86] Cousins, *Indian Womanhood Today*, p. 71.

saw the energy, courage, and ability women displayed; of the girls of his own household he spoke with affectionate pride. The author Edward Thompson told Jawaharlal: 'You Nehrus have been very, very lucky in many ways, and lucky most of all in your charming and splendid women.'

One day, the Nehrus were enjoying a rich dark cake, chocolate through and through, with chocolate swirls on top. Just then, policemen arrived to arrest Motilal. The family kissed him good-bye and watched him leave, talking cheerfully to the policemen. They ate their chocolate cake and, in the infant minds, prison became in a mysterious way associated with chocolate cake.[87] Where there were no cakes, people made do with garlands and carried the prisongoer to jail amidst shouts of 'Jai'.[88] When so many armed men came to arrest Vijaya Lakshmi Pandit, her daughter Chandralekha said they would be fighting the British outside while she was in. The mother saw before herself 'a new Lekha with a new purpose in her eyes ...'[89] She described her daughter's arrest in *Prison Days*.

> The story of her [Lekha's] arrest is the usual comic opera affair—police, armed guards, CID men and the usual paraphernalia went to Anand Bhawan about 9 p.m. yesterday. The girls had gone out with friends to a picnic at Ram Bagh. The Inspector asked for Lekha and was informed that she was out. They waited and meanwhile produced a warrant for the search of her room. When this was over and nothing incriminating found, Lekha was still not back so they went away. This morning the arrest took place at 8 o'clock. Lekha informs us that although she was seething with excitement, she was determined to appear casual and actually ate an extra piece of toast for breakfast just to make the police wait and show them that she regarded this event as of no special importance! Obviously an attempt to imitate Mamaji (Jawaharlal).[90]

Once in jail, Chandralekha and her mother read George Bernard Shaw (1856–1950) and a comedy, *Drawing Room*, by Thomas Browne

---

[87] N. Sahgal, *Prison and Chocolate Cake*, p. 34.

[88] He was sentenced to a year's imprisonment and a fine of rupees one hundred by Fategarh's district magistrate (Bhargava, *Ganesh Shankar Vidyarthi*, pp. 65–6).

[89] 30 August 1947, *Prison Days*, p. 49.

[90] Vijaya Lakshmi Pandit, *Prison Days*, p. 53.

(1605–82) that depicted some things strikingly similar to those in their own family, and they had a good many laughs over it.

Seeing themselves as people of their times,[91] women courted arrest voluntarily, accepted imprisonment gladly, and treated jailgoing as a gala occasion, not a sombre one. Their lives were accompanied by a great deal of laughter and mutual back-slapping. Jailgoers were no silent sufferers but pilgrims armed with the song 'Raghupati Raghava Raja Ram'. Even though jail's dreary monotony and harshness played havoc with their health, they did not give up. Thus, when Jawaharlal and Sadiq Ali (1910–2001), a Bihar politician, broke the salt law, Nehru's wife, Kamala, and his sister, Krishna, joined the first batch of satyagrahis. Krishna, who lived in Bombay, recalled:

> The streets were crowded and thousands turned up to see the salt being made. I have seldom seen such enormous crowds. It is believed that there were 20 thousand people or even more. For miles you could see nothing but heads of the thousands there. On the way the procession was stopped every now and then and people came and garlanded us and put *tika* and *chandan* on our foreheads.[92]

'Across the landscape of this moving family,' Sarojini Naidu remarked, 'fall the brighter lights and the half lights, the dimmer and the deepest shadows inseparable from human destiny.'[93]

Vijaya Lakshmi Pandit had three rounds of imprisonment, the last when she waited in the dead of night to be taken away. Three cheers for jail, Bhai (Jawaharlal) complimented her. He thought prison was the best of universities, if only one knew how to take its courses. Vijaya Lakshmi Pandit thought otherwise. While she adjusted nicely to jail routine in 1932, she felt numb a decade later, as if the power to feel or think had gone. The stifling heat and mosquitoes added to her woes, while the ants got into the sugar and the cat drank the milk. She and

[91] Nayantara Sahgal, *Jawaharlal Nehru: Civilizing a Savage World* (New Delhi: Viking, 2010), p. 3.

[92] Krishna Jawaharlal to Deen Dayal Bhargava, 13 April 1930, file no. 176, Misc., AICC Papers.

[93] 'Foreword', Krishna Hutheesing, *With No Regrets* (Bombay: Oxford University Press, 1952), p. vii.

others were deprived of sleep because they were counted every fifteen minutes throughout the night. She was frustrated with the brief and infrequent meetings with Ranjit, who was in the same jail growing nasturtiums. He was a man of learning and fastidious scholarship, and a lover of art.[94] Vijaya Lakshmi Pandit missed Rita's birthday for the third time, and this one was her thirteenth. At such times she felt torn between her duty to the children on the one hand and that of serving the country on the other. At the end of 1942 she wondered: 'What does 1943 hold for us…. More sorrow and suffering, or a glimpse of the promised land?'[95] It was better for her not to look to dates or count days.[96] 'We are an abnormal family,' wrote Jawaharlal, 'or rather force of circumstances has made us lead rather abnormal lives, and the emphasis of these lives is more and more cherished, though it is hidden from the public gaze.'[97]

Indira Priyadarshini

One missed many things in prison, but perhaps most of all Jawaharlal missed Indu, which means 'moon', or 'Indira', and longed to see her. His life's greatest joy was to communicate with her, whether face to face or by letter.[98] He wrote his first letter to her on her thirteenth birthday, offering 'the air and the mind and spirit, such as a good fairy might have bestowed on you—things that even the high walls of prison cannot stop'. He ended up composing 176 letters, running into 1849 foolscap pages, to Indu alone. 'What a mountain of letters I have written! And what a lot of good *swadeshi* ink I have spread out on *swadeshi* paper!'[99] He pinned the pages and put them neatly in a stack, not knowing when Indu would read them.

Born to a world of 'storm and trouble',[100] Indira was lonesome without her father. This could have made her shy, reticent,

94 3 May 1943, *Prison Days*, pp. 119–20.
95 21 December 1942, *Prison Days*, p. 105.
96 25 August 1942, *Prison Days*, p. 41.
97 22 April 1938, *Nehru's Letters to His Sister*, p. 55.
98 Lamb, *Nehrus of India*, p. 112.
99 *SWJN*, vol. 5, p. 494.
100 Katherine Frank, *Indira: The Life of Indira Nehru Gandhi* (Delhi: HarperCollins, 2001), p. 14.

and glum in her youth, and could have led her to see life in a solemn perspective, 'cast in an austere mould, shorn of lightness, as if lightness were a weakness, a trap to be avoided'.[101] And yet, she vigorously protested when the local police raided Anand Bhawan ostensibly to collect the money for various fines levied on Motilal and Jawaharlal. Reading about Joan of Arc by night, she lectured the servants by day and, in between, founded the Monkey Army to carry messages in and out of jail. She was even seen drilling the children's *vanar sena* (children's 'army'). She returned an embroidered frock that her aunt had brought from Paris, and set fire to a 'foreign doll'. The strong patriotic fervour did not leave her.

At first, she ignored the tumult around her, but too many things were happening—political visitors storming in, protest rallies, and arrests. In December 1929, she read the Purna Swaraj Resolution at Lahore, and felt part of the excitement. Her father's speech itself unfolded a great picture of nationalism spreading over India and Asia. He inherited the doctrine which some of his predecessors had preached, that the formation of large aggregates was in the interest of India's stability. On 20 September 1932, Indira held prayers when Gandhi fasted. She had a taste of prison life as well. 'My inside is steadily getting tougher. And I think I can honestly thank whatever gods may be for my unconquerable soul.' She talked of a 'lovely dream ... walking on a broad path'.

I had a feeling that it was suspended in the air although there was nothing to show it positively. And in a perfect circle all around—far away as if there was no obstacle to prevent me seeing the whole horizon at the same time—there was a chain of mountains. All sorts of mountains: high towering into the sky besides smaller ones, ragged and smooth, snow covered and bare. And on a single peak in front of me there was a dazzlingly beautiful light. It seemed like a spotlight from above although the sky was pitch dark, neither sun, nor moon, nor stars. It was awe-inspiring. I was looking at it and walking on and on when the road became narrow and covered with deep snow like a mountain pass. I woke up feeling exhilarated and fresh, as if I had been to the Mont Blanc or the Matterhorn at least.[102]

[101] Nayantara Sahgal quoted in *Mother India*.
[102] Hasan, *The Nehrus*, p. 228.

In jail, Indira made merry on Vasanta Panchami and Holi, and wore a new sari on Nauroz.[103] She and Chandralekha saved up their rations to host a party in the 'Blue Drawing Room'—a section of the prison barracks so named by them because of the blue rug placed at the centre which Vijaya Lakshmi Pandit had brought with her from Anand Bhawan. They could not decide whether to write the menu in French or not. After lock-up, they read plays; Nan looked on and listened. They even held a party to celebrate Indira's birthday on 19 November 1942. When they were unexpectedly liberated on 13 May 1943, they felt as if they were coming out of a dark passage. Indira shed a few tears of excitement. She was growing to be a Nehru worthy of the name.[104] She possessed exceptional courage and initiative, and the family support stood her in good stead when she confronted a turbulent world.

It had not been the same with Feroze Gandhi, Indira's fellow prisoner. The two spent a few days at a hill station near Bombay. Jawaharlal thought well of him, entrusted him with family and other errands, and commended his dynamism in running *The National Herald*. After Independence, the voters of Pratapgarh and Rae Bareli elected him to the first Lok Sabha. He died prematurely on 8 September 1960. By this time, he had separated from his wife. Thereafter, she played in Jawaharlal's life the role that Kamala had played with such endurance and dignity. She had amazing stamina and staying power. Like Kamala who faced police lathis without batting an eyelid, she faced her adversaries on their own turf. Indira dealt with the 'Syndicate' decisively with the help of her advisers, and her two sons, Sanjay and Rajiv, gave her strength.

Mother Kamala

Kamala Kaul bore the burden of running the house without forging a close bond with the jewel of the Nehru clan. In Anand Bhawan, sisters and close relatives encircled Jawaharlal. Kamala found it hard to cope with their sophisticated lifestyle, especially that of the

[103] 'To Darling Papu' (from Naini Central Jail), 19 April 1943, in *Two Alone, Two Together*, edited by Sonia Gandhi (New Delhi: Penguin Books India, 2004), p. 355.
[104] S. Gandhi, *Two Alone, Two Together*, p. 17.

sisters-in-law who were intelligent, articulate, and brimming with confidence. She was no pushover, though: she was bright and beautiful and her grandfather, Pandit Kishan Lall Atal, had been adviser to the royal families of Jaipur, Jodhpur, and Rewa. On her own, however, she did not know much about social niceties and worldly ways, and had no incentive to learn more. This may well explain why she suffered silently at the hands of the 'acid-tongued' Vijaya Lakshmi Pandit.[105] Indira, born twenty months after Jawaharlal and Kamala married, fought for and quarrelled for her mother with others.[106] Sadly, Kamala suffered from pulmonary tuberculosis and other ailments on and off for more than a decade. For this she had to spend over a year at Montana in Switzerland, a well-known town along with Davos and Leysin that specialized in treating pulmonary tuberculosis patients. Yet Kamala met her domestic responsibilities stoically and spent over three weeks in jail from 1 January to 26 January 1931. She parted with her jewellery. The family silver also went. Jawaharlal had no regrets, for he would have been familiar with Gandhi's view that 'man falls from the pursuit of the ideal of plain living and high thinking the moment he wants to multiply his daily needs.'[107]

Kamala's health deteriorated in September 1934. The doctor felt that her husband's presence would cheer her up during the last few months of her life.[108] There was something inhuman in the situation which kept a political prisoner who had not committed an act of violence, only a very short distance away from his dying wife, without providing any opportunity of seeing her or being with her.[109] Andrews tried in vain to secure Jawaharlal's unconditional release. But the Viceroy was told: 'I have known him [Andrews] now for 22 years and can hardly remember a time when he was not putting forward some more or less emotional proposition for a gesture, promising that if it were made the most astonishing results would

---

[105] Gupte, *Mother India*, pp. 129–31.

[106] Gupte, *Mother India*, p. 131.

[107] *Harijan*, 1 January 1940, *CWMG*, vol. LXXIII, p. 94.

[108] Jivraj Mehta to Home Member, 20 September 1934, Home Dept, Political, file no. 38/7, 1934.

[109] Andrews to Hallet, 21 September 1934, Home Dept, Political, file no. 38/7, 1934.

follow. His advice has once or twice been accepted, but the results have never been realized.'

Rajani Palme Dutt (1896–1974), the Marxist intellectual, and Jawaharlal met each other in 1907 as members of the Cambridge Majlis. They met yet again in 1936 in a sanatorium in Lausanne, the second largest city on Lake Geneva. Kamala was a 'wonderful woman', who gave Jawaharlal much of his inspiration and breadth of outlook'.[110] She died on 28 February 1936. In 1962, a plaque was put outside the house where she stayed. Jawaharlal relived the feelings he had endured previously, and was sadly surprised at their continued sharpness. He lamented that two long prison terms of two years each had come between them just when their need for each other was the greatest, just when they had come so near each other. He dedicated his autobiography, then in a London press, to her. He stopped working for a time, and only returned to the book when the necessity arose.

In sum, the family as a unit fulfilled Jawaharlal's psychological needs. The birth of a new member (Rajiv Gandhi, his first grandson) reminded him of his childhood days and other births. The growth of the little ones was 'an unending panorama of human life with its sweet and bitterness, its ups and downs'.[111] Always caring with a soft heart and gentle mind, prison made him value more deeply his parents, his daughter, his sisters, and others in the extended family.[112] He listened to them and respected their views instead of brushing them aside, and paid attention to their hardships. The plight of his mother, in particular, saddened him. She had to adapt to a new mode of living, one of simplicity and thrift, but she did so without any sign of distress or reluctance.[113] Nehru could not imagine his frail old mother beaten repeatedly with heavy canes by the police, bleeding on the dusty road. He could not tolerate an affront or an insult to her in the lock-up. Towards the end of August 1933 he stayed by her bedside until her recovery.

[110]   Rajani Palme Dutt, Oral History Transcript (141), NMML.

[111]   To Krishna, 29 August 1944, *Nehru's Letters to His Sister*, p. 162.

[112]   Judith M. Brown, *Nehru: A Political Life* (New Delhi: Oxford University Press, 2003), p. 110.

[113]   Hutheesing, *Nehru's Letters to His Sister*, p. 17.

'You are a brave little darling,' Motilal told Vijayalakshmi Pandit. 'I was remarking last night at the dinner table that you alone of my children have inherited my spirit.' It was this fusion of professional commitment and family pride that he bequeathed to his children. Jawaharlal had, in fact, great affection for his self-willed and proud sister. She reciprocated on Bhaiya Duj, 19 November 1942, with the remark: 'Out of the many good things fate gave me at my birth, one of the best was surely my brother. To have known and loved him and been so near to him would have been ample justification for having been born.'[114] Similarly, Jawaharlal treated Krishna more like his daughter. On her birthday on 19 October 1930, he asked her to buy books, 'the belated but loving gift of a somewhat absent-minded brother who thinks often of his little sister'. Out of the books, he wanted her to construct 'a magic city full of dream castles and flowering gardens and running brooks where beauty and happiness dwell ...'[115] Later, when it came to dividing Motilal's property, Jawaharlal assured her that she had as much right, indeed more, to the property as he did.[116] In his eloquent Will, he recorded: 'In the course of a life which has had its share of trial and difficulty, the love and tender care for me of both my sisters ... has been of the greatest solace to me.' Krishna, in turn, looked up to her brother, and admired and respected him. The bond between them grew with the years.[117]

Friends in Chains

It was odd and sometimes irritating that a mixed group of prisoners were herded together. At the same time, Jawaharlal was pleased with the opportunity of getting to know them better in the close companionship of prison. He pointed out: 'Often we appreciate others the more, in spite of the obvious differences, for which each tries to fit in with the others.'[118] Singularly alike, it did not make much difference to Jawaharlal what the shape and colour were of the prison walls

[114] 10 November 1942, *Prison Days*, p. 91.
[115] November 1930, *SWJN*, vol. 4, p. 422.
[116] To Krishna, October 1931, *Nehru's Letters to His Sister*, p. 17.
[117] Hutheesing, 'Introduction', *Nehru's Letters to His Sister*, p. 8.
[118] 3 October 1942, *Nehru's Letters to His Sister*, p. 91.

that enclosed him.[119] What made the difference, nonetheless, was the separation of friends from the Ahmadnagar Fort.[120] Oscar Wilde was ashamed of his friendships, Jawaharlal was proud of them. Edward Thompson, the historian, noticed that he had time to maintain his personal relationships.[121]

An official wrote of a largish collection of literature mostly addressed to Jawaharlal and suggested forwarding of the stuff to the addresses, except in individual cases where the book or magazine concerned was objectionable.[122] Letters and books came from friends who shared Jawaharlal's dreams, or from those who followed him to the public platform and the prison. Young lawyers, barristers, pleaders, and university teachers also wrote to him. Despite being averse to the idea of persons of varying habits and tastes being herded together, the Nehrus made a fairly decent family strictly regulated by the code of *varnashrama*.[123]

The Nehrus revered Tagore. Jawaharlal met him in 1921, and Indira, at her father's suggestion, spent time at Santiniketan. Politically, they had very little in common, but Tagore was the nation's pride, and the symbol of its reawakening. He did not go to jail but renounced the knighthood after the bloodbath at Jallianwala Bagh. People loved him before, but now they adored him, and his melodious tunes haunted them for many nights and days.[124] After receiving the news of Tagore's death, Jawaharlal, in the solitude of the Dehra Dun Jail, remarked how his ideas and attitudes strengthened an emotional bond between them.[125] After Independence, during a debate in the Lok Sabha over the linguistic reorganization of states, Nehru argued against monolingualism (and the homogeneity of culture it engenders). He told the

[119] To Nan, 13 March 1945, *Nehru's Letters to His Sister*, p. 363.
[120] Azad was in Bankura (Bengal), Asaf Ali in Gurdaspur Jail in Punjab, Acharya Kripalani was sent to Karachi Jail, and Vallabhbhai to Yervada.
[121] E. P. Thompson, Oral History Transcript (689), NMML.
[122] Home Dept, Political (1), file no. 156.
[123] *SWJN*, vol. 3, p. 21; Iyenger and Zackariah, *Together They Fought*, p. 175.
[124] S. Mazumdar, *Memoirs of an Indian Woman*, p. 169.
[125] Jawaharlal Nehru, 'Introduction', *Rabindranath Tagore: A Centenary Volume, 1861–1961* (New Delhi: Sahitya Academy, 1961), pp. xiii to xvi.

House that he had sent his daughter, Indira, to Santiniketan so that she could imbibe the culture of Bengal. But it is in his tribute to Tagore on his birth centenary at Visva-Bharati that one gets a sense of the reasons that led Jawaharlal to have Indira educated at Santiniketan. The institution built by Tagore, or Gurudev, exemplified the values that he himself held dearly: the confluence of nationalism and international-ism, tradition and modernity, the importance of developing the spirit over sheer material gains, the necessity of breaking down the narrow barriers of caste, race, and creed. 'I have a fear,' he said, 'that in this year of Gurudev's birth centenary his message and ideals might be swept away in the flood of words and eloquence and that we may imagine that we have done our duty by him. That is a dangerous delusion which comes over us often. I should like you specially here at Santiniketan and the Visva-Bharati to remember that the test of your homage is not what you may say about him but the way you live, the way you grow, and the way you act up to his message.'

In 1937, Tagore pleaded for changing the mindset to move to a new era of the Hindu–Muslim relationship. He noted: 'In the manner in which Europe emerged from the Middle Ages and entered the modern era through the pursuit of truth and by expanding the frontiers of knowledge, Hindus and Muslims will have to venture forth from the walls hemming them in.'[126] Tagore tried to balance the affirmation of separate identities and a sense of the universal human community, and, using his extraordinary imagination and breadth of vision, he sought to identify areas of East–West cooperation.

Like Tagore, Maulana Abul Kalam Azad embodied the synthesis of cultures: the Persian, Arabic, and Indian. He personified dignity, self-respect, and restraint,[127] as opposed to the prevalent violence and vulgar self-assertiveness, and unctuous and odious self-righ-teousness. Azad and Jawaharlal were in many ways as unlike each other as two men can be, but they were alike in their belief in times past, and in their capacity to inspire. They resembled each other in

[126] Fakrul Alam and Radha Chakravarty (eds), *The Essential Tagore* (Cambridge, MA: Belknap and Harvard University Press, 2011), p. 182.

[127] To Nan, 9 April 1943, *Before Freedom, 1909–1947: Nehru's Letters to His Sister*, edited by Nayantara Sahgal (New Delhi: Roli Books, 2004), p. 319.

the bridges they built between religions and cultures, and spoke of intermixing through marriage, migration, and settlement. Their writings offer us a glimpse into an entirely new world, which opens to us endless points of view, and which wing our spirit for bold flights into unexplored regions. Most of all, they shared each other's exuberant inclusiveness. Meeting a person like Azad succeeded in rubbing off most of Jawaharlal's rough edges. Jawaharlal mourned Azad's death not simply as the passing away of a man, but the passing away of an age, characterized by a certain grace, tolerance, patience, and courtesy, which he felt was dissipating fast. In a warm remembrance speech in the Lok Sabha, the Prime Minister compared Azad to the 'great men of the Renaissance' or the 'Encyclopaedists who preceded the French Revolution'.

From *The Golden Threshold*

The Golden Threshold, Sarojini Naidu's home in Hyderabad, was a spacious bungalow with a walled-in compound. Like Anand Bhawan, it had a lovely garden with fully grown trees. On 11 May 1925, Sarojini Naidu shared with Jawaharlal the pleasure of the sun-birds and honeybirds making music in the garden among the flowering gulmohars and scarlet roses.[128] She attracted and inspired other strong and independent minds, who turned the house into 'an oasis of stimulating personalities, talk and activity'. 'Why don't you too go on strike and hide here?' she once suggested to Jawaharlal.

The Nehrus they grew more and more to admire Sarojini Naidu and to think of her as a rich and rare being. An outspoken opponent of religious rituals and superstitions, Motilal did not harp on trifles and eschewed religious controversies. Sarojini Naidu shared his 'modern' sensibilities and his spacious and unprejudiced viewpoint on past and present; together with him she added a cosmopolitan thrust to Congress activities. They were both faithful to their wider political interests, and, while their politics shifted somewhat, their vigour was unabated to the end. What is more, they strove for dignity in public life. During the Home Rule protests and the Rowlatt

---

[128] J. Nehru, *A Bunch of Old Letters*, p. 42.

Satyagraha, Sarojini Naidu bore hardships with much stoicism and humour. Once seen, she could not be forgotten because of her verbal ingenuity and powerful oratory. Most either warmed to her instantly or were spellbound by her talent and vitality. Her exuberance was such that she would put all her strength into whatever she said. To speak was as easy for her as it was for a fish to swim. Though deflected from the highway of poetry by her engagement in politics, her three anthologies—*The Golden Threshold* (1905), *The Bird of Time* (1912) and later *The Broken Wing* (1917)—received acclaim in India and England.

In early 1913, Sarojini Naidu attended a Muslim League meeting. Gokhale had told her that Jinnah 'has true stuff in him, and that freedom from all sectarian prejudice which will make him the best ambassador of Hindu–Muslim unity'.[129] In 1915, she honoured Jinnah from the Congress platform, in her poem 'Awake', and called him the ambassador of Hindu–Muslim unity a year later. This followed the Lucknow Pact (December 1916). She trusted his searching and quintessentially 'secular' mind, and relied on his credentials to close the breach with Congress.[130] When the Nehru Report was drafted in August 1928, Motilal sought Sarojini Naidu's intervention to bring Jinnah back for talks.[131] Years later, she spoke of Jinnah as Lucifer, a fallen angel, one who had once promised to be 'a great leader of Indian freedom, but had instead, cast himself out of the Congress heaven'.[132]

When it came to political affairs, Jawaharlal and Sarojini Naidu were on the same side—'the invincible faith of one's spirit kindles the flame of another in radiance that illumines the world'. Jawaharlal was sometimes amused by her almost wayward impatience, but equally touched by her intellectual serenity in a crisis. Sarojini Naidu, in

[129] Stanley A. Wolpert, *Jinnah of Pakistan* (Delhi: Oxford University Press, 1984), p. 35.

[130] Kanji Dwarkadas, *India's Fight for Freedom, 1913–1937: An Eyewitness Story* (Bombay: Popular Prakashan, 1966), pp. 63–4.

[131] Ansari to Jawaharlal Nehru, 29 March 1928, file no. G 60/1928, AICC Papers; Motilal to Thakurdas, 28, 29 April 1928, Thakurdas Papers (71), NMML.

[132] Wolpert, *Jinnah of Pakistan*, p. 289.

turn, had an abiding faith in his 'incorruptible sincerity and passion for liberty'.[133] She reminded him towards the closing months of the year 1937 that 'liberty is the ultimate crown of all your sacrifice ... but you will not walk alone'.[134] And, on his fiftieth birthday, she remarked that he would transmute sorrow, suffering, sacrifice, anguish, and strife 'into the very substance of ecstasy and victory—and freedom'. He was 'a man of destiny born to be alone in the midst of crowds, deeply loved and but little understood...'[135] In July 1938, Jawaharlal and Krishna went to Ceylon. They broke journey in Hyderabad to enjoy a delightful lunch at the Golden Threshold, the home of the Naidus. The Nightingale's voice was stilled on 2 March 1949. 'I am a Governess,' she used to say. As in life, she would have faced death with a light heart and with a song on the lips and smile on the face. Jawaharlal affirmed that 'just as the Father of the Nation had infused moral grandeur and greatness into the struggle, Sarojini Naidu gave it artistry and poetry'.[136]

Sarojini Naidu exhibited, in a high degree, the perceptiveness of a poet and its corollary, a fine sense of humour and irony. The Indian bourgeoisie was in many cases Western; but Jawaharlal, who waited for years for his 'discovery' to take place, respected Sarojini Naidu's adaptation to and acceptance of Indian traditions. He thought that her speeches were 'all nationalism and patriotism',[137] and that she was quite free from all pretentiousness and snobbery. She built bridges of cooperation, harmony, and tolerance—a necessity for human survival.[138] Her approach became an essential foundation for a strong secular democracy and, even more, a necessary part of a multicultural society. Jawaharlal, too, exerted himself to recognize the 'Western' point of view and approaches in the concrete task of nation-building.

[133] Sarojini Naidu to Jawaharlal Nehru, 29 September 1929, *A Bunch of Old Letters*, p. 75.
[134] Sarojini Naidu to Jawaharlal Nehru, 13 November 1937, *A Bunch of Old Letters*, p. 255.
[135] Sarojini Naidu to Jawaharlal Nehru, Diwali 1939, p. 407.
[136] Edib, *Inside India*, p. 28.
[137] J. Nehru, *An Autobiography*, p. 35.
[138] J. Nehru, *An Autobiography*, p. 594.

Mohamed Ali

'Awful creature I must have been then with my "education" and "snobbishness", Jawaharlal once remarked. That he was not. He valued loyalty and friends. Meeting them in or out of jail bolstered his spirits. Among the former Aligarh graduates, Jawaharlal had warm feelings towards Mohamed Ali until his outpourings against the Nehru Report and Civil Disobedience came to his knowledge in the Naini Prison. This led him to suggest that India's Muslims could do nothing more disastrous for their own interests than to keep away from the freedom movement.[139] However, when it came to naming a street or park in Allahabad, he shared his appreciation of Mohamed Ali's role with the Municipal Board.[140]

Anand Bhawan sheltered aspiring lawyers, journalists, and teachers. It attracted well-to-do Muslims as well: A. M. Khwaja (1882–1962), Nehru's contemporary at Cambridge, Sherwani, and Khaliquzzaman (1889–1973), and Syed Mahmud. They were at ease in the company of the Nehrus. The Saprus and the Kunzrus led the same lifestyle, but they could not cultivate the young Muslims who were looking to make their political career. Jawaharlal was, on the other hand, a product of north India's pluralist culture, which was greatly dominated by Indo-Muslim symbols.

When in jail, Jawaharlal sent for two books from the Anand Bhawan library on Western Tibet and the Borderland. He thought of a long pilgrimage with Khaliquzzaman that would take them to Kashmir and Ladakh and Tibet, to the Mansarovar Lake and Mount Kailash, and to the famous cities of Central Asia, Afghanistan, Iran, Arabia, and the West.[141] He took delight in narrating how Khaliquzzaman neither had a beard nor a moustache. To a maulvi who gently reminded him about not conforming to the Sunnat (a practice observed by the Prophet), Khaliquzzaman replied with great fervour: 'Don't say anything at all about a beard. I have the greatest possible respect for it, therefore I have allowed it to grow in my heart.'[142]

---

[139] Prison Diary, 30 April 1930, SWJN, vol. 4, p. 335.

[140] To the Chairman, Municipal Board, (before) 14 March 1931, SWJN, vol. 4, p. 588; J. Nehru, An Autobiography, p. 117.

[141] B. R. Nanda, The Nehrus, pp. 213–14.

[142] J. Nehru, An Autobiography, p. 117.

Khan Abdul Ghaffar Khan

In the NWFP, Khan Abdul Ghaffar Khan tamed the fiery and rebellious spirit of his followers only to use their energies creatively to build
an anti-British ideology. Without being a revolutionary or an innovative
reformer, he transformed them. He never talked down to them, knowing
what they could understand and phrasing his arguments accordingly. He
did not throw his weight about, but established the principle, which the
League fiercely contested, that nationalism was compatible with Islam
and that Indian citizenship did not come in conflict with the concept of
umma. *Qaum* (nation and not community) and *umma* were indivisible.

Jawaharlal's attachment to the serene and amiable Ghaffar Khan
took the form of a dream; in the heat of a summer afternoon, he saw
him being attacked and himself fighting to defend him. He woke up
in an exhausted state, 'feeling very miserable'. He recalled, 'That surprised me, for in my waking state I was not liable to such emotional
outbursts'. Gandhi spoke at a prayer meeting in early January 1932 on
the fears in man's mind—fear of death and fear of loss of material possession. A man of prayer and self-purification, he said, 'will shed the
fear of death and embrace death as a boon companion and will regard
all earthly possessions as fleeting and of no account'.[143] The 'Frontier
Gandhi' did just that. One can safely link him with the whole body
of subterranean forces and energies that were geared up to wage *jihad*
against foreign rule. Officials refused to deal with 'a fanatic or honest fanatic, whose fanaticism got the better of him'. On 'first principle',
one of them asserted, 'it seems to me that government must maintain its position as the final and authoritative arbiter and must not
submit to being placed on trial before any independent individual or
organisation—however eminent'.[144] Gandhi committed himself very
deeply on the side of the innocence and non-violence of the Red Shirts.
C. F. Andrews tried to soften the official stance towards them, but the
government failed to realize how much Ghaffar Khan had done to
imbue the concept of non-violence into the Frontier people. In this
respect, as also in many others, the 'Frontier Gandhi' was, undoubt-
edly, one of the makers of history.[145] Andrews met the Home Member
in December 1934 to explain that Ghaffar Khan and his Red Shirt

---

[143] 3 January 1932, *CWMG*, vol. XLVIII, p. 489.
[144] Home Dept, Political, file no. 11/14, 1934.
[145] Arrested on 24 December 1931.

followers were misrepresented as a dangerously violent force akin to Russian communism.

In the Hazaribagh Jail, Ghaffar Khan had no access to letters—he spent more than forty years of his life in detention, having been first arrested in 1914. Visitors were kept out on the plea that they would conspire, if together, against the civil administration. Naturally, Ghaffar Khan felt miserable,[146] but followed Gandhi in eschewing the favours offered to him by the jailors.[147] He thought always of his children and felt anxious—one son studied in the United States, two others were at school in Dehra Dun, and a daughter went to a convent in Murree. He confided in Ansari:

> I live alone in a third-class barrack. I am closed up at night time. Neither somebody can come to me nor can I go to somebody. There is neither volleyball nor badminton nor rules nor regulations nor a letter nor interview in spite of the fact that I am a state prisoner. Administer [sic] justice yourself. I consider 'C' class prisoners better off than myself. In my opinion this law had been constituted for taking revenge. What should I write more? If I do so, perhaps you would be deprived of this letter and so consider this 'A grain from the heap.' But well, we too have a God who might be seeing our oppressedness [sic] and we are also seeing what He will do. I am quite healthy. Morning and evening I take good exercise in walking. I have formed a small beautiful garden by which my time passes well. Perhaps you may appreciate my garden if you see it. It is bigger and better than that of Zafar Ali Khan. You should pray for me and I will pray for you.[148]

[146] He felt strongly that he had not been allowed to receive any letters and apparently all letters from him were with the Inspector General of Police, NWFP.

[147] Yunus, Letters from Prison, p. 15.

[148] 4 February 1932. The police intercepted the letter (Police Home Dept. Political, file no. 31/107, 1932). Maulana Zafar Ali Khan, poet and journalist of Lahore, was one of the early victims of the government's repressive policy. On 12 January 1914, the Punjab government forfeited the security of Zamindar, and in December that year, restricted him to his village near Sialkot. This was followed in May 1915 by the arrests of the Ali brothers, Azad, and Hasrat Mohani. In December 1916, Maulana Mahmud Hasan and his four companions of Deoband were arrested for their part in the 'Silk Letter Conspiracy' (Tehrik-e Reshmi Rumal), a scheme that Ubaidullah Sindhi and his chief disciple, Mahmud Hasan, had devised to destroy British rule.

Owing to his being practically in solitary confinement and exhibiting a tendency to brood over his grievances, the Bihar and Orissa governments allowed his brother, Khan Sahib, to join him at the Naini Prison on 2 June 1932.[149] 'The blood of the martyr is the deed of the church.' This eternal law prevailed in the case of the 'Frontier Gandhi'. Legends of all kinds quickly crystallized around his fetters grinding prison labour. He would have cited Ghalib to the effect:

Where's the second step of desire, O God?
The desert of possibilities was only a footprint.

'On the summit of deep, universal, tumultuous movements,' ran Ranke's last dictated words, 'appear natures cast in a gigantic mould, which rivet the attention of the centuries. General tendencies do not alone decide; great personalities are always necessary to make them effective.'[150] We have dealt with a number of great personalities who had a certain romance in life and a certain vision to nurture. They did not fear imprisonment or death; instead they defied British laws and challenged the raison d'etre of British rule. In much the same vein, Jawaharlal told the judge at his trial on 3 November 1940: 'Perhaps it may be that, though I am standing before you on my trial, it is the British Empire itself that is on its trial before the bar of the world.'[151] We also hear Mohamed Ali declaring that he had no defence to offer, and that it was the government itself that was on trial. Indeed, it was the judge himself on trial. We can hardly overestimate the impact of this state of mind: it got rid of whatever scepticism and despair afflicted the mind of the political actors.

Prison was a place where each day was like a year, a year whose days were long, wrote Oscar Wilde. Being oppressed, ill-treated, and brutalized, the inmates felt sad, abandoned, and weary. Some of them, though, lived with their thoughts, dreams and ideas, and having long, dreary months and years ahead of them, they all the same

[149] Home Dept, Political, file no. 30/70, 1932.
[150] G. P. Gooch, *History and Historians in the Nineteenth Century* (Boston: Beacon Press, 1959), p. 95.
[151] Jawaharlal Nehru, *The Unity of India: Collected Writings, 1937–1940* (London: Lindsay Drummond, 1948), p. 399.

wanted to live. They lived with one thought, one desire—to further the cause of freedom, and, without drawing any hard and sharp lines, their personal and political identities were continuously shaped and restructured to generate opposition towards British rule. One had to accept everything as it came, both in social life and in private life with a smile. Rosa Luxemburg, the revolutionary, whose life spanned a great historical epoch until her murder in Berlin in 1919, lived with the conviction that things would take the correct turn after a period of terrible human suffering.[152] In the subcontinent, audacious men and women were grinding corn or working on 'oil presses' in sweltering heat. Rajaji saw so many cheerfully toiling away like men 'to the manner born', who had accepted hard labour as an alternative to merely giving security.[153] He saw Sesha Reddy and two brave Nellore youths, broomsticks in hand, sweeping the grounds in front of his cell, and heard them say, 'Are we not scavengers?' Gandhi had promised swaraj within a year. One non-cooperator learnt somewhere that it had come and depended on three years' good conduct.[154] Jawaharlal was determined to break through and demolish all the prison walls that 'encompass our bodies and mind, and function as a free nation'.

[152] Waters, *Rosa Luxemburg Speaks*.
[153] He was locked up in Vellore's Central Jail from 21 December 1921 to 20 March 1922.
[154] 25 December 1921, Rajagopalachari, *Jail Diary*, p. 8.

11. Crafting History in a Cell

The French political theorist Alexis de Tocqueville (1805–1859) talked about the part played in French political thinking by men of letters. In the second half of the nineteenth century, Bengal witnessed a 'renaissance' to which literary men, reformers, and journalists contributed their bit. In the 1920s and '30s, literary works in Urdu and Hindi had a striking impact in raising mass awakening. Jawaharlal Nehru wrote a great deal during this period: prison life brought both leisure and a measure of detachment.[1] While Jawaharlal was jailed, a great deal happened that affected the whole gamut of his emotions and touched off thoughts. A sensitive person like him had to put them down in words that came with graceful spontaneity.[2] 'In India today,' Jawaharlal wrote to Indira on her thirteenth birthday,

---

[1] Jawaharlal Nehru, Preface to the original edition, *Glimpses of World History* (Allahabad: Kitabistan, 1942 edn), p. vii.

[2] Hirendranath Mukherjee, *The Gentle Colossus: A Study of Jawaharlal Nehru* (Delhi: Oxford University Press, 1968), p. 35.

'we are making history, and you and I are fortunate to see this happening before our eyes and to take some part ourselves in this great drama.'[3] Without comparing his own role with that of the famous jailbirds— Miguel de Cervantes (1547–1616) and John Bunyan (1628–1688)—he learnt lessons from the history of a generation, indeed the interpretation of a whole liberation struggle.[4] Reading history is good, but even more interesting and fascinating is to help make history.[5]

Love of learning is too strong to be quenched by the disadvantages of prison life. Jawaharlal read fifty-five books from 21 May 1922 to 29 January 1923 alone. Oscar Wilde's *The Ballad of Reading Gaol* had a magical sway over him. Plato's *Republic* stimulated him, whereas *To the Lighthouse* by Virginia Woolf (1882–1941) opened his eyes to many scenes of life. As a person with socialist leanings, he perused Beatrice Webb (1858–1943), a Fabian socialist, and Sidney Webb (1859–1947). Besides, he delved into philosophy, and turned the pages of history to illuminate his understanding of the ideas and movements that stood apart as catalysts for momentous changes. As with the French Revolution or the Bolshevik revolution, he wanted to know what lay behind the people's upsurge. He glanced through Romesh Chandra Dutt (*Economic History of India under British Rule*, 1902), William Digby ('*Prosperous*' *British India: A Revelation from Official Records*, 1901), and R. Palme Dutt (*India Today*).[6] Their reflections enabled him to understand how simple, ordinary men and women became heroes, and how history became stirring and epoch-making.

Benjamin Disraeli (1809–1881), the British statesman, had written the following words about the Dutch philosopher Hugo Grotius (1583–1645): 'Other men condemned to exile and captivity if they survive, despair; the man of letters may reckon those days as the

---

[3] J. Nehru, *Glimpses of World History*, p. 2.

[4] Mulk Raj Anand, 'Self-Actualization in the Writings of Nehru', in *Jawaharlal Nehru: Centenary Volume*, edited by Sheila Dikshit, K. Natwar Singh, G. Parthasarathi, H.Y. Sharada Prasad, S. Gopal, and Ravinder Kumar (New Delhi: Oxford University Press and the Implementation Committee for the Commemoration of the Jawaharlal Nehru Centenary, 1989), p. 7.

[5] Anand, 'Self-Actualization in the Writings of Nehru', in *Jawaharlal Nehru: Centenary Volume*, p. 4.

[6] J. Nehru, *Glimpses of World History*, p. 429.

sweetest of his life.' Jawaharlal's imagination ran high in a solitary cell. He had no library or reference books at hand, but he imagined books lined up, 'row after row, with the wisdom of ages locked up in them, serene and untroubled in a changing and distracted world, looking down silently on the mortals that come and go'.[7] About *Prison Days and Other Poems* by S. H. Vatsyayan, he commented: 'Something of that dreaming comes out in these poems, something of that yearning when the arms stretched out in search for what was not and clutched at empty space.... There was always a sorrow to hope for, a tomorrow which might bring deliverance.'[8]

Felix Dzerzhinsky found it impossible to explain everything in a letter so that people could turn over in their minds all that the soul had undergone in the long and excruciating years of wandering.[9] Jawaharlal secured some space to contemplate and write behind stone walls and iron bars. Putting pen to paper was an antidote to isolation and helped him harness his creative energies. He flattered himself that he kept himself very well in jail.[10]

In the course of self-introspection, Jawaharlal asked himself what he was heir to, and answered that he was heir to all that humanity had achieved over tens of thousands of years, to all that it had thought and felt and suffered and taken joy in, to its cries of triumph and its bitter agonies of defeat, to that astonishing adventure which had begun so long ago and yet continued and beckoned to man. He put pen to paper on the wisdom of India's past, on its great inexhaustible spiritual heritage, and on the vital necessity to apply it intelligently and reasonably to the present and the future.[11] With toleration and peace as the essence of the Indian outlook, he expected his countrymen to adjust to a new scheme of things.[12] He put in plain words: 'In prison I was away from facts and reality and was charged with the reactions

---

[7] 'A Dialogue with Jawaharlal Nehru' by Mohamed H. Heikal.

[8] Jawaharlal Nehru, 'Prison Days', *SWJN*, vol. 8, p. 877.

[9] To A. E. Bulhak, 15 April 1919, *Prison Diary and Letters*, p. 293.

[10] Nehru to Krishna, 11 December 1940, *Nehru's Letters to His Sister*, p. 70.

[11] Gorev and Zimyanin, *Jawaharlal Nehru*, pp. 226–7.

[12] To Nan (from Ahmadnagar Fort), 27 February 1945, in *Before Freedom, 1909–1947*, p. 361.

and illusions created by compulsory confinement behind prison bars. My feelings were unbridled and my frustration was intense. Perhaps I wanted violence outside to be an outlet to my confinement behind prison bars.' But the frail old man in the loincloth told him not to be troubled by the outside world but to read, write, or to learn any handicraft.

The memorandum on UP's land tenure system evoked his interest towards an uncharted sea. 'Whither India?', an important piece of his writing, called for radically transforming social relations and economic structures. The UP Chief Secretary wondered what might be its impact and how far Congress was prepared to go on the road to Communism.[13] In other writings, Jawaharlal roused enthusiasm in ideas that, quite apart from their economic aspect, contemplated the overthrow of the Raj. He raised issues of poverty, of people in distress, infinitely worse than the difficulties of the comfortable bourgeois and leading a muddied and grimy existence. His conviction that their condition was mirrored in the colonial institutions struck notes of thoughtful response. He sought to understand what lay behind the eyes that stared at him. Glimpses came to him that illumined his vision and made him realize the immensity of their problems. Those troubles absorbed not only past experiences and ignominious failures, but also outlined his impulses for a new life. He wanted India to be in pursuit of transition, regeneration, and transformation and not be in the throes of a conflict. At the same time, his dialectic of change and development was strongly rooted in past accomplishments.

Jawaharlal Nehru did not claim to be a historian but, taking his cue from Gandhi, he put in writing some of his thoughts in *Glimpses of World History*.[14] The work was received with a chorus of admiration. It consists of letters to Indira written in different prisons between October 1930 and August 1933. They were gathered together before Jawaharlal's arrest on 12 February 1934 and published by his sister, Vijaya Lakshmi Pandit. A revised version appeared in 1939. Prison gave its author the chance he needed, and he seized it. Decades of

[13] Home Dept, Political, file no. 4/8, 1933.
[14] 'A Dialogue with Jawaharlal Nehru' by Mohamed H. Heikal.

research and discussion have questioned or modified many of his con-
clusions, but whatever else is read, parts of *Glimpses* must be read also.
It is not one of the great historical books of the world, but few works
make such an impression of sustained intellectual power.

The letters were meant to acquaint Indira with the milestones
in world history, the creative thrust and splendour of mankind, the
theory and practice of statecraft, the multiple influences of events, and
the fate of societies that have been constructed in a narrow and superficial spirit. They reflect on the Indian situation and its bearing on the
outside world, so that she could 'see a mighty procession of living men
and women and children in every age and every clime, different from
us and yet very like us, with much the same human virtues and human
feelings'. History is not a magic show, but there is plenty of magic in it
for those who have eyes to see.[15]

Historiography, according to Leopold von Ranke followed the great
impulses of public life. Jawaharlal identified the stirring and epoch-
making past events, and reflected on those who spurred the masses
on to great deeds—Lenin who inspired his people to write a noble
and never-to-be-forgotten chapter in history; Giuseppe Garibaldi
(1807–1888) and the Italian Risorgimento; Count Camillo Cavour
(1810–1861), the first Prime Minister of Italy; Giuiseppe Mazzini
(1805–1872); Mustafa Kemal Ataturk; and, above all, Gandhi, who
was in prison but the 'magic of his message' stole into 'the hearts of
India's millions.' He admitted that it was not for him to evaluate the
Mahatma's role in the long story of humanity, given his personal close-
ness to the man; but neither could those who remained untouched
by the magic of his charisma and personality accomplish this task.
Nonetheless, he recounted his leadership, his ideas, his conception of
truth, and his ability to mould and move people. Certain that much ink
and paper would be expended on discussing and critiquing Gandhi's
life theories and activities, he insisted that he would remain forever
'a radiant and beloved figure'. He imaged Gandhi leading the Dandi
March, determined, staff in his hand.

In his glimpses of the great moments in the career of Gandhi
and of many more people, he brought to the fore their treasures

---

[15] J. Nehru, *Glimpses of World History*, p. 951.

of knowledge, learning, heroism, and devotion. He is generous, understanding, and kindly in evaluating the freedom struggle in Asia and Africa. Likewise, he dealt with the ideals and aspirations of liberal nationalism in Turkey and in the Middle Eastern countries. Jawaharlal's Asian pride was hurt by Europe's machinations in the region, and he drew comparisons between those countries and India, and aspired for their freedom. In this way, he recovered his own voice, his own enthusiasm, and strengthened his own hands in the service of his people. On his fiftieth birthday, his article in the *Modern Review* illuminates his sense of leading a critical mission:

> From the far North to Cape Comorin, he has gone like some triumphant Caesar, passing by, leaving a trail of glory and a legend behind him. Is all this for him just a passing fancy which amuses him? .... Is it his will to power ... that is driving him from crowd to crowd and making him whisper to himself, 'I drew these tides of men into my hands and wrote my will across the sky in stars'? (*Seven Pillars of Wisdom* by T. E. Lawrence)[16]

Jawaharlal displays a unity of outlook and a command of facts that would do credit to any professional writer. Without the dust and tumble of politics, they are clear, emphatic, neat, and without a trace of pedantry.[17] The *Glimpses* provoked a good deal of criticism, even among those who praised the book. Yet, it stands by itself as 'a demonstration of human intellectual capacity'.[18] In it, he looks at the entire world with a fresh eye and gives a balanced view of man's life on many continents. His was a global view—not an Asian view any more than it was a European one.[19] As a lover of words and phrases, which he expressed intelligently and in ordered sequence, he outlined an approach to life compounded of buoyancy and optimism, a humorous tolerance towards life's foibles, and even its trials. He showed 'great

[16] On the article and its interpretation, see Benjamin Zachariah, *Nehru* (London: Routledge, 2004), pp. 88–9.

[17] Sarvepalli Gopal, *Jawaharlal Nehru, 1889–1947* (Delhi: Oxford University Press, 1975), vol. 1, p. 147.

[18] Norman Cousins, in *Jawaharlal Nehru: Centenary Volume*, p. 133.

[19] Lamb, *Nehrus of India*, p. 114.

sensitivity' and an artist's perception of feeling that a novelist or a painter has. [20]

Jawaharlal's writings possess artistic and dramatic unity. A running thread is discernible within his diverse interests, because of his awareness of the continuity between the past and the present, and his hopes and vision for the future. And because his object was to reveal to his countrymen the wealth they possessed in their chronicles, he refers to the weight of the past, the greatness of the civilization he inherited, not as a burden to be borne but as a reference point for judging the moral worth and wisdom of his decisions. He brings people to light, and then lets the reader draw any conclusion that he likes. In this respect, it is hard to find much fault with his general conception of ideas or to deny the limitations of an otherwise wide canvas. A reviewer in the *American Current History* thought that *Glimpses of World History* was a better survey of world history than H.G. Wells's *Outline*. Fenner Brockway praised it. His daughter, Indira, claimed that she learnt more from *Glimpses of World History* than any history book she studied at school.[21] Passages from it were read out in the Aga Khan Detention Camp. Gandhi felt like translating them.[22] Since then, new editions succeeded one another and many have appeared after Jawaharlal's death. Besides public men, lawyers, and judges who thought highly of the *Glimpses*,[23] few works of the time require so little adaptation to satisfy students today.

The Great Rebellion

Jawaharlal read in the pages of stone and brick and mortar what his ancestors did in days of old. For a man whose mind had been formed in the anti-imperialist climate of early industrial, competitive capitalism, the 1857 Rebellion was an important part of a protracted struggle against British colonialism.

---

[20] Begum Iftikharuddin, Oral History Transcript (53), NMML.
[21] Lord Brockway, Oral History Transcript (18), NMML.
[22] 2 November 1943; Nayyar, *Mahatma Gandhi's Last Imprisonment*, p. 309.
[23] Husain B. Tyabji, Oral History Transcript (166), NMML.

Jawaharlal's ancestors and some of the other Kashmiri Pandit families had lived through the horror of 1857. The family experienced many vicissitudes during the unsettled times that followed and the *jagir* dwindled and vanished.[24] Forced by cicumstances, the Nehrus joined the vast numbers fleeing to Agra. Motilal's Munshi, Mubarak Ali, whose own family in Budaun had suffered at the hands of the British, familiarized the young Jawaharlal with the happenings. Stories of entire villages being burnt down as punishment filled him with anger. He narrated how the world of his ancestors had darkened after the British occupied Delhi:

> The family, having lost nearly all it possessed, joined the numerous fugitives who were leaving the old imperial city and went to Agra. My father was not born then but my two uncles were already young men and possessed some knowledge of English. This knowledge saved the younger of the two uncles, as well as some other members of the family, from a sudden and ignominious end. He was journeying from Delhi with some family members, among whom was his young sister, a little girl who was very fair, as some Kashmiri children are. Some English soldiers met them on the way and they suspected this little aunt of mine to be an English girl and accused my uncle of kidnapping her. From an accusation, to summary justice and punishment, was usually a matter of minutes in those days, and my uncles and others of the family might well have found themselves hanging on the nearest tree. Fortunately for them, my uncle's knowledge of English delayed matters a little and then someone who knew him passed that way and rescued him and the others.

Jawaharlal attributed the people's anger to the ignorance and rapacity of officers, and the bitterness of feudal chiefs.[25] He linked colonialism with racism, observing how the combine had corrupted Britain's public life and made her forget the lessons of her own history and literature.[26] He compared Jesus preaching non-violence and *ahimsa* with his loud-voiced followers of that time, with their imperialism and armaments and wars and worship of wealth. The Sermon on the Mount and modern European and American Christianity—how amazingly dissimilar

---

[24] J. Nehru, *An Autobiography*, p. 2.
[25] J. Nehru, *Glimpses of World History*, p. 414.
[26] J. Nehru, *Glimpses of World History*, p. 326.

they are!' he observed.[27] He denounced the British for spreading terror, for shooting down people in cold blood, for hanging thousands from the wayside trees, and for destroying prosperous villages.[28] Making a special mention of General Neill,[29] a Madras officer who converted every tree by the roadside, from Allahabad to Kanpur—into a gibbet, he detailed the horrors:

> It is all a terrible and most painful story, and I hardly dare tell you all the bitter truth. If Nana Sahab had behaved barbarously and treacherously, many an English officer exceeded his barbarity a hundred-fold. If mobs of mutinous Indian soldiers, without officers or leaders, had been guilty of cruel and revolting deeds, the trained British soldiers, led by their officers, exceeded them in cruelty and barbarity. I do not want to compare the two. It is a sorry business on both sides, but our perverted histories tell us a lot about the treachery and cruelty on the Indian side, and hardly mention the other side. It is also well to remember that the cruelty of a mob is nothing compared to the cruelty of an organized government when it begins to behave like a mob. Even to-day, if you go to many of the villages in our province, you will find that the people have still got a vivid and ghastly memory of the horrors that befell them during the crushing of the Rebellion.[30]

Later, Jawaharlal invoked Buddha Purnima to remind his audience of the virtues of reconciliation and eschewing violence. He disapproved of extremism and of bombs being thrown on English officers; instead, he returned to Gandhi 'to remind ourselves that unless we see reason and defeat violence, it will bring ruin to mankind'.[31] The Gandhian way had acquired greater relevance in the atomic age with its potential for unimaginable violence.[32] Indeed, he considered the stirring of a

[27] J. Nehru, *Glimpses of World History*, p. 87.
[28] Also mentions the 'barbarous behaviour' of some rebels who sullied their cause by massacres of the British.
[29] He 'dimmed his glory by deeds of dark vengeance' (Percival Spear, *The Oxford History of Modern India, 1740–1947*, Oxford: Clarendon Press, 1965, p. 226).
[30] J. Nehru, *Glimpses of World History*, p. 415.
[31] *SWJN*, vol. 38, p. 15.
[32] *SWJN*, vol. 38, p. 14.

fierce hatred towards the enemy to be inconsistent with the Indian tradition so that saints and seers, poets and writers, dancers and musicians could challenge the might of the British Empire without invoking the war symbols. Often, they could soothe frayed tempers. Thus Gandhi launched satyagraha without calling for savage reprisals.

Jawaharlal did not want the past to be a burden on a community or the nation. As opposed to the British who glorified their heroes—there were 50,700 recipients of the Indian Mutiny Medal alone[33]—he did not believe in pining for the past. He wanted the ghastly and horrible picture showing man at his worst to be forgotten, or remembered in a detached, impersonal way. According to him, 'So long as the connecting links and reminders are present, and the spirit behind those events survives and shows itself, that memory also will endure and influence our people. Attempts to suppress that picture do not destroy it but drive it deeper in the mind. Only by dealing with it normally can its effect be lessened.'[34] It was hateful to have to refer to this past history, but the spirit behind those events did not end with them.[35]

Great personalities have something in them that inspires a whole people to do great deeds. In *Glimpses*, Jawaharlal dwelt on the role of Lakshmi Bai (1828–1858), the young and impulsive Rani of Jhansi, and 'fine guerrilla leaders' like Firoz Shah and Tantya Tope (1814–1859).[36] In another context, he talked of 'a whole people [becoming] full of faith for a great cause, and then even simple, ordinary men and women become heroes, and history becomes stirring and epoch-making.'[37]

Why did the Rebellion fail? Jawaharlal blamed the feudal chiefs, who, besides being disorganized, desired to preserve their own privileges.[38] They had no clear signs of a constructive ideal. Hence, the 'mutinous rabble' created the very condition of anarchy that offered the East India Company the excuse to gain a foothold in India in the first

[33] Pramod K. Nayyar (ed.), *The Trial of Bahadur Shah Zafar* (New Delhi: Orient Blackswan, 2007), p. xxiii.

[34] J. Nehru, *Discovery of India*, pp. 324–5.

[35] J. Nehru, *Discovery of India*, pp. 324–5.

[36] J. Nehru, *Discovery of India*, p. 324.

[37] Gupte, *Mother India*.

[38] J. Nehru, *Discovery of India*, p. 324.

place. Historians agree that modern nationalism had yet to come—India had still to go through much sorrow and travail before learning the lesson that would give her real freedom.[39] Bickering over petty matters, he warned, would mean 'betraying the sacrifices and courage of all the people who fought for freedom, and betraying Gandhiji, Gautam Budhha, and, finally, ourselves.'[40]

Hindu–Muslim unity occupied centrality in Jawaharlal's schema. Speaking at Delhi's Ramlila Grounds a hundred years after the fire ignited in Meerut, he emphasized that the two communities had shared the fruits of victory and the disappointment of defeat.[41] The air resounded with slogans of Hindu–Muslim unity. G. W. Forrest, author of the military operations, had warned that one of the lessons of the 'Rebellion' was that the Hindus and Muslims could be united against the British: 'It reminds us,' he observed, 'that our dominions rest on a thin crust ever likely to be rent by titanic fires of social changes and religious revolutions.'[42]

Scores of proclamations backed Jawaharlal's contention that Hindus and Muslims acted in unison. The Lucknow Proclamation of 5–17 July pleaded for unity against the 'inhuman and ungodly Christians'. Those who wrote it were in all likelihood inspired by Maulvi Ahmadullah Shah, a Sufi who led both the Hindu and Muslim sepoys at the battle of Chinhat, a village on the Fyzabad road. Every other proclamation mentioned Hindus and Muslims and their respective religions in the same breath; Bahadur Shah, the Mughal Emperor, emphasized the standard of the Prophet of Islam and the standard of Mahavir, the founder of Jainism.

The Hindus and Muslims acted in unison from the time a detachment of the 34th Native Infantry marched into Behrampore, 116 miles north of Calcutta, until death, desolation, and despair afflicted Delhi and Lucknow. The prevalent spirit of harmony was manifested in the rebels hailing Birjis Qadr as Lord Krishna, and in Bahadur Shah celebrating Holi at Mehrauli (Kottab-sahib). When some zealots hoisted the green standard of holy war at the Jama Masjid on

[39] J. Nehru, *Discovery of India* p. 325.

[40] *SWJN*, vol. 38, p. 15.

[41] Mushirul Hasan (ed.), *SWJN*, vol. 39, p. 7.

[42] Quoted in S. B. Chaudhuri, *Civil Rebellion in the Indian Mutinies, 1857–1859* (Calcutta: Word Press, 1957), p. 282.

19 May 1857, he ordered its removal. To the beat of drums he decreed the death penalty for those sacrificing cows and goats during Bakr-Id.

People often speak of 'the verdict of history', 'the philosophy of history', 'the science of history'. G. P. Gooch, the historian, declared that there is no agreed verdict; no agreed philosophy, only 'a welter of conflicts'. 'We continue our eager and never-ending search for truth,' he said, and added, 'but the sphinx smiles at us and keeps her secrets'. He went on to ask: 'Are there or will there ever be final answers to the questions prompted by our study of the human endeavours?' 'If so,' he answered, 'they have not yet been found.'[43] Jawaharlal would have agreed with this formulation. What he offered was the barest outline of the 1857 Revolt and just fleeting glimpses of India's colonial past.

The Self in Nationalism

Bertrand Russell (1872–1970), whom Jawaharlal admired, wrote fiction to release his hitherto unexpressed feelings. Jawaharlal's *Autobiography* (written almost entirely in prison from June 1931 to February 1935) was probably the most revealing thing he ever produced for it bears 'the mark of a passionate, albeit humane, nationalism'.[44] Others have also put pen to paper on their life and times,[45] but his work compares favourably, to give one instance, with Gandhi's *My Experiments with Truth*. Glowing with patriotic feeling, it mirrors his breadth of view and patient learning. There is no cover-up, no concealment of facts. As for the 'self', the influences are too subtle and too diffused to be easily identified or measured. He loved India tenderly, and, in the words of Monod, to him that loved, much may be forgiven.

Even though autobiographical confessions cannot be regarded as accurate descriptions of a consistent life, the *Autobiography* is out of the ordinary precisely for its tropes and figures of thought, without

[43] G. P. Gooch, *History and Historians of the Nineteenth Century* (Boston: Beacon Hill Press, 1959), p. i.

[44] B. R. Nanda, *The Nehrus*, p. 362.

[45] Vijay Ramasawamy and Yogesh Sharma (eds), *Biography as History: Indian Perspective* (New Delhi: Sage, 2009); Udaya Kumar, 'Autobiography as a Way of Writing History: Personal Narratives from Kerala and the Inhabitation of Modernity', in *History in the Vernacular*, edited by Raziuddin Aquil and Partha Chatterjee (New Delhi: Permanent Black, 2005).

which Jawaharlal would not have turned real-life events into a narrative and nor would he have transformed them from a chronicle into a story. He recognizes the role of nationalist ideas, and pays attention to the popular upsurge that transformed the face of the rural world in parts of Awadh. He applies his mind to literature and manners, explores culture and its rich manifestations, and holds together the alternative and complementary themes by an underlying devotion to objective writing. Hence Tagore discerned 'a deep current of humanity which overpasses the tangle of facts and leads us to the person who is greater than his deeds, and truer than his surroundings'.

Partha Chatterjee, the political scientist, dismissed the *Autobiography* and *The Discovery of India* as 'rambling, bristling with the most obvious contradictions, and grossly overwritten'. But he concedes, nonetheless, that Jawaharlal spelt out clearly the key ideological elements and relations of nationalist thought at its moment of arrival.[46] Others comment on the subtle, complex, discriminating, infinitely cultivated nature of the book that is suffused with intellectual passion. They underlined Jawaharlal's rationality, breadth of learning, and the fluent lucidity of his writings.[47]

The *Autobiography*'s success exceeded all expectations. The younger readers devoured rather than read it, and there was nothing to criticize and nothing to desire. They were drawn to the author as a duck to water.[48] The union of prophecy and autobiography released energies

---

[46] Partha Chatterjee, *Nationalist Thought and the Colonial World: A Derivative Discourse* (New Delhi: Oxford University Press, 1986), p. 132.

[47] Shashi Tharoor, *Nehru: The Invention of India* (UK: Viking, 2007).

[48] In his foreword to the second Hebrew edition, published in 1957, he recalled: 'This book was written when we in India were in the middle of our struggle for freedom. That struggle was long-drawn-out and it brought many experiences of joy and sorrow, of hope and despair. But the despair didn't last long because of the inspiration that came to us from our leader, Mahatma Gandhi, and the deep delight of working for a cause that took us out of our little shells.... All of us are older now and our days of youth are long past. Yet, even now, when we face the troubles and torments that encompasses, something of that old memory of our leader gives us strength' (H. Mukherjee, *The Gentle Colossus*, p. 35; Brown, *Jawaharlal Nehru*, p. 109).

that were to flow into them.[49] Without Jawaharlal, the freedom movement would have lacked the vital intellectual and aesthetic dimension. It was he who saved it from aggressive philistines getting the upper hand.[50] One is regaled by the literary quality of his words: they come across clear and honest. Now you hear him delighted, now solemn, now youthful and energetic, full of hopes for his country, and now piqued at the delays in the fruition of his ideas. It is a voice that we shall gain much by returning to more often.

However, many others who stood outside the Congress camp found him wanting in his analysis and interpretation. The Liberals, who talked of the British love of fair play and their tolerance, were enraged by his partisan view.[51] They did not approve of his contrasting the patriotism of the masses with the coldness and opportunism of the Liberals. He chastised them as 'old women—weeping and howling and feeling terribly oppressed about everything.' During UP's No-Tax Campaign, he feared that they were ranged against his group.[52] This confirmed the impression that even the secular formations outside the Congress could not trust Jawaharlal.

Jawaharlal made short shrift of the Muslim League as well. Instead of engaging with its leaders, he presumed that Jinnah desired to prevent radical changes not because of a Hindu majority but because the radical elements would put an end to semi-feudal privileges.[53] Instead of charting all the crests and troughs of the past, he dedicated space only to those events that enhanced his ability to distinguish

[49] Anand, 'Self-Actualization in the Writings of Nehru', in *Jawaharlal Nehru: Centenary Volume*, p. 10.

[50] *Jawaharlal: Centenary Volume*, p. 430.

[51] 'Am I a lunatic or is India full of lunatics that they can tolerate the Sastris and Saprus, not to mention those who grovel even more abjectly before the imperial power?' (18 June 1933, *SWJN*, vol. 5, p. 484). Srinivas Sastri (1869–1946), who joined the Servants of India Society and succeeded Gokhale as President, poured scorn on the Liberal efforts to reach a deal with Irwin, the Viceroy (S. Gopal, *Jawaharlal Nehru*, vol. 1, p. 145; Mansergh, ed., *Transfer of Power*, pp. 87–8).

[52] 31 May 1930, *SWJN*, vol. 4, p. 357. They visited the Nehrus in Naini Jail on 27 July 1930. Earlier, they met with Gandhi in Yeravda between 21 and 24 July.

[53] 2 February 1942, in *A Nationalist Muslim and Indian Politics*, p. 219.

between the 'progressive' Congress and the 'reactionary' League. He understood the reality of power politics, but not how it affected the minorities. Muslim nationalism was a bitter pill that Jawaharlal could not swallow.

The Discovery

Written in Ahmadnagar Fort Prison from April to September 1944, *The Discovery of India* is Jawaharlal's mental voyage of exploration. He brought

> not just political ambition but all of the intellectual means at his command—journalistic reportage, anthropological fieldwork, electoral campaigning, the intimate and affectionate tutelage of Gandhi and Tagore, the reading of literature, the writing of history, and spells of deep personal reflection, especially over the ten years or so that he was locked up in jail in the course of his career—to construct India as an object that he and his compatriots can relate to in some fundamental way.[54]

The *Discovery* is a hymn to the glories of India. India appears in the narrative as a space of ceaseless cultural mixing, and the past a celebration of the soiling effects of cultural miscegenation and accretion.[55] Other Indian writers who underlined change and continuity in Indian history did so from a rather narrow, sectarian perspective,[56] but India's infinite charm, variety, and oneness grew upon Jawaharlal more and more, and the romantic in him drew on old and new interpretations to buttress ecumenical and universalistic points of view. Sanskrit triggered discoveries in mathematics, astronomy, medicine, and metallurgy. Jawaharlal worked ceaselessly for a synthesis, drawing on the best, and breaking with the worst.[57] He consciously follows Gandhi and Tagore in the direction of the universal.[58]

[54] Vajpeyi, *Righteous Republic*, p. 182.

[55] Sunil Khilnani, *The Idea of India* (London: Hamish Hamilton, 1997), p. 169.

[56] Dayanand Saraswati (1824–1883) and Swami Vivekananda (1863–1902) belong to this group.

[57] To Betty, 10 November 1942, *SWJN*, vol. 3, p. 27.

[58] Albert Memmi, *The Colonizer and the Colonized* (Boston: Beacon Press, 1965), p. xxii.

Jawaharlal mapped the metaphysical and philosophic approach to life, and paid tribute to the countless sages who laid down their lives performing penance. Probably, he attributed to them more historical substance than they possessed. In other respects, he could not emancipate himself from idealizing ancient India as a world apart, independent of and superior to the rest of the civilizations, toning down the barbarism of the caste system and throwing the warm colours of fancy around his narrative. The fact is that the *Discovery* was not so much an attempt to glorify, but to suggest a departure into new modes of feeling and thought, necessarily admitting the knowledge of the European Renaissance, with a view to absorbing the lessons of the third industrial revolution and asking, what, now, is the destiny of man.[59]

Endowed with a prodigious literary gift, Jawaharlal's intellectual style was self-consciously dispassionate and philosophical. Reading him is, therefore, a very distinctive experience, different in all kinds of ways from reading Gandhi, Tagore, and Ambedkar.[60] While he recreates the atmosphere of the Middle Ages and provides tableaux rather than a record of events, his account of the twentieth century is humane and sympathetic towards the torment of the colonized, which it breathes throughout. He conducts the reader through the labyrinth of the colonial era, recounts the most complex events, and recreates portraits of outstanding fellow-countrymen. By and large, his writings make public the spirit and substance of his many-sidedness, the deep-seated urge to freedom, and the negative response to the concomitants and consequences of colonial rule.

It is true that Jawaharlal looked right through the nasty and brutal aspects of Indian life, rationalized social and cultural practices, covered up the mistakes of the Congress, allowed the obscurantist elements and the right-wingers to have a field day in the party, and failed to translate his concern for the poor and the oppressed into action. He tried to hunt with the hounds and run with the hares. As a result, the high priest of communal peace committed serious errors on the eve of the transfer of power.

[59] Anand, 'Self-Actualization in the Writings of Nehru', in *Jawaharlal Nehru: Centenary Volume*, p. 11.

[60] Vajpeyi, *Righteous Republic*, p. 170.

Jawaharlal concluded his *Autobiography* in jail with the following remark: 'But this year too will pass, and I shall go out—and then? I do not know, but I have a feeling that a chapter of my life is over and another chapter will begin. What this is going to be I cannot clearly guess. The leaves of the book of life are closed.'[61]

---

[61] J. Nehru, *An Autobiography*, p. 588.

12. Conclusion

The Price of Freedom

In the golden days to come when the history of our times and our country comes to be written, the present will occupy a glorious chapter. And shall we not think of the good old days? Shall we not remember the great men who showed us the way, and filled us with the fire of faith? In the words of Meredith (changing but one word, 'Italia' for 'India'):

'We who have seen India in the throes
Half-risen but to be hurled to the ground, and now,
Like a ripe field of wheat where once drove plough,
All bounteous as she is fair, we think
Of those who blew the breath of life into her frame.'[1]

The colonial system refused to recognize the bravest and most daring fighters because it suffered from what the historian C. A. Bayly calls

---

[1] Jawaharlal Nehru, *An Autobiography.*

'information panic'. The government, wrapped up in its ruling concerns, raised the whirlwind without being able to ride out the storm. What is more, the colonial situation could not be adjusted to; like an iron pillar, it could only be broken.[2] 'As long as we continue to be afraid of bloodshed,' says Prabhu Sevak in Munshi Premchand's *Rangbhumi*, 'our rights too will continue to be afraid to come to us. They too can only be protected by bloodshed. The region of politics is no less terrible than a battlefield. To enter into it fearing bloodshed is cowardice.'[3] In another passage, Vinay goes to Rajasthan with Seva Dal volunteers, and is promptly put in jail.[4]

New ideas sowed the seeds of discontent that transformed itself into a revolution. For all that, freedom fighters were strong, determined, and dedicated, willing to make a better world for the toiling masses. Most delved deeply into life, were determined to battle for it, and turned their immense energies to rev up their spirits. The experience of imprisonment opened up new windows of thought and vision. The distinction between 'tomorrow' and 'yesterday' vanished, so that sometimes a moment seemed like an eternity and things that happened a century ago seemed to have happened only the day before. In the leisure of isolation from the world outside, Faiz Ahmed Faiz found time for thought and study, and time to devote attention to adorning the bride of poetry—in other words, time for polishing one's verse.[5] In his own words:

If ink and pen are snatched from me, shall I
Who have dipped my fingers in my heart's blood complain—
Or if they seal my tongue, when I have made
A mouth of every round link of my chain?[6]

Vijaya Lakshmi Pandit paid a huge compliment to the constant pilgrimages to prison. She talked of the favoured few whom prison could not break because their passion for freedom enabled them to soar beyond the locks and bars of jail.[7] This 'sovereign virtue', as

[2] Memmi, *Colonizer and the Colonized*, p. 128.
[3] Premchand, *Rangbhumi*, p. 234.
[4] Premchand, *Rangbhumi*, p. ix.
[5] Hameed, *Daybreak*, p. 45.
[6] Hameed, *Daybreak*, p. 45.
[7] 1 January 1943, Vijaya Lakshmi Pandit *Prison Days*, p. 109.

Jawaharlal called it, led them to find good things in jail. To purchase one's continued existence by compromising with illegality and injustice went against the grain of the likes of Subhas Chandra Bose, the 'Bengal Tiger'.[8] In other words, it was necessary to have the conviction of the need to suffer, to go to prison for freedom, and to have the strength to experience the horrors of life. Mohamed Ali called jail the 'gateway to freedom', and took pride in frequenting many of them (*Poochhte kya ho bood-o-baash ka haal; hum hain baashinde jailkhaane ke*). He thus found a haven of refuge in the Karachi Prison, where 'the wicked cease from troubling', and from that of 'the wicked', the weary had some rest.[9] He had been imprisoned, he said, for denouncing the injustices that had been perpetrated on India and on Islam by the British, and now he must denounce them still, even if it meant returning to prison.

Indian nationalism often ended where it started: glorification of jailgoing as a commanding value. Writers remembered the 'finest specimens' of nationalists, who courted arrest only out of a sense of gallantry. The British were too strongly entrenched to give them any expectation of emoluments or worldly gains.[10] Hence the Congress and the other parties organized relief for political victims,[11] and idealized prisoners, their courage, their principles, and their boldness. They lauded the four satyagrahis from Kistna district in Andhra who refused to apologize for their conduct, and also M. P. Narayana Menon of Kerala who spurned the offer of unconditional release in mid-January 1929.[12] 'Men may break,' Gandhi was to say on the eve of the Quit India Movement, 'but they should not bend beyond brute force.'[13] What of Indian civil servants? The nationalists did not quite know what to make of those

---

[8] Panikkar, *Towards Freedom, 1940*, part 1, p. 344.

[9] Mohamed Ali, *My Life—A Fragment*, p. 169.

[10] Khaliquzzaman, *Pathway to Pakistan*, p. 65.

[11] Such as the UP Political Workers' Family Aid Association, the UP Political Prisoners' Relief Committee, and the Political Prisoners' Distressed Family Relief Fund created in 1945 out of the donations presented to Rajendra Prasad on his Bihar tour.

[12] File no. G 35/1928–29, AICC Papers; file no. 31, part 2, 1931, AICC Papers.

[13] To Bholanath, 3 November 1940, *CWMG*, vol. LXXIII, p. 149.

highly paid minions of the government who though Indians by nation-ality were expected to serve the British loyally.[14]

The values permeating the prisoner's world provided an attractive alternative to the cold and hierarchical prison structures. Some main-tained the greatest serenity,[15] faced bereavement without flinching, and embodied the finest aspects of their cultural heritage. Quite a few received the sentence of rigorous imprisonment with a smile;[16] their wounds healed on the very first day of freedom.[17] 'How with heads erect they walked along the street,' a Calcutta newspaper remarked.[18] Without a doubt, a great many had faith in what Gandhi said to them: 'We should consider it our good luck if we are sent to jail for the good of our country, for preserving our honour, for observing our religion.'[19] Some prisoners who lived behind iron-barred cages did not care much for the life denied to them.[20]

What is worthy of note in such descriptions is the eternal illusion that India would cease to move without them; so they stood on its shoulders and were eager to make others follow their path. Aurobindo Ghose claimed that he had earned a high place in society owing to his birth, training, public role, imprisonment, and especially because God had chosen him for the glorious and important work. In prison, he learnt from an inner voice that he was to have a worldwide purpose. His visions and communications with God were the good that came out of confinement and were the basis for his claim that a new man, a new Aurobindo had emerged from the Alipore Ashram in May 1909.[21] In like manner, Tilak thought that higher powers ruled the destinies of men and nations, and his incarcerations would serve the country's interests better. Others talked of the 'most cultured classes'

---

[14] Dharma Vira, 'The Indian Civil Service', *Indo-British Review*, The Indian Civil Service, part 2, vol. 13, no. 1, p. 137.

[15] 21 April 1943, Vijaya Lakshmi Pandit, *Prison Days*, p. 115.

[16] Panikkar, *Towards Freedom*, 1940, part 1, p. 331.

[17] Savarkar, *The Story of My Transportation For Life*, pp. 571–2.

[18] *Pravarkar* (Calcutta), 17 January 1922, *Report*, Bengal, week ending 22 January 1922.

[19] Holmes, Bridge, and James, *Mahatma Gandhi*, p. 147.

[20] Paranjape, *Sarojini Naidu*, p. 282.

[21] Gordon, *Bengal*, pp. 128–9.

going through its rigours,[22] claiming that it was not them but the British Empire itself that was on trial before the world. Thus Bose idealized his own burning desire for freedom:

> What greater solace can there be than the feeling that one has lived and died for a principle? What higher satisfaction can a man possess than the knowledge that his spirit will beget kindred spirits to carry on his unfinished task? What better reward can a soul desire than the certainty that his message will be wafted over hills and dales and over the broad plains to every corner of his land and across the seas to distant lands? What higher consummation can life attain than peaceful self-immolation at the altar of one's Cause?[23]

At the same time, 'sacrifice' was often a cloak for many actions that did not always stem from the highest motive. In fact, many wore it to hide what lay beneath.[24] This is indeed true of some civil servants who claimed that they did their very best to serve the national cause. Whether they did or did not is a contentious issue, but people did ask: 'How were the lackeys of the erstwhile white foreign rule going to be treated in independent India?' Many wondered what would be the fate of those who had sent freedom fighters to prison for violent activities? The fact is that they did well in free India, perhaps even better than before. The first Congress government did nothing to clip their wings. In fact, it signalled its intention by appointing G. S. Bajpai as the first Secretary-General of the Ministry of External Affairs. The Madras government gave the British members of the ICS the option to stay on for an indefinite period on the same terms as before. Thus Peter Gwynn was stationed in the Nilgiris district from mid-1947 to the end of 1949, first as Sub-Collector, Coonoor, and then as Collector, Ootacamund.

[22] 'When we are out to conquer our enemy by showing up the worthlessness of his weapons, it is best to grapple with his worst weapons and disarm him straightaway' (2 March 1922, Rajagopalachari, *Jail Diary*, p. 84).

[23] Panikkar, *Towards Freedom, 1940*, part 1, pp. 344–5. Sentenced to death on 23 March 1931 (along with Rajguru and Sukhdev), Madan Lal Dhingra saluted in military fashion and said, 'Thank you my Lord. I am glad to have the honour of dying for my country.'

[24] Vijaya Lakshmi Pandit, *The Scope of Happiness: A Personal Memoir* (New Delhi: Vikas Publishing House, 1979).

On the other hand, the fate of the freedom fighters was a rather mixed one. Some were justly honoured and rewarded, but many like Indulal Yagnik eschewed the exhibition of formal sentiments as well as appearances of honour.[25] With the world appearing insubstantial and the colour of politics false, Indulal Yagnik was not only *aniket* (homeless) but also *akinchen*—without any material possessions. For Saifuddin Kitchlew, Jawaharlal's contemporary at Cambridge, Independence was the consummation of Indian history; it was her proud destiny, having won freedom for herself, to inaugurate the era of democracy, which is liberty incarnate. But he did not reach for anything beyond his grasp, bagged no prized trophies, and secured no offfice. While Jawaharlal loaned him some cash and recommended a reduction of his rent at 12 Willingdon Crescent and 2 Aurangzeb Road,[26] he bowed out of history with Partition and the ensuing blood-bath. In the words of Akhtar-ul-Iman, the Urdu poet:

> The earth is not the same, nor the sky,
> Not the day and night.
> The boundaries of grief sometimes shrink,
> Sometimes expand.
> The world has stopped
> Where no day and night,
> No stagnation or frenzy are found.
> The stars call and the earth beckons.
> My existence still flees from everything
> I hope that life would not become
> An autumn-tainted spring, or poisoned wine.[27]

'India is a strange land,' Subhas Chandra Bose observed on 19 April 1939, 'where people are loved not because they have power, but because they give up power.'[28] As a matter of fact, scores of people

---

[25] Yagnik, *Autobiography*, pp. 189, 199; C. Mehta, *Freedom's Child*, p. xxii.

[26] Toufique Kitchlew, *Saifuddin Kitchlew: Hero of Jallianwala Bagh* (Delhi: National Book Trust, 1987), p. 140.

[27] Akhtar-ul-Iman, *Query of the Road*, pp. 191–2.

[28] Sisir Kumar Bose and Sugata Bose (eds), *Subhas Chandra Bose: Letters to Emilie Schenkl, 1934–1942* (Calcutta: Netaji Research Bureau/Permanent Black, 2004, paperback), p. xix.

avoided the highways of service and fame and treaded the mud-tracks of humble service. Vinoba Bhave ranks high among them. So does J. C. Kumarappa, the economist who went to jail twice for his pungent criticism of British economic policies. When Vinoba visited his hut in Madurai district in 1956, he saw Gandhi's picture. 'He is my master,' he said, and, pointing at another one he said: 'And here is my master's master.' That picture was that of a poor farmer.

Marxist writers, poets, and publicists marched on with wounded fingers and bloodied bodies. They discarded the hat, suit, and boots and the mental habiliments of the dominant classes. Amir Haider Khan (1900–1989) returned to his village in Rawalpindi district and gave up his share of land and property to start a school.[29] P. C. Joshi stayed in a small room on Asaf Ali Road in Delhi, and wore half-pants and half-shirts.[30] After his expulsion from the Party, he and Kalpana Dutt moved to Calcutta where they stayed at Howrah in a rented house. Muqimuddin Faruqi, National Secretary of the CPI for twenty-five years, wore white homespun pyjamas and kurta, or long shirt, and lived in a couple of dingy, airless rooms above the party office in the heart of the city [Delhi], eating frugally, always willing to help anyone in trouble.[31] Similarly, Muzaffar Ahmad led a materially precarious and marginalized social existence. The picture of daily life he led is one of chronic poverty, overcrowded living spaces, ill-health, lack of funds, house searches, police raids, and arrest.[32] The loss of freedom was deeply embedded in his mind. As for Firaq, when he came home after his release from jail, he found his family in severe financial distress. Jawaharlal sent him to Allahabad to run the Congress office.

[29] Mirza, *A Legendary Communist*, p. 241.

[30] G. Chakravarty, *P. C. Joshi*, p. 112.

[31] Born in 1920 in a small town in Saharanpur district in northern Uttar Pradesh, Muqimuddin Faruqi moved to Delhi's St Stephen's College for his master's. degree. In 1940, he was expelled for organizing a university strike against Jawaharlal's arrest. The university forfeited his MA degree, but restored it at a special convocation in 1989. As the first General Secretary of the All-India Students' Federation, he was jailed thrice for his part in the Quit India Movement.

[32] S. Chattopadhyay, *Muzaffar Ahmad*, p. 210.

Hasrat Mohani, too, spoke passionately against the unforgivable cases of petit bourgeois vacillation and absenteeism. His Aligarh College mates remembered how, in 1899, he had got down from an *ekka* (horse carriage) wearing flared pyjamas and his wedding *sherwani*, holding a *pandan* (betel-leaf container) in one hand.[33] But *Khalajan* (aunt), as he was nicknamed by the Aligarh boys, gave up his *taluqdari* habits to lead a plain and unembellished existence. Early in life, he gave away his properties to Hazrat Shah Wajih, a Sufi, to his *murshid* Maulana Abdul Wahab of Firangi Mahal, and to his daughter. He preferred to walk even when he called on the rajas of Mahmudabad and Salempur, and the Firangi Mahali ulama. In April 1939, he travelled third class (£12 or Rs 160) to London to meet the Secretary of State for India and Ramsay MacDonald, the former British Prime Minister. And while attending the Constituent Assembly, this man of idealistic mind, deliberate habits, imperturbable optimism, and steadfast will stayed in a nearby mosque at no cost to the nation.[34]

Pride and Prejudice

> Sitting here [in jail in 1942] I find it very difficult to understand or excuse that group of people which live between two worlds—the world of conflict for the sake of ideals and that other world which seeks to crush truth and light and beauty and lowers human dignity and makes a mockery of civilization. Such people seem to grow in numbers. Neither the tragedy of their own country nor the terrible world conflict seems to affect them. (Vijaya Lakshmi Pandit, *Prison Days*)

For years the fetters that bound India to the British had been drawn tighter and tighter. When deliverance came, the moment of opportunity was put to good use. The final results were all that one could expect. The government granted remission to or released some prisoners, both political and non-political, on 15 August 1947 and 26 January 1950 (Republic Day).[35] And UP freed 513 of them on

---

[33] A. Siddiqi, *Adabiyat*, p. 97; Naim, 'The Maulana Who Loved Krishna'.
[34] Naim, 'The Maulana Who Loved Krishna'.
[35] Home Dept. (Judicial), file no. 40/ 66, 1955.

Gandhi Jayanti, 2 October 1955. Majrooh Sultanpuri (1919–2000) waxed lyrical, *Mujhe sehl ho gain manzilen; wo hawa ke rukh bhi badal gaye/Tera haath haath me aa gaya; ke chiragh raah me jal gaye* (It has become easy to reach the destination now/The stormy winds have changed their direction/With your hand in my hand, the long path/is illuminated with lighted lamps).

Jailgoing, trials, and executions are essential endowments of a popular hero in South Asia.[36] Thus Udham Singh (1899–1940), whom the British tried and executed in 1940 for assassinating Michael O'Dwyer (1864–1940), Punjab's Lieutenant-Governor from 1912 until 1919, received the coveted *Nishan-e Khalsa* and his life story became the theme of a film in December 1999. In the mid- to late-1960s, the tale of his grand self-sacrifice circulated widely, exhorting Punjabis to remember him in a way befitting martyrs and heroes.[37] This kind of adulation extended to public figures in free India, such as Jayaprakash Narayan (JP) who was arrested during the Emergency in 1975.[38] One of the main episodes in his life had occurred in 1942, when he climbed down the prison wall on a rope made of *dhotis*. In neighbouring Pakistan, Faiz Ahmed Faiz's imprisonment as one of the accused in the Rawalpindi Conspiracy Case enhanced his fame, and when he came out of jail, he had a larger and more appreciative public than when he went in.[39] Decades later, thousands applauded Benazir Bhutto on 10 April 1986 on her return after years of exile: 'the sea of humanity lining the roads, jammed on balconies and roofs, wedged in trees and on lamp-posts, walking alongside the truck and stretching back across the fields, was more like an ocean.'[40] She, in turn, threw

[36] Nirad C. Chaudhuri, *Thy Hand, Great Anarch! India 1921–1952* (New Delhi: Time Book International, 1987), p. 476.

[37] Louis E. Fenech, 'Contested Nationalism; The Neglected Terrains: The Way Sikhs Remember Udham Singh', *Modern Asian Studies*, vol. 36, no. 4 (2002).

[38] There exist quite a few accounts of the Emergency years, 1975–7; M. G. Devasalayan, *JP in Jail: An Uncensored Account* (New Delhi: Roli Books, 2006); Kuldip Nayyar, *In Jail* (New Delhi: Vikas Publishing House, 1978), and his *Beyond the Lines*.

[39] Hameed, *Daybreak*, p. 51.

[40] Benazir Bhutto, *Daughter of the East: An Autobiography* (London: Hamish Hamilton, 1988), p. 279.

flowers and embroidered cloth on the prisoners she recognized in the throng. This is not the end of the story. India celebrated, along with the rest of the world, the end of South Africa's white minority rule and of the military dictatorship in Mynamar. Nelson Mandela and Aung San Suu Kyi walking out of prison to liberate the oppressed and the oppressor both have been moments of immeasurable joy and utmost relief.[41]

'No one knows where the final destination stands; All we know is that the bell of the caravan is ringing,' wrote the Persian poet Hafiz Shirazi. After liberation, what? What about those who received lathi blows with patience, put up with the slights and indignities, or walked gallantly to the cell or the gallows? In their partisan view, historians have forgotten their part in restoring the liberal foundations of the modern state. India's gold-diggers in the political arena have done the same. The Ministry of Culture observes a choice of commemorative events: during the last couple of years it has spent crores to remind us of the creativity of the existence of Rabindranath Tagore and Swami Vivekananda (1863–1902). With innocent children and lazy-looking government servants being herded into Delhi's plush Vigyan Bhawan, one begins to question the purpose and utility of such extravaganzas fed on the diet of departed leaders or patriots. Often, as George Rudé suggests in the context of food riots in England, those who appeared for trial were not so much leaders in any commonly accepted sense of the term as those whose momentary enthusiasm or daring marked them out for arrest.[42] Amidst all this we must not forget the people's anger and frustration, for the tide may change. As Ghalib prophesied long ago:

Rang layegi humari faqa masti ek din.[43]

---

[41] Mandela remarked: 'The truth is that we are not yet free; we have merely achieved the freedom to be free, the right not to be oppressed ... to be free is not merely to cast off one's chains, but to live in a way that respects and enhances the freedom of others' (Mandela, *Long Walk to Freedom*, p. 751).

[42] George Rudé, *Ideology and Popular Protest* (London: Lawrence and Wishart, 1980), p. 142.

[43] And they think that their cheerfulness in middle of adversity will bring about a miraculous transformation some day.

Appendix I

Aseer-e Zindan—*Poems from Prison*

1

Dare kya qahr-e-dushman se bhala dil
Qawi hai wada-e-haq se mera dil
Sahara kya nahin kafi tumhara
Na dhoonde ab kisi ka asra dil
Laga do aag uzre-maslehat ko
Ke hai bezaar is shai se mera dil
Lada kar ankh us jane jahan se
Na hoga ab kisi se ashna dil
Mite azkar-e-gu-na-gun ke jhagde
Tere gham ko na de kyun kar dua dil
Terey dard-e-muhabbat ki badaulat
Hua hai manzil-e-sidq-o-safa dil
Badi dargah ka sayel hun hasrat
Badi ummeed hai meri bada dil

Why should I fear the enemy's terror
When strength of truth fills my heart
Your support is enough for me my Lord
I do not seek any other comfort
Let wise words go down the drain
I care not for such prudent thought
After falling in love with that dear one
To anyone else, I cannot give my heart
All conflicts have come to an end
Why shouldn't my heart bless your love?
It is the sorrow of your love due to which
Truth and virtue have entered my heart.
I am a beggar at the gate of the Highest
My hopes are high, I have a big heart.

     —Hasrat Mohani[1] (Translated by Nishat Zaidi.)

2

Qawi dil, shadman dil, ba-safa dil
Terey ashiq ne bhi paya hai kya dil
Jafakari hai tasleem-e-sitam bhi
Na hoga taba-e jaur-o-jafa dil
Ghalat hai qual-e-aql-e-maslehat kosh
Na is janib karega etena dil
Na manuga nasihat main kisi ki
Ke naseh sab se behtar hai mera dil
Tawana-e-sadaqat hai to hasrat
Na hoga pairave batil tera dil

Your lover is blessed with such a heart
A heart that is strong, happy and smart
Acceptance of cruelty is no less a tyranny
These excesses will never bend my heart
All efforts of reason are futile, wrong
Such arguments will never win my heart
I will not listen to any advice

[1] Siddiqi, *Begam Hasrat Mohani aur Unke Khutoot.*

O preacher, what I trust best is my heart.
If you have the strength of truth, O Hasrat!
Never will thee side with the wrong, nor thy heart.
                        —Hasrat Mohani[2] (Translated by Nishat Zaidi.)

3

Sar Yeh Hazir Hai Jo Irshad Ho Mar Jane Ko
Kaun Talega Bhala Aap Ke Farmane Ko
Danish-e-Bakht Hai Be-Danishi-e-Shauq Ka Nam
Log Diwana Na Samjhen Terey Diwane Ko
Bhool Jaun Main UnheN Ho NahiN Sakta Naseh
Aag Lag Jaiyo Zalim Tere Samjhane Ko
Dekh Len Shama Ko Taseer-e-wafa Ke Munkir
Jal Bujhi Khud Bhi Jalaya Jo Thha Parvane Ko
Hoke Serab-e-karam Dil Se Dua DuN Saqi
Ek Baar Aur bhi Bhar De Merey Paimane Ko
Furqat-e-yaar Men Ghanghor Uthi Hai Jo Ghata
Ashk-e-Khun Ankh Bhi Aamada Hai Barsane Ko
Barq Ka Qaul Mujhe Yaad Hai Abtak Hasrat
'Zindagi Kahten Hain Duniya Se Guzar Jane Ko'

I offer my head if only you command, 'Die'
Who can your command ever defy?
Naiveté of passion is the wisdom of destiny
Let none take your lover as a mad well-nigh
It is impossible for me to forget her, O Preacher!
May your preaching go up in flames, I sigh
Let those who deny the power of love come and witness the candle
After consuming the moth in its flames, it douses to die.
The roaring dark cloud rises in separation's sorrow
Craving to shed the tears of blood is my eye.
I still remember the words of 'Barq', O Hasrat
'Life is nothing but in this world just passing by.'
                        —Hasrat Mohani[3] (Translated by Nishat Zaidi.)

---

[2] Siddiqi, *Begam Hasrat Mohani aur Unke Khutoot.*
[3] Siddiqi, *Begam Hasrat Mohani aur Unke Khutoot.*

4

The flag of our liberty will wave in India

Do not become agitated for that day will come.
When the flag of our liberty will wave in India.
The leaders of the nation are now saying this in prison.
The troops of the leaders will come with *swaraj*.
Let them do oppression and tyranny; our desire is peace.
O tyrant! Will tyranny stand before patience?
Those sacred places will now bring on ruin.
The unity of the enemies of religion will be humble unto dust.
The heretics had made Thrace bloody through oppression.
The blood of the innocent Moslems will come like a chastisement.
It is nothing if we have been made to grind the mill in the jail.
We will not feel agitated even if we are ground down.
The innocents of the Punjab have shrieked out in Paradise.
Your tyranny, O Dyer! will now make you feel the consequence of it.
O tyrant! How can the unjust shedding of blood be hid by concealing it?
Now you will have to feel the consequence of making us quiver.
Now await that which the Congress will do.
The method in which you move will be changed by it.
Learn this lesson after carefully going through it again.
To-morrow you will be made to learn a more difficult lesson than this.
Go on making efforts and never be off your guard, O Ahqar!
What a thing *swaraj* is, O God! You will get it.

—Zahurud-din Ahqar Sherekoti[4]

[4] *Ihrar* (Calcutta) 12 January 1922; *Report*, Bengal, 21 January 1922.

Appendix II

Tables

Table A.1 Political Prisoners from Punjab

No.	Name	Year of Conviction	Section of Indian Penal Code	Sentence	Remarks
38149	Bishen Singh	1912	302, 302-149	Life	Reported to have been concerned in a plot to break open the Lahore Central Jail and release all those concerned in the Lahore Conspiracy Case
38184	Udham Singh	1915	121, 121-A, 131	"	Lahore Conspiracy Case
38360	Chatar Singh	1914	307	"	Reported as a violent seditionist. Attempted to murder Professor of Khalsa College

(Contd.)

Table (*Contd.*)

No.	Name	Year of Conviction	Section of Indian Penal Code	Sentence	Remarks
38365	Wasawa Singh	1915	121, 121-A, 124A, 396, 109	"	Lahore Conspiracy Case
38366	Harnam Singh	1915	121, 121-A, 131	"	Ditto
38367	Sohan Singh	1915	121, 121-A, 124-A, 131	"	Ditto
38368	Sawan Singh	1915	121, 121-A, 396	"	Ditto
38370	Ram Saran Das	1915	121, 121-A	"	Ditto
38371	Pirthi Singh	1915	121, 121-A, 124-A, 307	"	Ditto
38372	Permanand	1915	121, 121-A, 122, 124A	"	Ditto
38374	Nidhan Singh	1915	121, 121-A, 122, 124A, 131, 395-109, 326	"	Ditto
38375	Nand Singh	1915	121, 121-A, 122, 395, 394	"	Ditto
38376	Kesar Singh	1915	121, 121-A, 124A, 131	"	Ditto
38377	Khushal Singh	1915	121, 121-A, 396	"	Ditto
38378	Hirdha Ram	1915	121, 121-A, 122, 131, 295, 397, 398, 102, 302, 109	"	Ditto
38380	Jagat Ram	1915	121, 121-A, 131, 122, 124-A	"	Ditto
38504	Gurmukh Singh	1915	121, 121-B, 131, 395	Life	Lahore Conspiracy Case
38109	Sher Singh	1915	121, 121-A, 124-A, 131	"	Ditto

Table (*Contd.*)

No.	Name	Year of Conviction	Section of Indian Penal Code	Sentence	Remarks
38514	Rur Singh	1915	121, 121-A, 131	"	Ditto
38517	Madan Singh	1915	121, 121-A	"	Ditto
38520	Jawala Singh	1915	121, 121-A, 124-A, 131	"	Ditto
38825	Chuhar Singh	1915	121, 121-A, 122, 395, 397, 398	"	Ditto
43338	Sunder Singh	1919	121, 307, 149-307, 189	"	Amritsar Riot. Miss Sherwood's Case
43339	Mehr Din	1919	121	"	Amritsar National Bank murder Case
43340	Jalal Din	1919	121	"	Amritsar Riot. Alliance Bank Case
43543	Wilaiti	1919	121, 147, 307, 149	"	Amritsar Riot. Miss Sherwood's Case
43544	Karam Chand	1919	121	"	Amritsar National Bank Murder Case
43630	Ratan Chand	1919	121	"	Ditto
43631	Buga	1919	121	"	Ditto
43632	Manohar Singh	1919	121	"	Ditto
43633	Raja Ram	1919	121	"	Malakwal Riot Case (Gujarat District)
43634	Jai Ram Singh	1919	121	"	Amritsar National Bank Murder Case
43843	Allah Din	1919	121	"	Kasur Riot Case
43844	Muhamadi	1919	121	"	Amritsar National Bank Murder Case
43845	Sadiq	1919	121	"	Amritsar Riot. Alliance Bank Case
			of		
44200	Nadir Ali Shah	1919	121	Life	Kasur Riot Case

(*Contd.*)

Table (*Contd.*)

No.	Name	Year of Conviction	Section of Indian Penal Code	Sentence	Remarks
44201	Girdhari Lal	1919	121	"	Gujranwala Riot Case
44202	Harnam Singh, etc.	1919	121	"	Amritsar Riot National Bank Case
44203	Diina	1919	121	"	Amritsar Riot Alliance Bank Case
44327	Sandhi	1919	121	"	Ditto
44328	Harnam Singh	1919	307, 121	"	Judgment called for not received yet
39528	Kapoor Singh	1916	121, 121-A	"	Burma Conspiracy Case
39529	Hardit Singh	1916	121, 121-A	"	Ditto
39530	Kirpa Ram	1916	121-A	"	Ditto
41052	Amar Singh	1917	121-A	"	Ditto
41053	Ali Ahmed Sadique	1917	121-A	"	Ditto
41055	Mohammed Mujtaba, etc	1917	121-A	"	Ditto
38178	Chanan Singh	1915	131	"	Lahore Conspiracy Case
38179	Kehar Singh	1915	131	"	Ditto
38182	Bishen Singh	1915	131	"	Ditto
38177	Bishan Singh	1915	131	10 years	Ditto

Source: Home Dept., Political, file no. 69-4, 1922.

Table A.2 Allowances for State Prisoners and Families

S. No.	Name	Date of Arrest	Amount of Allowances Sanctioned for		
			Prisoner in Jail	His Family and Dependants	Other Purposes
Regulation III of 1818					
1	Abdul Waris alias Bashir Ahmad	28.8.30	Rs. 1/6 per diem for diet	Nil	
			Rs. 32/ monthly for necessaries		
			Rs. 60/ lump allowance on first admission to jail		
2	Fazal Elahi alias Qurban	-do-	-do-	Nil	
3	Ghulam Muhammad alias Aziz Hindi	-do-	-do-	Nil	
4	Ihsan Elahi	9.2.1931	-do-	-do-	
5	Harjap Singh	14.9.1931	-do-	Rs. 25/- p.m. for his wife	
6	Karam Singh	21.5.1931	-do-	Nil	
7	Jiban Lal Chaterji	23.11.1931	Rs. 1/4 a day for diet	Rs. 40/ p.m	
			Rs. 32 monthly		
8	Surendra Mohan Ghosh	23.11.1931	-do-	Rs. 30/ p.m	
9	Pratul Chandra Ganguli	-do-	-do-	Rs. 50/ p.m	
10	Trailokhya Nath Chakrabartti	-do-	-do-	-do-	
11	Ramesh Chandra Acharji	25.11.31	-do-	Rs. 55/ p.m	
12	Rabindra Mohan Sen Gupta	-do-	-do-	Nil	

(Contd.)

Table (*Contd.*)

S. No.	Name	Date of Arrest	Amount of Allowances Sanctioned for		
			Prisoner in Jail	His Family and Dependants	Other Purposes
13	Pratul Chandra Bhattacharji	23.11.31	-do-	Nil	
14	Benoyendra Roy Roy Chaudhury	23.11.31	Rs. 1/4 a day for diet Rs. 32/ monthly	Rs. 20 p.m	
15	Satya Bhusan Gupta	24.11.31	Rs. 1/6 a day for diet	Rs. 50 p.m	
16	Manoranjan Gupta	-do-	-do-	Nil	Rs. 36/7 half yearly premium on insurance policy
17	Bhupendra Kumar Datta	-do-	-do-	Rs. 20 p.m	Rs. 59/12 quarterly
18	Arun Chandra Guha	24.11.31	Rs. 1/6 a day for diet Rs. 32 monthly	Nil	Insurance policy Rs. 58/1 quarterly Rs. 53/5- Half-yearly respectively as premia on two insurance policies
19	Bhupendra Kishore Rakshit Roy	2.1.1932	Rs. 12/ a day for diet Rs. 32 monthly	Rs. 75 p.m	
20	Rasik Lal Das	-do-	-do-	Nil	
21	Jyotish Chandra Ghosh	1.1.1932	Rs. 1/8 a day for diet Rs. 32/- monthly	Rs. 60/- p.m	

Table (*Contd.*)

S. No.	Name	Date of Arrest	Amount of Allowances Sanctioned for		
			Prisoner in Jail	His Family and Dependants	Other Purposes
22	Suresh Chandra Dass	2.1.1932	-do-	Rs. 100/- p.m	
23	Pruna Chandra Das	1.1.1932	-do-	Rs. 60/ p.m	
24	Bhupati Mazumdar	2.1.1932	-do-	Rs. 165 p.m	Rs 140/8 half yearly premium on insurance policy Rs. 8/4/6 quarterly municipal tax. Rs. 8 annual Union Board Tax
25	Subhash Chandra Bose	3.1.32	Rs. 3/8 a day for diet Rs. 32 monthly Rs. 100 lump sum on first admission to jail	Nil	
26	Sarat Chandra	4.2.1932	Rs. 3/8 a day for diet Rs. 32 monthly Rs. 100 lump sum on first admission to jail	Rs. 1,200 p.m	Payment until a certain policy acquires surrender value of premia amounting to Rs. 1334 per annum plus Rs. 1157/13 as a single payment in respect of one other policy

(*Contd.*)

Table (*Contd.*)

S. No.	Name	Date of Arrest	Amount of Allowances Sanctioned for		
			Prisoner in Jail	His Family and Dependants	Other Purposes
27	Jatindra Mohan Sen Gupta	20.1.1932	Rs. 4/8 a day for diet Rs. 32- monthly Rs. 100/ lump sum on first admission to jail	Rs. 1,000 p.m.	Rs. 255 quarterly premium on insurance policy
28	Abdul Ghaffar Khan	24.12.31	Rs. 200 p.m. consolidated allowance	Nil	
29	Saadullah Khan	-do-	Rs. 150 p.m.	-do-	Nil
30	Qazi Ataullah Khan	-do-	Rs. 150 p.m -do-	Rs. 400 p.m	
31	Dr. Khan Sahib	-do-	Rs. 200 p.m	Rs. 500 p.m plus an additional 200 p.m. during the period his son and daughter by his English wife lived in England for their education	
32	M. K. Gandhi	4.1.32	Rs. 100 p.m. consolidated allowance	Nil	
33	Vallabbhai Jhaverbhai Patel	-do-	-do-	Nil	

Table (*Contd.*)

S. No.	Name	Date of Arrest	Amount of Allowances Sanctioned for		
			Prisoner in Jail	His Family and Dependants	Other Purposes

Regulation III of 1818

	Bhawani Sahai	26.4.32	12/ a day for diet	Nil	
			Rs. 10- monthly allowance		
			Rs. 60 lump sum on first admission to jail		

Source: Home Dept., Political, file no. 31/85, 1932.

Index

Revolutionary Socialist Republican
  Army, 12
Rifah-e Am Press, Lahore, 81
Roshnai (*The Light*), 104
Round Table Conference (RTC),
  London, 37, 54, 77, 155, 160,
  203
Rowlatt Committee, 178n111
Rowlatt Satyagraha, 26, 155,
  216–17
Roy, M. N., 38, 124–31; comments
  on 'intellectual stagnation', 127;
  Historical Role of Islam, The, 129
Roy, Raja Rammohun, 80, 84
Rude, George, 250
Russell, Bertrand, 235
Russian Revolution (1917), 125

Sabri-Chishti school of Islamic
  mysticism, 116
Sahajanand, Swami, 24, 140
Sahay, Raghupati, 'Firaq', 138–9
Sahgal, Nayantara, 180, 184
Sahitya Akademi, 96
Salt Laws, breaking of, 164–5
Santiniketan, 128, 214
Sapru, Tej Bahadur, 160
Sarabhai, Mridula, 131, 175
satyagraha, 69, 131, 158, 177, 207,
  243
Savarkar, Ganesh, 10
Savarkar, Vinayak, 10
Saxena, Shibban Lal, 54
security prisoners, 27, 33, 147, 165
Sedition Committee's Report
  (1918), 25, 28
Sehgal, Zohra, 100
Sen, Surya, 143
'Serial' jails in Gujarat and Kasur, 26
Servants of India Society, 169
Sesh Prasna, 128

Sevak, Prabhu, 242
Shah, Firoz, 233
Shah, Maulvi Ahmadullah, 234
Shikast-e zindan ka khwab, 100–1
Shikoh, Dara, 88
Shikohabadi, Munir, 7
Shirazi, Hafiz, 138, 250
Short History of the Saracens, A, 163
Sihah-e Sitah, 66
Simon Commission, 11, 12n48
Singh, Bhagat, 11, 52–4
Singh, Udham, 249
Slocombe, George, 164
Sohrabji, Dadabhai, 100
Soviet Union, 37, 113, 123
Spirit of Islam, The, 163
Spratt, Philip, 189
Stalin, Joseph, 122, 136
Storm over India, 163
Sufism, 7, 156
Sultanpuri, Majrooh, 249
Sultans of Delhi (1206–1526), 129
Sunna, 83
Sunnat, 142
Suu Kyi, Aung San, 250
Swadeshi Movement, Bengal, 4
Swaraj Shastras, 172

Tagore, Rabindranath, 43, 128, 214,
  250
Tandon, Purshottamdas, 138
Tanvir, Habib, 100
Tarjuman al-Quran, 84–5, 92
Tavernier, J. B., 20
Tazkira, 84, 92
Tegart, Charles, 204
tehsildars, 21
Tihar Jail, Delhi, 4
Tilak, Bal Gangadhar, 52, 201
Tolstoy, Leo, 151
Tonki, Syed Mohammad, 124, 138

About the Author

Mushirul Hasan is former Professor of History and Vice-Chancellor of Jamia Millia Islamia (2004–9). He has also served as the Director General of the National Archives of India (2010–13) and was appointed the Jawaharlal Nehru Fellow (2013–15). He has been a Visiting Professor at the Central European University, Budapest; the International Institute of Languages and Civilizations, Paris; the University of Virginia; the University of Rome; Fondation Maison des Sciences del' Homme, Paris; a Fellow at the Institute of Advanced Study, Shimla; and a Professorial Fellow at the Nehru Memorial Museum and Library, New Delhi. He was elected President of the Indian History Congress (Modern India) in 2002 and its General President in 2014. He was a recipient of the Padma Shri in 2007. He is the author of several books, including *Faith and Freedom: Gandhi in History* (2013), *A Moral Reckoning: Muslim Intellectuals in Nineteenth-Century Delhi* (Oxford University Press, 2005),

From Pluralism to Separatism: Qasbas in Colonial Awadh (Oxford University Press, 2004), *Legacy of a Divided Nation: India's Muslims since Independence* (Oxford University Press, 1997), *India's Partition: Process, Strategy, and Mobilization* (Oxford University Press, 1993), and *India Partitioned: The Other Face of Freedom*, volumes 1 and 2 (Oxford University Press, 1995 and 1997), among others.